WORLD
PREHISTORY

WORLD PREHISTORY
A Brief Introduction
SECOND EDITION

Brian M. Fagan
University of California, Santa Barbara

■ HarperCollins*College*Publishers ■

Acquisitions Editor: Alan McClare
Project Editor: Steven Pisano
Design Supervisor and Cover Design: Paul Agresti
Cover Illustration: Anasazi shaman figure courtesy of Danilo Agresti
Photo Researcher: Mira Schachne
Production Manager/Assistant: Willie Lane/Sunaina Sehwani
Compositor: Digitype, Inc.
Printer and Binder: R. R. Donnelley & Sons Company
Cover Printer: New England Book Components

World Prehistory: A Brief Introduction, Second Edition

Library of Congress Cataloging-in-Publication Data

Fagan, Brian M.
 World prehistory: a brief introduction / Brian M. Fagan. — 2nd
 ed.
 p. cm.
 Includes bibliographical references and index.
 ISBN 0-673-52262-8
 1. Man, Prehistoric. 2. Anthropology, Prehistoric. 3. Human
evolution. I. Title.
GN740.F34 1993
573.2—dc20   92-40999
                                                             CIP

93 94 95 96   9 8 7 6 5 4 3 2 1

To Victoria Pryor
with thanks for creative inspiration and many kindnesses

There is not yet one person, one animal. . . . Only the sky alone is there; the face of the earth is not clear. Only the sea alone is pooled under all the sky; there is nothing whatever gathered together. It is at rest; not a single thing stirs. . . . Whatever there is that might be is simply not there: only the pooled water. . . .

From the Quiche Maya legend of the creation. (Dennis Tedlock, *Popol Vuh.* New York: Doubleday, 1985, p. 127)

Contents

To the Reader

*T*his book introduces you to the exciting story of human prehistory, from the earliest times up to the advent of cities, writing, and the earliest civilizations. The 2.5 million years covered by our narrative encompass not only human origins and the peopling of the globe, but the beginnings of agriculture and the origins of states. Some of the archaeological sites mentioned in these pages are household names — like Olduvai Gorge, the Pyramids of Giza, and Teotihuacan. But, despite these familiar names, many people are surprised to learn that archaeologists have reconstructed so many details of the earliest chapters of human existence. I hope that this book provides you with an interesting summary of what we do know about ancient times.

No prior knowledge of archaeology is needed to take this journey through prehistory. Technical terms and theoretical arguments are kept to a minimum. Chapters 1 and 2 describe some of the basic principles of archaeological research and provide insight into how archaeologists date the past and interpret the major developments of prehistory. The remainder of the volume takes you on a narrative journey from the beginnings of human existence to recent times. Strategically placed maps and chronological tables provide you with a time and space framework. The Timelines columns at the beginning of Chapters 3 through 13 (except for Chapter 8) place each part of the story on a linear time scale. And a Guide to Further Reading at the end of the book provides you with convenient references if you want to delve more deeply into the major topics covered in this book.

Good luck with your exploration of archaeology and the fascinating realm of human prehistory.

To the Instructor

World Prehistory attempts a daunting task—a narrative summary of human prehistory within the compass of just under 300 pages. It is designed as a supplementary text for basic anthropology courses. As such, it assumes that your students have no background in archaeology and just two or three weeks to cover world prehistory. It attempts to give the reader a summary grounding in archaeology and major approaches to prehistory, then examines the major developments in our early past.

By no stretch of the imagination can this book be called complete. Many fierce academic controversies lurk in these pages and are glossed over here. My feeling is that it is sometimes best to overstate some tentative scenarios at this stage in learning rather than present an inconclusive piece of reasoning, which will tend to confuse the beginner. One can always correct errors of overstatement in class or at a later stage. For more complete coverage, I recommend you turn to one of the widely available prehistory texts listed in the "Guide to Further Reading."

World Prehistory is written within a generalized evolutionary framework and is more of a cultural history than an interpretative treatment of prehistory. As a conscious decision, I have played down discussions of archaeological theory at the expense of providing an overall narrative, according to the argument that extended discussions of such topics are usually introduced in more advanced courses.

An attempt is made to provide balanced coverage for as many different areas of the world as possible. We live in a multicultural, diverse world. I believe that a book of this nature must reflect that diversity, even if some better-known areas, like, say, Europe or Mesoamerica, receive more cursory treatment than some instructors might like. I recommend that you use your own expertise and case studies, also theoretical biases, to amplify the narrative that follows. For this reason, and because of space considerations, I have kept detailed examples to a minimum. After all, each class situation is different, and the degree of detail thought appropriate changes from class to class. In short, *World Prehistory* is designed as a simple pedagogical tool to provide a context for presenting archaeology and human prehistory in many different ways.

Several colleagues provided reviews of the manuscript in draft. I am grateful for their trenchant criticism and useful insights. Thanks especially to William Breece, Orange Coast College; Gary Feinman, University of Wisconsin; Tom Foor, University of Montana; and John Rick, Stanford University. Alan McClare, my editor at HarperCollins, was a constant inspiration and a source of useful ideas. Grateful thanks, also, to Steven Pisano, who saw the book through production.

Any comments or ideas for improving future editions of the book would be much appreciated, and should be addressed to the author at the Department of Anthropology, University of California, Santa Barbara, CA 93106.

Brian M. Fagan

A Note on Chronologies

*T*he narrative of prehistory in these pages is organized in as linear a fashion chronologically as is practicable. It is based on radiocarbon, potassium–argon, and tree-ring dates, as well as historical documents. Although every effort has been made to make dates accurate, many of them should be recognized for what they are — statistical approximations.

The time scales of prehistory are presented in two ways:

- At the beginning of each chapter (except Chapters 1, 2, and 8), a "Timelines" column shows the reader the relative position of the developments described in that chapter within the broad time frame of prehistoric times.
- Chronological tables placed at strategic points in the book provide a comparative view of developments in different areas of the world. Each is linked to its predecessors and successors, so that they provide background continuity for the narrative.

The following conventions are used:

- Dates before 10,000 years ago are expressed in years Before Present (B.P.)

Dates after 10,000 years ago are expressed in years Before Christ (B.C.) or Anno Domini (A.D.)

Please note that all radiocarbon dates and potassium–argon dates should be understood to have a plus and minus factor that is omitted from this book in the interests of clarity. They are statistical approximations.

PART
One

PREHISTORY

It is a capital mistake to theorize before one has data. Insensibly, one begins to wish facts to suit theories, instead of theories to suit facts. . . .

Sherlock Holmes
A Scandal in Bohemia

Chapter
1

The Study of
World Prehistory

Since time immemorial, humans have been intensely curious about their origins, about the mysterious and sometimes threatening world in which they exist. They know that earlier generations lived before them, that their children, grandchildren, and their progeny in turn will, in due course, dwell on earth. But how did this world come about? Who created the familiar landscape of rivers, fields, mountains, plants, and animals? Who fashioned the oceans and sea coasts, deep lakes and fast-flowing streams? Above all, how did the first men and women settle the land? Who created them, how did they come into being? Archaeology and biological anthropology have replaced legend with an intricate account of human evolution and cultural development that extends back more than two-and-a-half million years into the remote past. This book is a brief account of human prehistory, of these two-and-a-half million years.

"IN THE BEGINNING . . . "

After the Great Fire destroyed the world and before the little bird Icanchu flew away, he roamed the wasteland in search of First Place. The homeland lay beyond recognition, but Icanchu's index finger, of its own accord, pointed to the spot. There he unearthed the charcoal stump that he pounded as his drum. Playing without stopping, he chanted with the dark drum's sounds . . . At dawn on the New Day, a green shoot sprang from the coal

3

drum and soon flowered as Firstborn Tree . . . From its branches bloomed the forms of life that flourished in the New World. . . . [1]

We Westerners take the past for granted, accept human evolution as something that extends back many thousands, even millions, of years. Science provides us with a long perspective on ancient times. In contrast, the story of Icanchu's drum is a classic origin myth of the cosmic fire told by the Mataco Indians from South America. Like all such accounts, the tale begins with a primordium (the very beginning) where a mythic being, in this case Icanchu, works to create the familiar animals, landscape, and plants of the world, and then the human inhabitants. Icanchu, and his equivalents in a myriad of human cultures throughout the world, create order from primeval chaos, as God does in Genesis, Chapter 1.

Myths, and the rituals and religious rite associated with them, function to create a context for the entire symbolic life of a human society, a symbolic life that is the very cornerstone of human existence. The first human beings establish the sacred order through which life endures from one generation to the next. This kind of history, based on legend and myth, is one of symbolic existence. Creation legends tell of unions between gods and monsters, of people emerging from holes in the earth after having climbed sacred trees that link the layers of the cosmos. They create indissoluble, symbolic bonds between human beings and other modes of being, such as plants, animals, and celestial beings.

The vivid and ever present symbolic world has influenced the course of human life ever since humans first acquired the power of creative thought and reasoning. The Cro-Magnons of western Europe depicted mythical animals and the symbolism of the Ice Age hunt in cave paintings more than 20,000 years ago (Chapter 5). They modeled clay bison in dark chambers deep beneath the earth. The sculptures seemed to flicker in the light of fire brands during powerful rituals carried out by shamans, tribal priests with the ability to voyage into the mysterious spiritual world. So compelling was the influence of the unknown powers of the cosmos and of the gods that inhabited it that the Maya and other Mesoamerican civilizations created entire ceremonial centers and cities in the form of symbolic landscapes to commemorate their mythic universe (Chapter 11).

Today, western science has chronicled more than 2.5 million years of prehistory, a narrative of human endeavor that extends back through hundreds of thousands of years of unfolding time. This story is one based on scientific research, something quite different from the creation legends that people use to define their complex relationships with the natural and spiritual world. These legends are deeply felt, important sources of cultural identity. They foster a quite different relationship with the past than

---

[1]Lawrence Sullivan, *Icanchu's Drum*. New York: Macmillan, 1988, p. 92.

that engendered by archaeology, which seeks to understand our common biological and cultural roots, and the great diversity of humanity.

PSEUDOARCHAEOLOGY

Golden Pharaohs, lost civilizations, buried treasure — archaeology seems like a romantic world of high adventure and exciting discovery. A century ago, archaeology was indeed a matter of exotic travel to remote places. It was still possible to find a hitherto unknown civilization with a few weeks of digging. Today, archaeology is a highly scientific discipline, concerned more with minute details of ancient life than with spectacular discoveries. But an aurora of unsolved mysteries and heroic peoples still surrounds the subject in many peoples' eyes — to the point of obsession.

The mysteries of the past attract many people, especially those with a taste for adventure, escapism, and science fiction. These people create elaborate adventure stories about the past — almost invariably epic journeys or voyages based on illusory data.

For example, in the 1970s a Swiss author named Erich von Daniken caused a furor when he wrote in a book *Chariot of the Gods* that human civilization was the result of long-forgotten visits by ancient astronauts to the planet Earth. Thousands of years ago, he wrote, these bold explorers from another world had landed their space ships in the Peruvian desert (and elsewhere) and encountered primitive peoples during their explorations. The visitors fertilized these savages and gave them the technology of civilization, everything from pyramid architecture to metalworking. Eventually they left, leaving only a few traces of their presence on earth for archaeologists (von Daniken) to find thousands of years later.

Von Daniken claimed, of course, that his theories were based on archaeological evidence, on the cracking of genetic codes, and other variant theories. In fact, they are complete fiction, a tapestry narrative created in his fertile imagination and tied to a handful of archaeological sites, usually thousands of miles apart. It is as if a scientist tried to reconstruct the contents of an American house using artifacts found in Denmark, New Zealand, South Africa, Spain, and Tahiti.

Nonscientific nonsense like this comes in many forms. There are those who believe that the Lost Continent of Atlantis once lay under the waters of the Bahamas, that Atlanteans fled their sunken homeland and settled the Americas thousands of years ago. Other fantasize about fleets of ancient Egyptian boats or Roman galleys that crossed the Atlantic long before Columbus. All these bizarre manifestations of archaeology have one thing in common: they are oversimple, convenient explanations of complex events in the past, explanations based on such archaeological data as their author cares to use.

These kinds of pseudoarchaeology belong to the realms of religious faith and science fiction. The real science of the past is based on rigorous procedures and meticulous data collection, its theorizing on constantly modified hypotheses tested against information collected in the field and laboratory—in short, archaeological, biological, and other evidence.

PREHISTORY, ARCHAEOLOGY, AND WORLD PREHISTORY

Human beings are unique and different from all other animals in both biological and cultural ways. We are the only animals that have a skeleton adapted for standing and walking upright—which leaves our hands free for other purposes than moving around. These physical traits are controlled by a powerful brain capable of abstract thought. The same brain allows us to communicate symbolically and orally through language and to develop highly diverse cultures—learned ways of behaving and adapting to our natural environments. The special features that make us human have evolved over hundreds of thousands of years.

The scientific study of the past is a search for answers to fundamental questions about human origins. How long ago did humans appear? When and how did they evolve? How can we account for the remarkable biological and cultural diversity of humankind? How did early humans settle the world and develop so many different societies at such different levels of complexity? Why did some societies cultivate the soil and herd cattle while others remained hunters and gatherers? Why did some peoples like, for example, the San hunter-gatherers of southern Africa or the Shoshone of the Great Basin in North America live in small family bands, while the ancient Egyptians and the Aztecs of Mexico developed highly elaborate civilizations (Figure 1.1)? When did more complex human societies evolve and why? The answers to these questions are the concern of scientists studying world prehistory.

Prehistory is defined by archaeologist as that portion of human history that extends back some 2.5 million years before the time of written documents and archives. In contrast, history, the study of human experience through documents, goes back only some 5,000 years in the Near East. Writing and written records came into use centuries later elsewhere in the world, in some parts of Africa and Asia only within the past century, when European powers annexed vast new territories and started to rule their new possessions. The study of prehistory is a multidisciplinary enterprise that involves not only archaeologists but scientists from many other disciplines, including biologists, botanists, geographers, geologists, and zoologists—to mention only a few. But archaeology is the primary source of information on human prehistory.

Archaeologist James Deetz calls the archaeologist a special type of anthropologist concerned not with living societies, but with ancient cul-

Figure 1.1 Temple of Amon at Karnak, Egypt. One of ancient Egypt's most important and spectacular temples.

tures. *Archaeology* consists of a broad range of scientific methods and techniques for studying the past, used carefully and in a disciplined way. The archaeologist studies the human societies of the remote and recent past, using the surviving material remains of their cultures to do so. Archaeology is a highly effective way of studying human cultures in the past and the ways in which they have changed over long periods of time. It covers the entire time span of human existence, from over 2.5 million years ago right up to the study of nineteenth century railroad stations and the garbage from modern industrial cities.

A century ago, most archaeologists worked in Europe and the Near East. They thought of human prehistory in very provincial terms, were convinced that all significant developments such as agriculture and civilization itself had originated in the area between Mesopotamia and the Nile. Today, archaeologists are at work all over the globe, in Africa, Alaska, and Australia. Thanks to universal dating methods like radiocarbon dating (page 17), we can date and compare prehistoric developments in widely separated parts of the world. We know, for example, that agriculture began in Syria in about 8000 B.C. and in central Africa about 2,000 years ago. We can date the first human occupation of Europe to about 700,000 years ago, and that of North America to about 15,000 years before present. This is the study of *world prehistory*, the prehistory of humankind evaluated not just from the perspective of a single region like the Near East, but from a global viewpoint.

MAJOR DEVELOPMENTS IN HUMAN PREHISTORY

World prehistory is concerned with the broad sweep of the human past, more specifically with four major developments (Table 1.1):

- The origins of humankind some 2.5 million years ago. We describe the ancestors of the first humans, the fossil evidence for our origins, and some of the behavioral changes and innovations that accompanied the appearance of our earliest forebears.
- The evolution of archaic *Homo erectus* and the origins of anatomically modern people, ourselves. These developments span a long period between about 1.5 million years ago and 15,000 years before present. We also describe the spread of *Homo sapiens* through the Old World and into the Americas, a process that ended about 15,000 years ago.

Table 1.1 MAJOR DEVELOPMENTS IN HUMAN PREHISTORY

A.D./B.C. Years B.P.	
A.D. 1532	Spanish conquest of Peru
A.D. 1	
3000 B.C.	Origins of civilization
	Metallurgy
10,000 B.P.	Origins of food production
15,000 B.P.	First settlement of the Americas
35,000 B.P.	First settlement of Australia
100,000 B.P.	Origins of modern humans
1.0 Million	Humans leave Africa
1.6 Million	*Homo erectus* in Africa
2.5 Million	Human origins

- The origins of more complex hunter-gatherer societies, of agriculture and animal domestication, sometimes called food production, after about 10,000 years ago. We evaluate the different theories developed to explain greater cultural and social complexity and why humans took up farming, and describe the early beginnings and spread of agriculture in the Near East, Europe, Asia, and the Americas.
- The origins of urbanized, literate civilization (state-organized societies) in about 3250 B.C. in the Near East and the development of similar, complex societies in other parts of the world in later millennia.

These major developments provide us with a broad framework for telling the story of prehistory. And central to this framework are the notions of time and space—the context of biological and cultural developments in the past. (For a brief summary of how archaeological research proceeds, see Figure 1.2.)[2]

LINEAR AND CYCLICAL TIME

Time. It rules our lives. We live by calendars, schedules, and clocks that measure it down to the smallest fraction of a second. To us, time unfolds inexorably in a kind of straight line, as it has since the beginning of human existence. The linear view of time seems entirely logical, even elementary, to Western eyes. We have a sense of linear, unraveling history that goes back through 5,000 years of recorded history to early Egypt and Mesopotamia. Ancient Egyptian civilization began in 3250 B.C.; Rome was founded in 753 B.C.; Christopher Columbus landed in the Bahamas on October 12, 1492; and The Declaration of Independence dates to July 4, 1776. These are landmarks along the ladder of historical chronology, which continues to unfold inexorably ever day, month, and year, as we live our lives.

Modern science calculates the total span of human existence to be about 2.5 million years, an imposing chronicle of ever more elaborate and diverse cultural experience. This perspective contrasts sharply with that of many non-Western peoples, both ancient and modern, who think of time not as a linear phenomenon, but as cyclical. In other words, history unfolds in an unending cycle to events that is destined to repeat itself again and again.

With this way of thinking, the past and the present are united, tied inextricably to one another in the same way that the spiritual and material

---

[2]Readers interested in archaeological method and theory should consult one of the standard texts on the subject listed in the Guide to Further Reading at the end of this book. No attempt is made to survey these methods in detail here.

A – The results of the research, the data, and interpretation are published in a scientific monograph or journal article. The site and research are now on permanent record for posterity.

B – Interpretation of the data is now undertaken, in the context of the research design, which is modified constantly as the research proceeds. This interpretation is based on the results of hypothesis testing during survey, excavation, and laboratory work.

C – The hypotheses generated at the beginning of the research are now tested against the analyzed data, again a process that takes place constantly as research and excavation proceed.

Analysis and data reduction are processes that begin as soon as archaeologists start collecting artifacts and other information in the field. While some of this work takes place in the field, most of it is undertaken back in the laboratory. It is now, too, that specialist data like animal bones, plant remains, or isotopic analysis or radiocarbon dating are sent out for examination by experts. Their reports form part of the analysis process and are critical to later stages of the research.

Publication

Interpretation

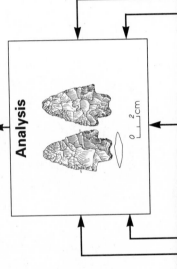

Analysis

0 2 cm

F – Guila Naquitz was published as a monograph edited by Kent Flannery: *Guila Naquitz: Archaic Foraging and Early Agriculture in Oaxaca, Mexico* (Academic Press, Orlando, 1986).

G – The core of the interpretation was an elaborate computer-based simulation that used the data from the excavations to test two hypotheses:

• What strategy led the occupants to select the mix of plants found on the living floors?

• How did this strategy change during the period of incipient agriculture?

Robert Reynolds developed an "adaptive computer model" for this purpose, incorporating the data from the excavations and laboratory work. His simulations showed that potential domesticates were probably first planted in wet years, and then, after they were proved reliable, in dry and average years. As time went on, plant cultivation assumed more importance in the diet and shifted from the thorn forest where people had originally concentrated their foraging activities into mesquite grassland, better suited for agriculture.

H – The cave was small enough to be excavated in its entirety, using small test trenches to identify the natural stratigraphy, then removing each living surface horizontally and separately. The entire site was excavated with trowels and brushes and the deposit passed through two screens of different sizes. Radiocarbon samples taken during the excavations dated the Guila Naquitz occupations to between 8750 and 6670 B.C.

Back in the laboratory, a team of nearly 20 specialists examined the finds, everything from chipped stone tools to tiny rodent bones. Others analyzed the distributions of artifacts on living surfaces, analyzed the division of labor at the site, assessed the nutritional value of the food remains.

I – Excavations were undertaken to develop a model to account for the underlying and more universal aspects of early plant domestication. They were also designed to tie this process into what was known about the cultures of the Valley of Oaxaca between 10,000 and 5000 B.C.

J – The site was discovered in January 1966 and excavated between February and May of the same year.

Data Collection

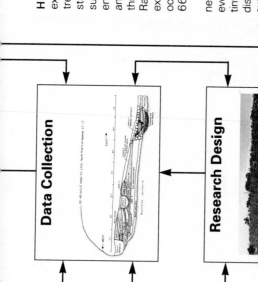

Research Design

Discovery

D – Data collection is a process that begins with initial site survey and continues right through excavations and all fieldwork. The excavation crew may include not only trained archaeologists but specialist experts on such topics as soil chemistry or animal bones. The collection process involves very accurate record keeping and the application of the initial research design. The hypotheses generated as part of this design are tested and modified constantly — as is the design — as data collection proceeds.

E – Archaeological research begins with the discovery of a site, or with a campaign of deliberate survey to find locations for later excavation. All research commences with the formulation of a formal research design, which includes not only background information, but objectives and hypotheses to be tested during the work, and a general theoretical framework for the fieldwork. A research design is the blueprint for survey and excavation, the working document for subsequent research. The best designs are highly flexible, designed to be easily modified as the work proceeds and objectives and hypotheses change.

Figure 1.2 **How archaeology works.** The process of archaeological research, as illustrated by excavations by Kent Flannery and a team of archaeologists at Guila Naquitz rockshelter, Valley of Oaxaca, Mexico.

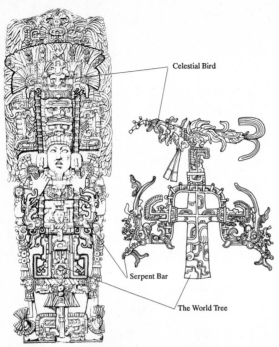

Celestial Bird

Serpent Bar

The World Tree

Figure 1.3 A Maya king from Mesoamerica dressed as the World Tree, which connected the spiritual Otherworld to the material world of humans.

worlds form a single plane of human existence (Figure 1.3). This cyclical view of time is based on the close relationship between hunters, foragers, and village farmers and their natural environments. It is also based on the eternal realities of human life: fertility and birth, life, growth, and death. The endlessly repeating seasons of planting and harvest, of game movements or salmon runs, and of ripening wild foods governed human existence in deeply significant ways. With such a dependence on the changes of seasons, it is hardly surprising that many ancient societies had cyclical views of time, albeit at times extremely long-term ones.

It is this cyclical view of the past that causes some non-Western societies to deny the importance of archaeology, of the view of the past reconstructed by scientific research. They believe that it is their close relationship to the natural world and the endless cycles of seasons that helps them define their existence, their place on earth and in the order of things. Such perspectives on the past are a matter of religious faith, not of science, which uses archaeological methods to reconstruct the long history of human biological and cultural diversity, of humanity as a whole.

DATING THE PAST

The chronology of world prehistory is based on stratigraphic observations (Figure 1.4), and on a variety of *chronometric* dating methods that take us far back into the past, long before the earliest historical records appear in the Near East about 5,000 years ago. Ninety-nine percent of all human existence lies in prehistoric times and can be measured only in millennia, and occasionally in centuries. The major chronological methods used by archaeologists span all of prehistory (Table 1.2):

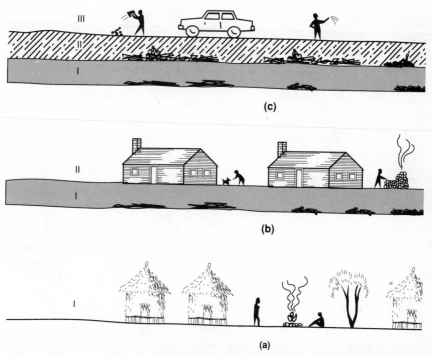

Figure 1.4 Superposition and stratigraphy. (a) A farming village built on virgin subsoil. After a time, the village is abandoned and the huts fall into disrepair. Their ruins are covered by accumulating soil and vegetation. (b) After an interval, a second village is built on the same site, with different architectural styles. This in turn is abandoned; the houses collapse into piles of rubble and are covered by accumulating soil. (c) Twentieth-century people park their cars on top of both village sites and drop litter and coins, which when uncovered reveal to the archaeologists that the top layer is modern.

An archaeologist digging this site would find that the modern layer is underlain by two prehistoric occupation levels; that square huts were in use in the upper of the two, which is the later under the law of superposition. Round huts are stratigraphically earlier than square ones here. Therefore village 1 is earlier than village 2, but the exact date of either, or how many years separate village 1 from village 2 cannot be known without further data.

Table 1.2   MAJOR CHRONOLOGICAL METHODS

Date	Method	Major developments
Modern times (after A.D. 1)	Historical documents; dendrochronology; imported objects	Columbus in the New World; Roman Empire
2,500 B.C.		
		Origins of cities
		Origins of agriculture
		Colonization of New World
40,000 B.C.	Radiocarbon dating (organic materials)	
75,000 B.C.	Still no chronometric dating method	
100,000 B.C.	Potassium-argon dating (volcanic materials)	*Homo sapiens sapiens*
500,000 B.C.		Early humans
5,000,000 B.C.		

Historical Records and Objects of Known Age (Present day back to about 3000 B.C. in some areas)

Historical records and objects of known age provide dates for recent centuries. In the Near East, 5,000 years of history are recorded in government archives and on thousands of clay tablets (Figure 9.2). But recorded history starts much later elsewhere — about 750 B.C. in the central Mediterranean, about 55 B.C. in Britain. The first written records for most of the New World began with the Spanish Conquest and parts of Africa entered "history" in A.D. 1890. In a few instances, the reading of ancient scripts has produced remarkably accurate time scales. For example, the decipherment of Maya hieroglyphs in the Mesoamerican lowlands has resulted in chronologies for powerful Maya lords that span many centuries.

Historical records span a tiny fraction of the human experience and cover very limited geographic areas. Fortunately, however, the literate civilizations of three or four thousand years ago traded their products far and wide. The ancient Egyptians exported fine ornaments to Crete; the

Cretans sent wine, olive oil, and painted pottery to the Nile. When archaeologist Arthur Evans excavated the magnificent Minoan civilization of Crete in 1900, he dated the labyrinthine Palace of Minos at Knossos by means of identical Minoan pottery fragments that had been excavated in faraway Egypt from levels whose precise date was known.

Similarly, coins and other objects of known age can be used to date buildings or refuse pits in which they were dropped centuries earlier. A bewildering array of dated objects are used by archaeologists dealing with the recent periods of prehistory. These include glass bottles and beads, seals, imported Chinese porcelain, even buttons from military uniforms. In each case the exact age of the object is known, so it can be used to establish the age of items associated with it.

Dendrochronology (Present day back to about 5000 B.C.)

Dendrochronology, or tree-ring dating, is another frequently used method of establishing chronology. Everyone is familiar with the concentric growth rings that can be seen in the cross section of a felled tree trunk. These rings of cambium between the wood and the bark appear in most trees. They are of special importance to archaeologists in areas such as the American Southwest, where the weather changes markedly with the seasons and growth is concentrated during a few months of the year. Each year's growth forms a distinct ring that varies in thickness, depending on the tree's age and on climatic variations. Climatic variations tend to occur in cycles of dry and wet years, which are reflected in patterns of thinner and thicker growth rings, respectively.

Tree-ring experts take borings (circular cores drilled out from the trunks) from living or felled trees. The ring sequences from the borer are then compared to each other and to a master chronology of rings built up from many trees with overlapping sequences tied to a log whose felling date is known. The patterns of thick and thin rings for the new sequence are matched to the master sequence (Figure 1.5). By using the California bristlecone pine, an extremely long-lived tree, tree-ring experts have developed a master chronology for the American Southwest extending more than 8,000 years into the past.

Tree-ring dating can be applied to long-felled wooden beams from Indian pueblos. Using this method, tree-ring experts have been able to construct an extremely accurate chronology for southwestern sites that extends as far back as 322 B.C. The ring sequences in the beams are linked to a master tree-ring chronology that is connected to modern times through living trees of known age. The dates of construction of such famed southwestern sites as Mesa Verde and Pueblo Bonito are known to within a few years (Chapter 7). Dendrochronology has also been used in other parts of North America, and with great success in Greece, Ireland, and Germany. The Irish tree-ring chronology goes back to before 5000 B.C.

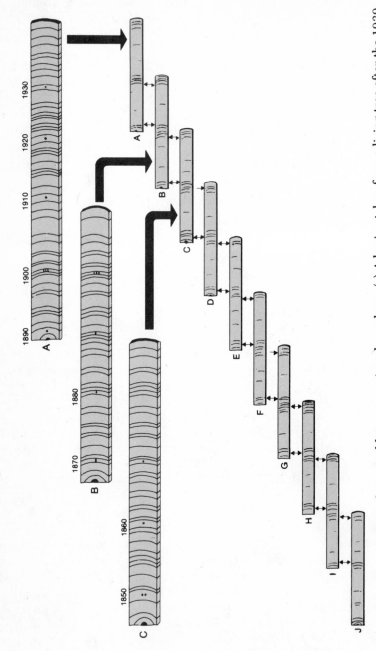

Figure 1.5 Dendrochronology. Building a tree-ring chronology. (a) A boring taken from a living tree after the 1939 growing season; (b)–(j) specimens taken from old houses and progressively older Southwestern ruins. The ring patterns match and overlap back into prehistoric times.

Radiocarbon (^{14}C) Dating (A.D. 1500 to about 40,000 years ago or earlier)

Radiocarbon (^{14}C) dating, developed by physicists J. R. Arnold and W. F. Libby in 1949, spans more than 40,000 years of later prehistory. Cosmic radiation produces neutrons that enter the earth's atmosphere and react with nitrogen to produce the isotope carbon -14 (^{14}C, or radiocarbon), which has eight rather than the usual six neutrons in its nucleus. With these additional neutrons, the nucleus is unstable and subject to radioactive decay. The *half-life*, the time it takes for half of the ^{14}C in any sample to decay, is 5,730 years.

The ^{14}C isotope is believed to behave just like ordinary carbon (^{12}C) from a chemical standpoint. Together with ^{12}C it enters the carbon dioxide of the atmosphere. Because living vegetation builds up its own organic matter by photosynthesis and by using atmospheric carbon dioxide, the ratio of ^{14}C to ^{12}C in living vegetation and in the animals that eat it is equal to that in the atmosphere. As soon as an organism dies, no further radiocarbon is incorporated in it. The radiocarbon present in the dead organism will continue to disintegrate, so that after 5,730 years half the original amount will be left; after about 11,400 years, one-quarter of the original amount will remain; and so on. Thus, measuring the amount of ^{14}C present in animal and plant remains enables us to determine the time that has elapsed since the death of the animal or plant. By calculating the difference between the amount of ^{14}C originally present and the amount now present, and comparing the difference with the known rate of decay, we can compute the elapsed time in years.

Radiocarbon samples can be taken from many ancient organic materials, including charcoal, burned bone, shell, hair, and other organic substances. Few artifacts made of these materials survive, so charcoal from hearths and other such features are commonly used. The samples themselves are collected with meticulous care from highly specific stratigraphic contexts so that precise locations can be dated.

The laboratory converts the sample to gas and pumps it into a proportional counter. The radioactive particle emissions are measured, usually for 24 hours. The results of the count are then converted to an age determination. The resulting date comes from the laboratory with a statistical plus or minus factor. For example 3600±200 years (200 years represents one standard deviation) means that the chances are two out of three that the correct date is between the span of 3400 and 3800. If we double the deviation, the chances are 19 out of 20 that the span 3200 to 4000 is correct. Thus, radiocarbon dates are statistical approximations rather than precise readings.

The conventional radiocarbon method relies on measurements of a beta ray decay rate to date the sample. A new approach uses accelerator mass spectrometry (AMS), which allows radiocarbon dating to be carried out by counting of ^{14}C atoms themselves rather than by counting radioactive disintegrations. This makes it possible to date tiny samples such as a speck of wood lodged inside a metal spear socket or an individual tree ring. In this way one can date, for example, a prehistoric corn cob from a southwestern cave. This is a much more precise way of dating early agricultural remains than merely using charcoal or wood from hearths or other features in the same layer as the corn fragments.

Arnold and Libby originally assumed that the concentration of radiocarbon in the atmosphere has remained constant through time, so that prehistoric samples, when they were alive, would contain the same amount of radiocarbon as living things do today. But in fact, we now know that changes in solar activity have considerably varied the concentration of radiocarbon in the atmosphere and in living things. Fortunately, however, it is possible to correct ^{14}C dates back to about 4500 B.C. by calibrating them with tree-ring chronologies. Some idea of the accuracy of ^{14}C dating over the past 6,000 years can be gathered from Figure 1.6.

Radiocarbon age A.D./B.C.	Calibrated age range A.D./B.C.
A.D. 1500	A.D. 1300 to 1515
1000	870 to 1230
500	265 to 640
1	420 to 5 B.C.
500 B.C.	820 to 400
1000	1530 to 905
1500	2345 to 1660
2000	2830 to 2305
2500	3505 to 2925
3000	3950 to 3640
3500	4545 to 3960
4000	5235 to 4575
4500	5705 to 5205
5000	6285 to 5445
5300	6585 to 5595
before 5500	Outside calibration range

Figure 1.6 Widely agreed upon calibrations for radiocarbon dates at 500-year intervals, from A.D. 1500 to 5300 B.C.

Calibration of dates earlier than 4500 b.c. is impossible because tree-ring chronologies are lacking so radiocarbon dates should be recognized for what they are — statistical approximations that date the deaths of once-living organisms.

Despite its limitations, radiocarbon dating is of great significance. ^{14}C samples have dated some Stone Age hunter-gatherer societies in tropical Africa to more than 40,000 years ago, and prehistoric bison kills on the North American plains to more than 9000 b.c. They have provided chronologies for the origins of agriculture and civilization all over the world. Radiocarbon dates provide a means for developing a truly global chronology that can equate major developments such as the origins of literate civilizations in such widely separated areas as China and Peru.

Potassium-Argon Dating (20,000 years ago to 2.5 million years before present and earlier)

Potassium-argon dating is another means of establishing chronology, used for dating archaeological sites earlier than 50,000 years ago.

Potassium (K) is one of the most abundant elements in the earth's crust and is present in nearly every mineral. In its natural form, potassium contains a small proportion of radioactive ^{40}K atoms. For every 100 ^{40}K atoms that decay, 11 percent become argon (Ar), an inert gas that can easily escape from its present material by diffusion when lava and other molten rocks are formed. As volcanic rocks form by crystallization, the concentration of Ar drops to almost nothing, but the decay of ^{40}K continues, and 11 percent of every 100 ^{40}K atoms will become ^{40}Ar. It is possible therefore, using a spectrometer, to measure the concentration of ^{40}Ar that has accumulated since the rock formed. Geologists use this method to date volcanic rocks ranging in age from 4 to 5 billion years old to 100,000 years before the present.

Many archaeological sites, such as those occupied by early humans at Olduvai Gorge in East Africa, were formed during periods of intense volcanic activity. Nearby volcanoes spewed ash and lava, which sometimes underlies and overlies places where human tools and broken animal bones lie. Potassium-argon samples from Olduvai dated early hominids to at least 1.75 million years ago. Even earlier dates come from fossil-bearing sites at Hadar in Ethiopia and from Koobi Fora in northern Kenya, where stone artifacts and animal bones have been dated to about 2.4 million years before the present.

Like ^{14}C dates, potassium-argon dates have a standard deviation, usually on the order of a few tens of thousands of years for early human sites. On the other hand, because many of the world's most important early archaeological sites are in volcanically active areas, we are fortunate in having at least a provisional chronology for the earliest chapters of human evolution.

These proven, and other more experimental, dating methods provide us with a provisional time scale for human prehistory. Potassium-argon dates place human origins at least as early as 2.5 million years ago and the appearance of more advanced humans, *Homo erectus*, at about 1.5 million years ago. Radiocarbon dates assign the appearance of modern humans in Europe to about 35,000 to 45,000 years ago, the earliest art traditions to about 30,000 years ago, and the origins of agriculture and animal domestication in the Near East to before 8000 B.C. We know that Mesopotamians were living in sizable city-states by 3200 B.C., and that the Olmec civilization of lowland Mexico was flourishing before 1000 B.C. Tree-ring chronologies date the Anasazi pueblos of Mesa Verde to about A.D. 1150, and historical dates and artifacts of known age enable us to date not only Maya civilization in Mesoamerica, but hundreds of late prehistoric sites in Europe and the Mediterranean. Hence, we have developed an approximate chronology for a truly global history and prehistory of humankind.

SPACE

Space—not the limitless space of the heavens, but a precisely defined location for every find made during an archaeological survey and excavation—is the other vital dimension of archaeological context. Every archaeological find, be it a tiny pin or a large palace, has an exact location in latitude, longitude, and depth, which together identify any point in space absolutely and uniquely. When carrying out surface surveys or excavations, archaeologists use special methods to record the precise positions of sites, artifacts, dwellings, and other finds. They locate the position of each site on an accurate survey map so that they can use the grid coordinates on the map to define the location in precise terms. When investigating a site, they lay out recording grids made up from equal squares over the entire site, using the grids to record the exact position of every object on the surface or in the trenches (Figure 1.7).

Distributions and Settlement Patterns

Spatial location is indispensable to archaeologist because it enables them to establish the distances between objects or dwellings, between entire settlements, or between settlements and key vegetational zones and landmarks. Such distances may amount to only a few inches, or they may extend for hundreds of miles as a team of fieldworkers traces the distribution of traded luxury goods in dozens of settlements. Thus, archaeologists think of space on two general scales: the distribution of artifacts within a settlement and the *settlement pattern*, the placement of the settlements themselves over the landscape.

Context in space is closely tied to people's behavior. Archaeologists examine both an artifact itself and its association with other artifacts to gain insight into human behavior. For example, Belgian archaeologists

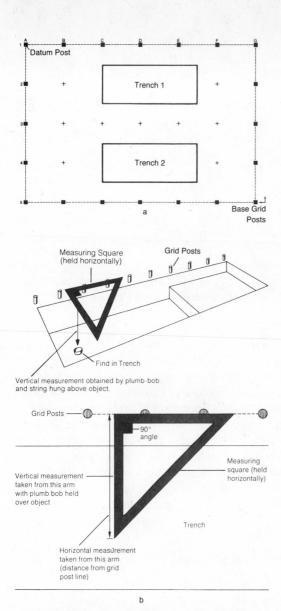

Figure 1.7 Recording the provenance of archaeological finds. (a) Two trenches laid out with a grid. (b) Three-dimensional recording of the position of an object using the grid squares.

investigated a 9,000-year-old hunting camp in a sandy clearing at Meer in northern Belgium. By plotting all of the stone fragments on the ancient ground surface, they were able to identify not only a camping area but an outlying scatter of stone fragments where one or two people had sat down and fashioned several flint artifacts. The spatial relationships among the stone chips enabled them to reconstruct what had happened 9,000 years ago in astounding detail. By fitting together the stone flakes, they were able to replicate the stoneworking technique, and even to show that one of the workers had been left-handed! Such investigations depend not only on meticulous excavation but also on the application of a fundamental principle of archaeology: the law of association.

The Law of Association

This law states that an artifact is contemporary with the other objects found in the archaeological level in which it is found (Figure 1.8). The proof that humanity was far older than the 6,000 years of Biblical chronology came when scientists found ancient stone hand axes in association with the bones of apparently older extinct animals. The mummy of the Egyptian Pharaoh Tutankhamun was associated with an astonishing treasury of household possessions and ceremonial objects. This association provided unique information about ancient Egyptian court life in 1323 B.C.

The law of association is of great importance when one is ordering artifacts in chronological sequences. Many prehistoric societies buried their dead with grave furniture — clay pots, bronze ornaments, seashells, or fine stone axes. In some cases, the objects buried with a corpse were obviously in use when their owner died. Occasionally they were heirlooms passed down from generation to generation. Together, they constitute an association of artifacts, a *grave group* that may be found duplicated in dozens of other contemporary sepulchers. But later graves may be found to contain quite different furniture or vessels of a slightly altered form. Obviously some cultural changes occurred in the interval between the burials. When dozens of grave groups are analyzed, the associations and changing styles of artifacts may provide a basis for classifying the burials according to different chronological styles (Figure 1.9).

Assemblages, Cultures, and Culture Areas

Human behavior can be individual and unique, shared with other members of one's family, or common to all members of the community. All these levels of cultural behavior should, theoretically, be reflected in artifact patterns and associations in the archaeological record (Table 1.3). For example, the iron projectile point found in the backbone of a British villager killed by a Roman legionary during a battle at Maiden Castle, England, in A.D. 43 is clearly the consequence of a single person's behavior, but that behavior is obviously related to the common cultural behavior of the warrior's society — the entire community at Maiden Castle resisted the Roman attack.

Shared human behavior on a larger scale is reflected not only in artifacts but also in the remains of houses and nonportable structures

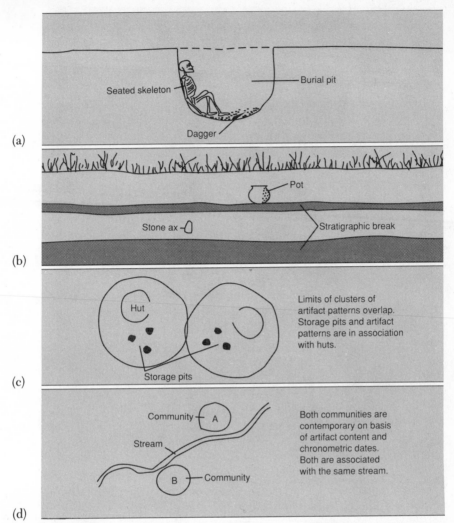

Figure 1.8 The law of association. (a) A skeleton associated with a single dagger and level II; (b) a pot and a stone ax, separated by a stratigraphic break, not in association; (c) two contemporary household clusters associated with each other; (d) an association of two communities that are contemporary.

associated with them, such as storage pits and ovens, hearths, and sleeping benches, and in community settlement patterns. For example, some early prehistoric Mexican villages in the Valley of Oaxaca consisted of groups of square, thatched houses. Each dwelling contained subassemblages that reflected the behavior of individual males and females. These included hearths and the artifacts lying around them that were evidence of domestic activity and areas where obsidian tools were manufactured. Together, the household groups in the village reflect the activities of the entire community (Figure 1.10).

Figure 1.9 A grave group. A Classic Maya collective burial at Gualan in the Motagua Valley of Guatemala. Clay vessels and ornaments were associated with the skeletons.

Many activities took place within human communities—butchering animals, cooking, sleeping, manufacture of stone tools, butchering of animals, shelling of nuts. Very often, each of these activities was carried out in a specific area. Many activities were associated with characteristic toolkits or artifact patterns that are preserved in the ground. By noting the locations of tools and other finds, archaeologists can map activity areas and use their plans to compare activities at different villages or within the quarters of, say, a large ancient Egyptian town.

Archaeological cultures consist of the material remains of human culture preserved at a specific space and time at several sites. They are the archaeological equivalent of a human society. Big-game hunting, long-distance trade, major religious ceremonies, and other activities are often shared by dozens of communities scattered over a large area. But these

Table 1.3 HUMAN BEHAVIOR AS REFLECTED IN ARCHAEOLOGICAL CLASSIFICATIONS

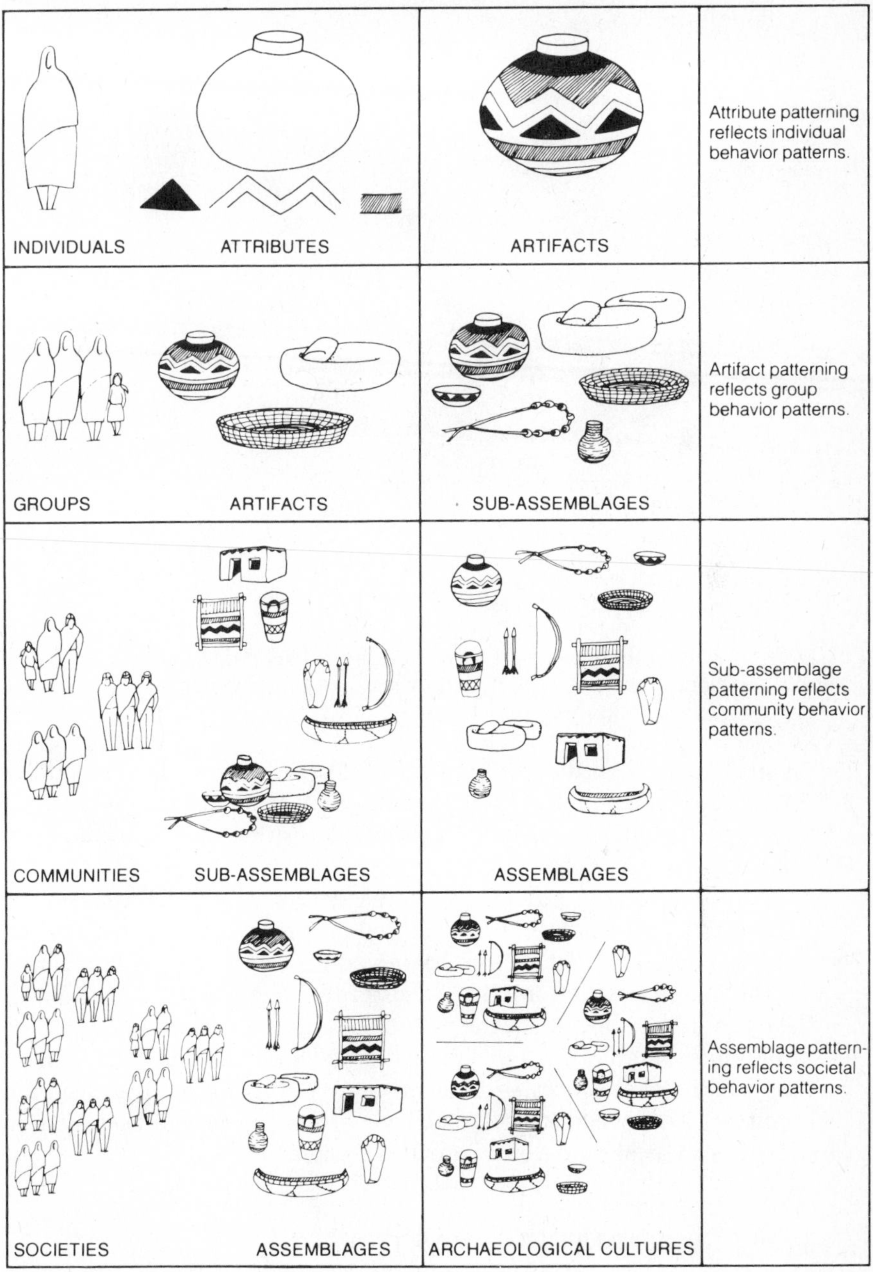

Figure 4.6 Human behavior as reflected in archaeological classifications. The hierarchy begins with attributes and artifacts and ends with entire archaeological cultures.

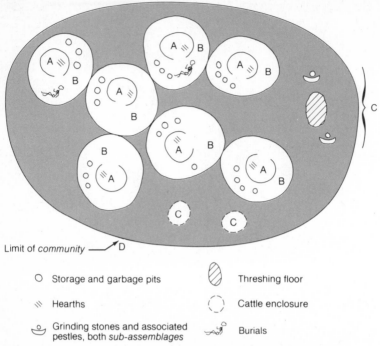

Limit of *community* ——D

O	Storage and garbage pits		Threshing floor
\\\\	Hearths		Cattle enclosure
	Grinding stones and associated pestles, both *sub-assemblages*		Burials

Figure 1.10 A hypothetical prehistoric farming village, showing (a) houses, (b) household areas, (c) activity areas, (d) the community.

behaviors can be identified only by the patterns of assemblages at different sites. Consistent patterns represent an archaeological culture, the archaeological equivalent of a human society. (For more on the concept of culture, see Chapter 2.)

A *culture area* is the geographic area within which the assemblages that make up a unique culture are defined in time and space. An example from New Zealand might be the Maori culture area, the region within which the characteristic toolkits of these remarkable people are found.

For the archaeologist, the concepts of culture, time, and space are absolutely inseparable. All our knowledge of human prehistory is based on the two critical concepts — time and space — that make up archaeological context. These concepts are derived from survey and excavation, investigations based on careful research design.

THE PRESENT AND THE PAST

The study of human prehistory extends back from modern times deep into the remote past. It is as if we are looking back into prehistoric times through the wrong end of a telescope. We can discern relatively recent cultures like those of the Aztecs or the sixteenth century Pueblo Indians of the Southwest with relative clarity, even if our knowledge is lamentably incomplete. Further back into the past the images become dimmer, more blurred, the scale smaller. We cannot use the lifeways of, say, modern arctic hunter-gatherers or Maya farmers from Guatemala to interpret this remoter past. The first native Americans of 15,000 years ago, the late Ice hunter-gatherers who flourished in Europe 25,000 years ago — these peoples lived in a world that is unimaginably remote from our own. And that of the archaic humans of earlier prehistory, of a quarter of a million years ago or more, is so far distant that is hard for us to comprehend in realistic terms. Such, then, is the objective of world prehistory — to understand prehistoric human behavior in a past separated from our own not only by thousands of years, but by environmental and social challenges very different to those we face today. In Chapter 2, we examine some of the ways in which archaeologists have tried to interpret prehistory and to recreate the prehistoric worlds of thousands, even millions, of years ago.

Chapter
2

Explaining Prehistory

World prehistory is the study of human cultural evolution over immensely long periods of time. Since the earliest days of archaeology, students of the past have tried not only to describe the past, but to interpret the major developments of human prehistory. This chapter examines some of the mechanisms and approaches that archaeologists have developed to explain ancient culture change.

CULTURE, CULTURE HISTORY, AND CULTURAL PROCESS

The concept of culture provides a framework that archaeologists can use to both describe and explain the prehistoric past. Most archaeologists define *culture* as the primary nonbiological means by which human societies adapt to and accommodate their natural environment. Under this definition, culture represents the cumulative intellectual resources of human societies. These resources are passed from one generation to the next by the spoken word and by example. Culture regulates relationships with natural environments through technology, social institutions, and belief systems.

When archaeologists study the tangible remains of the past and the ways in which they were discarded by their creators or users, they construct an image of the shared behavior of a group of prehistoric people.

Culture is an adaptive system. It is the interface between ourselves, the environment, and other human societies. Our unique biological traits and our culture are humanity's only means of adaptation. Culture is always adjusting to environmental, technological, and societal change. The key word, however, is system, for all human cultures have many interacting components, or subsystems, that interact with one another and with the natural environment.

A *cultural system* is "the means whereby a human society adapts to its physical and social environment. It is made up of many structurally different parts which articulate with one another within the system." The links between cultural and environmental systems are such that a change in one system is linked to changes in the other. Thus, a major objective of archaeology is to understand the linkage between the various parts of cultural and environmental systems as they are reflected in archaeological data. Archaeologists are profoundly interested in cultural systems within their environmental context. To be workable, any human cultural system depends on its ability to adapt to the natural environment.

A cultural system can be broken down into all manner of subsystems: religious and ritual subsystems, economic subsystems, and so on. Each of these is linked to the others. Changes in one system, such as a shift from cattle herding to wheat growing, will cause reactions in many others. Such relationships give the archaeologist a measure of the constant changes and variations in human culture that can accumulate over long periods, as cultural systems respond to external and internal stimuli. Many of the interacting components are highly perishable. So far, no one has been able to dig up a religious philosophy or an unwritten language. Archaeologists work with the *tangible* remains of human activity that still survive in the ground, such as clay potsherds and the foundations of dwellings. But these surviving remains of human activity are radically affected by *intangible* aspects of human culture. For instance, the Moche people of the Peruvian coast buried their great lords with elaborate gold and copper ornaments, with fine textiles and elaborate ceremonial regalia. Thanks to Walter Alva's excavations in the great mounds at Sipan, we know of one lord who was buried in A.D. 290 with a golden rattle that showed a Moche warrior in full regalia beating a prisoner on the head with his war club (Chapter 12). The artistic masterpieces buried with the Lord of Sipan reflected a culture with an elaborate symbolism and complex religious beliefs that formed part of the intangible world of the Moche.

When studying human prehistory, archaeologists study culture history, ancient lifeways, and cultural process.

Culture history is the *description* of human cultures that extends back thousands of years into the past. Culture history is derived from the study of archaeological sites, and the artifacts and structures in them, within the context of time and space. By investigating groups of sites and the artifacts found there, it is possible to construct local and regional sequences of human cultures that extend over centuries, even millennia.

The study of past lifeways — that is, how people have made their living in the past — involves the examination of prehistoric cultures within their environmental context. Environmental data come from many sources, including ancient plant remains, fossil pollen grains, and animal bones. Ancient subsistence patterns, and even diet, can be reconstructed from food residues such as animal bones, carbonized seeds, and fish remains. This is also descriptive archaeology, but it relates archaeological cultures to the complex and continually changing patterns of settlement, subsistence, and environmental influences.

Cultural process is the ways in which cultures change. The study of cultural process provokes intense theoretical debate among archaeologists, who assume that archaeology is far more than merely a descriptive activity and that it is possible to explain how cultural change occurred in the remote past.

Every cultural system is in a constant state of change. Its various political, social, and technological subsystems adjust to changing circumstances. We ourselves live in a time of rapid cultural change in which there are measurable differences between decades, let alone centuries. Consider the many small changes in automobile design that have occurred in the past few decades. In themselves, the changes often are not very significant, but the *cumulative* effect of several years of steady change toward safer cars is striking — air bags, energy-absorbing bumpers, padded steering wheels, and so on. The automobile of today is very different from that of the 1960s, and many of the changes are due to stricter government safety regulations, which in turn result from greater safety consciousness on the part of consumers. Here we see a major cumulative change in part of our enormous technological subsystem. By examining the relationships between these technological changes and the political and social subsystems, we can understand the processes through which culture has changed.

To study cultural process is to examine the processes by which human cultures change throughout time. Most processes of culture change in human prehistory were cumulative, occurring slowly over a long time period. They were the result of adaptations to constantly changing external environments. Cultural systems were constantly adjusting and evolving in response to internal and external feedback.

The fundamental questions about prehistory revolve around culture change. How did anatomically modern humans, *Homo sapiens*, evolve their more advanced cultures? What cultural processes came into play when people began to cultivate the soil, or when complex and elaborate urban societies developed in the Near East just over 5,000 years ago? Clearly, no single element in a cultural system is the primary cause of cultural change, because a complex range of factors — rainfall, vegetation, technology, social restrictions, and population density, to mention only a few — interact with one another and react to a change in any element in the system.

From the ecologist's point of view, therefore, human culture is merely one element of the ecosystem, a mechanism whereby people adapt to a particular environment. This viewpoint provides one common framework for much modern archaeological research and for world prehistory.

THE MECHANISMS OF CULTURE CHANGE

Culture history is a sound way of describing the past, but it is of minimal use for studying variations in different prehistoric cultures, for answering fundamental questions about the nature of culture change in the past. Culture history is based on what is called a *normative* view of culture, one that assumes that abstract rules govern what a human culture considers normal behavior. The normative view assumes that surviving artifacts such as stone tools and potsherds display stylistic and other changes that represent the changing norms of human behavior through time. But the archaeological record does not invariably reflect an orderly and smooth chronicle of culture change. A radically new artifact inventory may suddenly appear in contemporary occupation layers at several sites, while earlier toolkits suddenly vanish. A culture's economy may change rapidly within a century much as the plow revolutionized agricultural methods. How do such changes come about? What *mechanisms* of cultural change were at work to cause major and minor alterations in the archaeological record?

Four descriptive models are used to characterize culture change: inevitable variation, invention, diffusion, and migration.

Inevitable Variation

As people learn the behavior patterns of their society, inevitably some differences in learned behavior will appear from generation to generation. These, although minor in themselves, accumulate over a long period of time, especially in isolated populations. The snowball effect of inevitable variation among isolated, thinly scattered populations can be considerable. For example, projectile point forms varied considerably between different, isolated big-game hunting groups on the North American Great Plains in 4000 B.C., even though they all pursued the same animals with much the same techniques. But inevitable variation should not be confused with what happens when a society recognizes that certain culture changes or inventions may be advantageous, like, for example, cultivating the soil.

Invention

Humans are inquisitive, constantly innovating, having ideas. Invention is the creation or evolution of a new idea. The term invention refers to new ideas that originate in a human culture, either by accident or by design. All innovations in human society have their origin in such actions or chance occurrences, but only a very few inventions are truly unique and not introduced from outside by some other culture. In the early days of archaeology, scholars assumed that solitary geniuses developed the great ideas of prehistory. These innovations, such as agriculture, then spread all over the world as other societies realized how important the new ideas were. But as the importance of environment and adaptation in the development of human culture have become better understood, this simple view has been rejected. It is one thing to invent something, quite another to have it accepted by society as a whole. In general, technological innovations, like for example, the plow, are more readily accepted than social or religious innovations, for they are less likely to conflict with established value systems. The problem for the archaeologist is to recognize an original invention, something that can only be done by recognizing not only the invention itself but the prototypes that led to its final refinement— for example, a new form of axe head or simpler versions of a plow blade.

The genius of humanity was that it recognized opportunities when they came along and adapted to new circumstances, often in similar ways in widely separated areas, resulting in independent invention of very similar ideas.

Diffusion

The spread of ideas, over short or long distances, is termed diffusion. Ideas can be transmitted in many ways other than by the movements of entire societies or communities. Neither the exchange of ideas nor of technological innovations necessarily involve actual movements of people. Diffusion can result from regular trade between neighboring communities. Commerce of any kind implies a two-sided relationship, in which both parties exchange goods, services, and, of course, ideas such as a new religious belief. For instance, the highly distinctive Chavin religious beliefs and art style were diffused widely through highland and lowland Peru in about 900 B.C. (Figure 2.1) (Chapter 12).

Migration

Migration involves movements of entire societies that deliberately decide to expand their spheres of influence. Spanish conquistadors occupied Mexico, the Polynesians deliberately voyaged from island to island across the Pacific. In each case, new land masses were found by purposeful exploration, then colonized by small numbers of people.

Figure 2.1 Chavin art: sculpted head from the outer wall of the temple at Chavin de Huantar showing a shaman being transformed into a jaguar.

Smaller-scale migrations are more commonplace, such as when a group of foreigners move into another region and settle there as an organized group. Such was the case when a group of Oaxacan merchants from highland Mexico moved to the rival city of Teotihuacan in the first few centuries A.D. and settled in a residential area. Oaxacans lived in the same precinct for many centuries. There are other types of migrations, too, unorganized movements of slaves and artisans, and of people fleeing religious persecution.

Invention, diffusion, and migration are far too general cultural mechanisms to explain the ever-changing relationships between human cultures and their environments. The identification of these mechanisms is largely a descriptive activity, based on artifacts and other material remains. The explanation of culture change requires more sophisticated research models that reflect the interaction of cultural systems with the natural environment and other complex systems.

CULTURE AS ADAPTATION

In the 1950s, American anthropologists Julian Steward and Leslie White developed what they called *cultural ecology*, the study of the total way in which human populations adapt to and transform their environments. Archaeologists who study cultural ecology are concerned with how prehistoric cultures as systems interacted with other systems: with other human cultures, the biotic community (other living things around them), and their physical environment. This is what is often called *culture as adaptation*.

Culture as adaptation — this phrase is behind most contemporary interpretations of world prehistory. Leslie White called culture "man's extrasomatic [outside the body] means of adaptation." Culture is the result of human beings' unique ability to create and infuse events and objects with meaning that can be appreciated, decoded, and understood, with, among other things, ideology. Thus, human cultures differ greatly from place to place and from time to time, resulting in variations in prehistoric material culture — the data for studying prehistory.

Under the culture as adaptation rubric, human behavior is an adaptation not to a single site but to environmental regions. Thus, the archaeologist has to study not individual sites but entire regions. The archaeological record is not just a system of structured sites, but a continuous pattern of artifact distribution and density over the landscape. As individuals and groups hunt, forage, or farm their way across this landscape, they leave behind material remains of their presence, a record that reflects their continual behavior within the region.

MULTILINEAR CULTURAL EVOLUTION

The culture as adaptation approach attempts to interpret cultural variation and adaptation on a regional basis over long periods of time. This strategy means that the archaeologist must pay close attention to the relationships between ecological and social systems. Under this theory of *multilinear evolution* (evolution along multiple tracks), each human society pursues its own evolutionary course, determined by the long-term success of an adaptation, via technology and social institutions, to its natural environment. Multilinear evolution is widely used as a general framework for interpreting world prehistory, which witnessed occasional dramatic incidents of cultural change.

Some societies achieve a broad measure of equilibrium with their environment, in which adaptive changes consist of little more than some refinements in technology and the fine-tuning of organizational structures. Others become involved in cycles of growth that are triggered by external environmental change or from within society. If these changes involve either greater food supplies or population growth, there can be accelerated growth resulting from the need to feed more people or the deployment of an enlarged food surplus. Such was probably the case in parts of the Near East in 8000 B.C., when some communities living in favored regions began cultivating wild cereal grasses to expand their food supplies (Figure 2.2) (Chapter 6). Within generations of the first experiments with farming, many Near Eastern groups were depending heavily on cereal crops. Major technological and social changes followed. People

Figure 2.2 Experimental harvesting of wild-type einkorn, a widely domesticated cereal crop with a replica of an ancient Egyptian flint-bladed sickle.

now settled in permanent villages under entirely different social conditions.

Every society has its growth limits imposed by the environment and available technology, and some environments, like, say, Egypt's Nile Valley, have more potential for growth than others. Certain types of sociopolitical organization, such as centralized control of specialized labor, are more efficient than others. Adaptive changes triggered technological innovations that led to increased food supplies and higher population densities.

STAGES OF SOCIAL DEVELOPMENT

This sophisticated concept of multilinear evolution has led a number of archaeologists to talk of stages of social development in prehistory. These should not be thought of as universal stages through which all societies pass, as some Victorian anthropologists once argued, but as degrees of social development that are achieved by many groups quite independently, in many environments. Many scholars tend to think in terms of two broad categories: prestate societies and state-organized societies.

Prestate Societies

Prestate societies are societies on a small scale, based on the community, band, or village. They vary greatly in their degrees of political integration and are sometimes divided into three loosely defined categories (Figure 2.3):

1. *Bands* are associations of families that may not exceed 25 to 60 people. They are knit together by close social ties; they were the dominant form of social organization for most of prehistory, from the earliest times up to the origins of food production some 10,000 years ago.

2. *Tribes* are clusters of bands that are linked by clans (formal kin groups). A clan is not a tribe, which contains people from many kin groups, but a group of people linked by common ancestral ties, which serve as connections between widely scattered communities. Clans are important because they are a form of social linkage that gives people a sense of common identity with a wider world than their own immediate family and relatives. Many early farming societies throughout the world can be classified as tribal societies.

3. *Chiefdoms* are societies headed by individuals with unusual ritual, political, or entrepreneurial skills and are often hard to distinguish from tribes. Society is still kin-based but more hierarchical, with power concentrated in the hands of kin leaders responsible for acquiring and then redistributing food and other resources throughout the group.

Chiefdoms tend to have higher population densities and to display the first signs of social ranking, something that is a mark of a state-organized society. They vary greatly in their elaboration. For example, Chumash Indian chiefdoms in southern California were based on intensive exploitation of fish, sea mammals, and plant foods. Chumash chiefs were spiritual leaders who engaged in long-distance trade, and often lived in large, permanent communities. In contrast, the complex Mississippian chiefdoms of the Midwest and southeastern United States flourished during the early second millennium A.D. Their chiefs enjoyed political power and prestige over much larger areas than their Chumash contemporaries. They maintained trade networks and ritual contacts between different river valleys sometimes hundreds of miles apart (Chapter 7).

State-organized Societies

State-organized societies (civilizations) operated on a large scale, with centralized political and social organization. Such societies were ruled by a tiny elite, who held monopolies over strategic resources, including food surpluses, and used force to enforce authority. Their social organization can be likened to a pyramid, with a single ruler at the apex and stratified

	Prestate			
	Band	Tribe	Chiefdom	State-Organized Societies
Total numbers	Less than 100	Up to few thousand	5,000 – 20,000+	Generally 20,000+
Social Organization	Egalitarian Informal leadership	Segmentary society Pan-tribal associations Raids by small groups	Kinship-based ranking under hereditary leader High-ranking warriors	Class-based hierarchy under king or emperor Armies
Economic Organization	Mobile hunter-gathers	Settled farmers Pastoralist herders	Central accumulation and redistribution Some craft specialization	Centralized bureaucracy Tribute-based Taxation Laws
Settlement Pattern	Temporary camps	Permanent villages	Fortified centers Ritual centers	Urban: cities, towns Frontier defenses Roads
Religious Organization	Shamans	Religious elders Calendrical rituals	Hereditary chief with religious duties	Priestly class Pantheistic or monotheistic religion
Architecture	Temporary shelters	Permanent huts Burial mounds Shrines	Large-scale monuments	Palaces, temples, and other public buildings
	Paleolithic skin tents, Ukraine	*Neolithic shrine, Çatal Hüyük, Turkey*	*Stonehenge, England – final form*	*Pyramids at Giza* / *Castillo Chicén itzá, Mexico*
Archaeological Examples	All Paleolithic societies, including Paleo-Indians	All early farmers (Neolithic/Archaic)	Many early metalworking and Formative societies Mississippian, USA Smaller African kingdoms	All ancient civilizations e.g. in Mesoamerica, Andes Near East, India and China, Greece and Rome
Modern Examples	Eskimos Kalahari San Australian Aborigines	Pueblos, Southwest USA New Guinea Highlanders Nuer and Dinka in East Africa	Northwest Coast Indians, USA 18th-century Polynesian chiefdoms in Tonga, Tahiti, Hawaii	All modern states

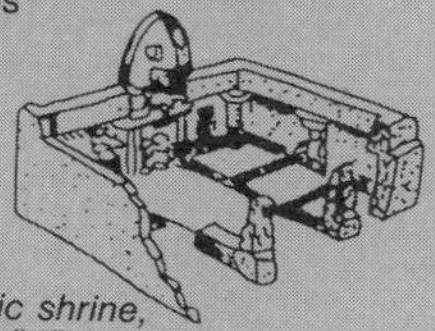

Figure 2.3 General categories of prehistoric human societies. (Modified from **Renfrew and Bahn**, 1991.)

classes of nobles, priests, bureaucrats, merchants, artisans, and commoners below. Some state-organized societies, like that of the Sumerians of Mesopotamia, were first ruled by priest-bureaucrats, then gradually came under the rule of secular kings, who sometimes became despotic monarchs, often with alleged divine powers. They presided over complex political structures and many permanent government institutions, including a priesthood and a standing army. Such societies were organized on the assumption of social inequality (Figure 2.4). Most were based in large cities, with populations that ranged upward from 5,000 people.

The state-organized society was based on intensive agricultural production, which often relied heavily on irrigation or swamp farming—carefully watered lands that yielded several bountiful crops a year. These carefully administered and controlled agricultural works were the means by which society supported thousands of nonfarmers, the artisans, officials, traders, and priests, also city-dwellers. State economies were based on the centralized accumulation of capital and social status through tribute and taxation. Long-distance trade and the division of labor, also craft

Figure 2.4 Assyrian King Assurbanipal rides out on a ceremonial lion hunt in the seventh century B.C. Assyrian monarchs were despotic rulers who presided over the fates of thousands of less privileged people.

specialization, were often characteristic of early states, as were advances toward record keeping, science, and mathematics, and usually some form of written script.

State organization was typical of the early literate civilizations—of the ancient Egyptians and Sumerians, the Harappan of the Indus Valley in Pakistan, of the Shang civilization of China, and the Olmec, Maya, Aztec, and Andean civilizations of the Americas (Chapters 9–12).

Civilizations

The term civilization has a ready, everyday meaning. According to the dictionary, it implies civility, a measure of decency in the behavior of an individual in a civilization. Such definitions invariably reflect ethnocentrism or value judgments, because what is civilized behavior in one society might be antisocial or baffling in another. For instance, the Aztecs of sixteenth century Mexico considered human sacrifice a socially acceptable custom, for it was deeply embedded in their belief in the need to nourish the sun god with human hearts. Spanish Catholics who witnessed these rites found them totally repulsive and uncivilized. By the same token, the Aztecs were baffled by Christian rituals and religious beliefs.

From the scientific point of view, such simplistic understandings are useless, for there were many early civilizations with quite different social and cultural institutions. For the purposes of this book, the term civilization coincides with a state-organized society, whose attributes were described above.

We should make one final distinction. *Pre-industrial civilizations* function with the aid of human and animal labor. *Industrial civilizations* use fossil fuels to drive machines to achieve many of the same tasks, and for mass production of goods. All early civilizations fall, of course, in the pre-industrial category.

MULTICAUSAL CULTURE CHANGE

Multilinear cultural evolution is the vital force that combines systems approaches to human culture and cultural ecology into a closely knit, highly flexible way of studying and explaining cultural process. The culture as adaptation approach requires that one look at cultural change in the context of the interrelationships among many variables. Thus, there is no one prime agent of cultural evolution that caused, say, food production in ancient Syria or Maya civilization in Mesoamerica (the area of Central America where prehistoric states flourished). Rather a series of important variables, all with complex interrelationships, acted together to trigger cultural change.

Kent Flannery of the University of Michigan applied this approach to early agriculture in Mexico's southern highlands. He discovered that between 10,000 and 4,000 years ago the highland peoples relied on five basic food sources—deer, rabbits, maguey cactus, tree legumes, and prickly pears—for their sustenance. By careful prediction of the seasons of each food, they could schedule their hunting and gathering at periods of abundance and before wild animals gained access to the ripe plants. Flannery assumed that the southern highlands and their inhabitants were part of a large environmental system consisting of many subsystems—economic, botanical, social, and so on—that interacted with one another. Then something happened to nudge the food procurement system toward the deliberate growing of wild grasses (for fuller discussion, see Chapter 6).

Flannery's excavations at dry caves dating to between 7,000 and 4,000 years ago showed wild maize cobs slowly increasing in size and other signs of genetic change. He suggested that the people began to experiment with the deliberate planting of maize and other grasses, intentionally expanding the areas where they would grow. After a long period of time, these intentional deviations in the food procurement system caused many changes in the cultural system. For example, the importance of wild grass collecting increased at the expense of other collecting activities until it became the dominant one. Eventually, the people created a self-perpetuating food procurement system, with its own vital scheduling demands of planting and harvesting, that competed with earlier systems and won out because it was more durable. By 4,000 years ago, the highly nutritious bean and corn diet of Mexican highland peoples was well established.

The Flannery research shows that, when we seek to explain the major and minor events of prehistory, we have to consider the ways in which change takes place, the processes and mechanisms of change, and the social and economic stresses (population pressure, game scarcity, and so on) that trigger these mechanisms. Such multicausal models are a far cry from theories that speak of ancient Egyptian voyages or brilliant, solitary inventors. They require rigorous methodologies for identifying the many factors involved, using data that consists, for the most part, of material remains such as potsherds and stone implements. These research methods are still in their infancy and depend, to a considerable extent, on data gathered from living, non-Western societies.

ANALOGY: THE ETHNOGRAPHIC PRESENT

Analogy, comparing the cultures and artifacts of living peoples with those of prehistoric ones, has long been a staple method for interpreting details of world prehistory. However, it is an approach fraught with difficulty.

Everywhere in the world, archaeologists work back from the known present into the past, from historic Pueblo Indian settlements, modern

African villages, from contemporary Australian Aboriginal camps. These historic societies, be they Aztec, Inca, Pueblo, or Zulu, represent something that is often referred to as the *ethnographic present,* prehistoric culture in its so-called pristine condition, before the contaminating influences of Western civilization transformed it forever. The ethnographic present is, however, an intellectual myth.

This point is best understood by considering an example. When Captain James Cook anchored in Nootka Bay on the west coast of Vancouver Island, Canada, in 1776, he encountered people who lived in communal log houses and were expert fisherfolk. They were as at home on the water as on land, venturing offshore in square-sterned, shovel-nosed canoes carved from large cedar logs. The Nootka people were expert traders and wood carvers with a rich ceremonial life. Cook sailed away to the accompaniment of ritual songs, while one elaborately masked man danced on a special platform mounted in the bow of the largest canoe.

In the years that followed, the peoples of the Northwest Coast came into contact with rapacious fur traders, then colonists and missionaries. All of them remarked on the complex culture enjoyed by the many groups who fished and hunted on this bountiful coast. Our knowledge of Northwest Coast Indian culture in all its elaboration was acquired by government officials, missionaries, and a few pioneer anthropologists in the late nineteenth century. By this time, the coastal peoples had been decimated by exotic diseases like smallpox and much of their traditional culture had changed beyond recognition as a result of the inexorable advance of European civilization. "I hear very little about olden times," wrote the great anthropologist Franz Boas after visiting the Pacific Northwest in the 1880s. Nevertheless, he recorded an elaborate traditional culture and rich oral traditions, which, to many scholars, have become the ethnographic present from which one draws analogies as to the nature of prehistoric Northwest Coast society.

In fact, except for a few sketchy accounts of coastal society written by Cook and other pioneers, we know almost nothing of eighteenth century Northwest cultures, which may well have become considerably elaborated as a result of the riches brought in by the European fur trade. Almost certainly, Northwest society changed radically between the first European contact and the late nineteenth century.

Elsewhere, too, the ethnographic present is a myth. Throughout North America, the American Indian societies encountered and described by Europeans had already suffered the effects of Western contact. Smallpox and other diseases spread far inland and decimated indigenous populations long before anyone physically encountered a foreigner. So even the first explorers of, say, the interior of the southeastern United States interacted with Indian societies that were often a shadow of their former selves.

One of the cornerstones of all archaeological research is the notion that one can use analogies, comparisons between the artifacts and culture of the ethnographic present and those of the prehistoric past, to help interpret at least the later millennia of prehistory. Of course, there are numerous, and sometimes obvious, analogies that can be made between ancient and modern hunting weapons, or grindstones (metates) used by modern Maya Indians and their remote ancestors. But to assume that prehistoric hunter-gatherers thought the same way about the environment as modern San peoples from southern Africa do, or to consider late Ice Age hunters living in arctic environments as similar in many respects to living Eskimos, is nonsensical. The ethnographic present has never existed, for all human cultures are in a constant state of change and there was never a moment, let alone one at European contact, where culture stood still, where it was pristine.

Ethnoarchaeology and Experimental Archaeology

Archaeologists use the testimony of the present to serve the past, but they do so by using two interlocking approaches that enable them to develop hypotheses about the archaeological record: ethnoarchaeology and controlled experimentation. They focus on the relationship between human behavior and material culture, using the latter to interpret the former.

Ethnoarchaeology, sometimes called living archaeology, is the study of living societies to aid in the understanding and interpretation of the archaeological record. By living in, say, an Australian Aboriginal camp and observing the activities of its occupants, the archaeologist hopes to record archaeologically observable patterns, knowing what activities brought them into existence.

For example, archaeologist John Yellen lived for many months among !Kung San hunter-gatherers in the Kalahari Desert in southern Africa. He went back to their campsites, recorded the scatters of abandoned artifacts, the remains of brush shelters, even hearths and sleeping places. Yellen even excavated some of the sites, gathering a valuable body of information for studying ancient hunter-gatherers. For instance, most artifact patternings at !Kung sites were the result of family activities, whereas communal events such as dancing and the first distribution of meat took place in open spaces and left no traces in the archaeological record.

Perhaps the most famous ethnoarchaeological study is that by Lewis Binford among the Nunamiut caribou hunters of northern Alaska. Eighty percent of their subsistence comes from hunting caribou. Binford set out to find out as much as he could about Nunamiut hunting, meat butchery, and flesh consumption. He then related these activities to the bone fragments the hunters abandoned at their various sites. He found that the Eskimo were very rational in their treatment of animal foods. Their lives depended on aggressive hunting of migrating caribou in spring and fall,

Figure 2.5 The Mask site, Nunamiut Eskimo hunting stand where caribou were hunted and butchered.

and on long-term storage of food to tide them over the lean months (Figure 2.5).

Binford showed how the Nunamiut had an intimate knowledge of caribou anatomy, which related directly to the meat yield and storage potential of different parts, and to their consumption needs. By carefully studying abandoned bone piles, he was able to show how their use of different parts of the caribou carcass would show up in a Nunamiut archaeological site. The Nunamiut study demonstrated just how skillfully hunter-gatherers adapt to very local conditions.

Ethnoarchaeology provides valuable information on modern adaptations, not only among living hunter-gatherers but among farmers as well. But the information such studies provide gives only general impressions of the dynamics of different lifeways and sobering reminders that human adaptations were as complicated in the past as they are today.

Lewis Binford and others have tried to develop a body of what they call Middle Range Theory, which seeks to bridge the gap between the archaeological record from the past and the living present. Middle Range Theory is based on the assumption that the archaeological record is a static phenomenon—what remains today of a once-dynamic past. What remains today was once a component in the constantly changing, dynamic life of human beings in ancient times. Thus, to understand and explain the past, one must comprehend the relationship between static, material properties common to both past and present and the long-extinct dynamic properties of the past. The only arena in which this relationship can be studied is in the present—which is why ethnoarchaeology and archaeology by experiment are important to our interpretation of world prehistory.

Experimental Archaeology is as old as archaeology itself. One ardent eighteenth-century experimenter blew an Irish Bronze Age horn so hard that he was able to produce "a deep bass note, resembling the bellowing of a bull." Unfortunately, he blew so vigorously that he burst a blood vessel and died. Most modern experiments have been conducted with much greater precision and with less life-threatening gusto.

Experimental archaeology seeks to replicate ancient technologies and lifeways under controlled scientific conditions. This means far more than merely flaking a precise replica of a prehistoric projectile point. Nor do such well-known instances of replication as explorer Thor Heyerdahl's *Kon-Tiki* voyage qualify as archaeology by experiment. Heyerdahl built a replica of a Peruvian balsa raft in 1947 and sailed it downwind to Polynesia with the aid of the trade winds and the Humboldt Current. He succeeded in reaching the islands, showing that long ocean voyages in rafts were possible, but he did not prove that the Peruvians settled Polynesia. Such proof could only come not from a sailing voyage, but from the discovery of indisputable Inca or earlier Peruvian artifacts on the Pacific Islands.

Most experimental archaeology is of limited scope and designed to solve specific technological questions. Experiments have involved the use of replicated polished stone axes to clear European forests, which showed that a man can clear one-half acre of forest in a week. Controlled tests with growing maize, beans, and other crops with prehistoric techniques at Mesa Verde in Colorado produced crops in all but two of seventeen seasons. In those two years drought killed the seedlings.

The replication of prehistoric stone tools is perhaps the most visible kind of experimental archaeology. A small army of often expert stone toolmakers has replicated everything from the earliest simple choppers and flake implements to elaborate North American projectile points (Figure 2.6). Such replicas are often indistinguishable from those of the original makers. Such experimentation is very valuable, especially when combined with other interpretative approaches such as retrofitting and edge wear analysis.

Both ethnoarchaeology and experimentation are part of a search for reliable ways of inferring past conditions from the archaeological record. All of prehistory is separated from us by countless generations, and much of it unfolded in environmental conditions very different from those of our own, densely populated world. This is one of the reasons that scholars are turning to modern evolutionary theory to explain developments in world prehistory (see below).

Figure 2.6 Lithic expert Jeffrey Flenniken preparing to remove a basal fluting flake from a Paleo-Indian projectile head.

THE MEANING OF THE PAST

The archaeological record consists of the material remains of the past, of artifacts, structures, food, remains, and their context in time and space. Many approaches to world prehistory are predominantly materialistic, that is to say, they are concerned with the complicated relationships between cultural and environmental change, with the processes of culture change. In recent years, there has been a reaction against the culture as adaptation approach, as archaeologists focus more attention on the meaning of the archaeological record, on ancient ideologies, and the symbolic context of prehistoric cultures.

Under the culture as adaptation approach, the main emphasis has been on identifying variations in ancient human cultures. This perspective, which, it must be confessed, is central to this book, focuses on adaptations of human culture in general, rather impersonal ways. The assumption is that prehistoric institutions were rational in their dealings with their environments. There is no doubt that this is partially right. However, some recent research has espoused a very different approach that tries to look behind the material aspects of the archaeological record at the intangible rules, as it were, which governed the ways in which prehistoric people went about their business.

This approach, sometimes known as structural archaeology, or post-processual archaeology, is an attempt to get at the ways in which the owners of ancient artifacts actually perceived them, at the wider symbolic meanings of material objects in their entire world of existence. Thus, ancient cultures, like that, say, of the Cro-Magnons of western Europe 20,000 years ago, were the result of an intangible logic of their own, which comes down to us only in material form, most vividly as of art or written scripts.

Structural archaeology is concerned with ideology, with the idea of complex dimensions. One of the few examples of such research is Linda Schele and David Friedel's remarkable work on Mayan iconography, based on a combination of deciphered glyphs and archaeological data. Although these two archaeologists do not consider themselves structuralists, their work does show how ritual life, shrines, and temple structures help shape peoples' lives (Chapter 11). "The Maya believed in a past which always returned, in . . . endless cycles repeating patterns already set into the fabric of time and space," they write in their book *A Forest of Kings* (p. 18). "Our challenge . . . is to interpret this history, recorded in their words, images and ruins, in a manner comprehensible to the modern mind, yet true to the Maya's perceptions of themselves."[1] This is no easy task, and is even harder when studying earlier periods of prehistory when there were no written records.

The study of ancient ideology, of the broader context of the material remains of the past, is still in its infancy, but promises to lead archaeology in new, exciting directions.

EVOLUTION AND HUMAN PREHISTORY

Where do theories of world prehistory go from here? The answer can only be that archaeologists are uncertain. We can be sure, however, that evolutionary theory will play an important part in the years to come.

The principle of natural selection has long been a central theme of evolutionary thought, accepted as a basic mechanism for evolution but little analyzed. Today, a whole new body of evolutionary theory has equipped biologists with methods of investigating the processes as well as the patterns of evolution. This wealth of new theory is having a major impact on prehistoric archaeology, for natural selection may prove to be a

---

[1]Linda Schele and David Friedel. 1990. *A Forest of Kings*. New York: William Morrow, p. 18.

means of explaining patterns of variation in human morphology and behavior. These issues are explored in more detail in later chapters, but
some of the themes and controversies should be mentioned at this
stage.

One major controversy surrounds the relationship between human
behavior and genetic makeup. Is human cultural expression, as some
biologists (known as sociobiologists) believe, a flimsy blanket for genetic
imperatives? In other words, are human actions more genetically directed
than we might think? Or was the greater part of human behavior produced by our unique culture, as many anthropologists believe?

In another of the growing links between anthropology and biology,
behavioral ecologists are using a comparative approach to biological evolution to place human characteristics within a general framework of animal variability. This and other emerging evolutionary approaches are
concerned with the analysis of human adaptation from a biological perspective. All assume that patterns of adaptation is prehistoric times were
the products of natural selection and can be interpreted in these terms.
These new approaches also assume that human biological evolution and
human prehistory cannot be isolated from one another. Human biological
and cultural evolution must be placed in two contexts: the evolution of the
animal community as a whole and that of local ecology. Human adaptation
in prehistory is the result of ecological and evolutionary adaptations between humans and other species that make up the biological community.

It is both useful and convincing to assume that natural selection conferred some reproductive advantage on some of the bearers of early
human culture. Their thoughts and actions evolved in directions that were
adaptive for an evolving humanity. As a result, very diverse human societies with very different institutions and beliefs tend to think and act in the
same general ways. Archaeologists of an evolutionary persuasion believe
that one can understand the ways in which people behave by compre-
hending the constraints placed on the human mind by a long evolutionary
heritage. It should be remembered, however, that the environment in
which humankind evolved is very different from that in which we have
lived for many thousands of years and still live today.

It follows that the common behavioral characteristics that are the
product of biological evolution serve to link modern humans with prehistoric, anatomically modern people, and ultimately with earlier hominids
as well. On these grounds alone, the validity of evolutionary approaches
to human prehistory is established beyond all reasonable doubt.

The modern evolutionary approach to prehistory considers adaptation
as a continual response to ever-changing environments. Thus, flexible
behavior and creative thought on the part of individuals are the driving
forces behind decisions to change social and physical environments. From
this perspective flows one major question: to what extent can one relate
short-term individual behavior on the part of opportunistic human beings

to the generalized data that is what scientists call the archaeological record?

The many attempts to explain the long, ever more complex prehistory of humankind are based on a woefully incomplete archaeological record that has accumulated from more than a century of archaeological research in all parts of the world. They form the explanatory framework for the prehistoric past, the story of which begins in Chapter 3.

PART
Two

THE WORLD OF
ARCHAIC HUMANS

And God said "let us create man in our own image, after our likeness:
and let them have dominion over the fish of the sea, and over the
cattle, and over all the earth, and over every creeping thing that
creepeth upon the earth. . . ."

Genesis 1:26

Chapter 3

Origins

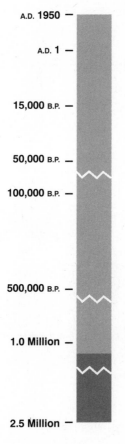

A.D. 1950 —

A.D. 1 —

15,000 B.P. —

50,000 B.P. —

100,000 B.P. —

500,000 B.P. —

1.0 Million —

2.5 Million —

*B*iologist Thomas Huxley called it "the question of questions," the nature of the exact relationship between humans and their closest living relatives such as the chimpanzee and the gorilla—the question of human origins. Ever since his day, scientists have been locked in controversy, as they trace the complex evolutionary history of humanity back to its very beginnings. In this chapter, we examine some of the controversies that surround the biological and cultural evolution of humankind and describe what we know about the behavior and lifeway of our earliest ancestors.

THE GREAT ICE AGE (1.6 million to 15,000 years ago)

The story of humanity begins deep in geological time, during the later part of the Cenozoic era, the age of mammals. For most of geological time, the world's climate was warmer than it is today. During the Oligocene epoch, some 35 million years ago, the first signs of glacial cooling appeared with the formation of a belt of pack ice around Antarctica. This development was followed by a major drop in world temperatures between 14 and 11 million years ago.

Chronological Table A

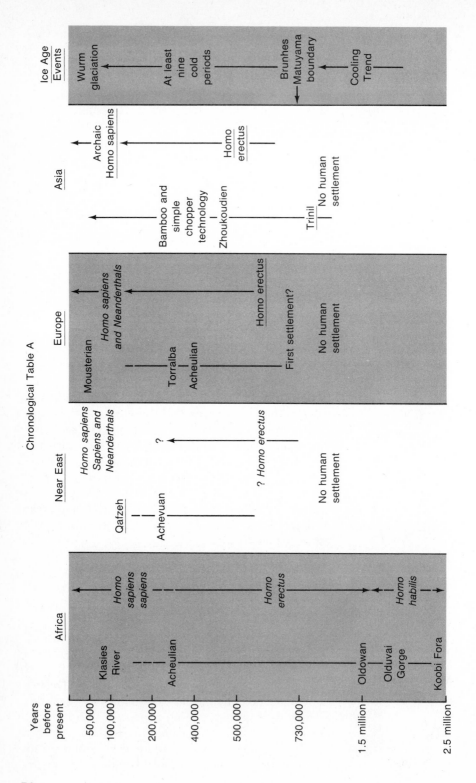

As temperatures fell, so large ice sheets formed on high ground in high latitudes. About 3.2 million years ago, large ice sheets formed on the northern continents. Then, some 2.5 million years ago, just as humans first appeared on tropical Africa, glaciation intensified even more and the earth entered its present period of constantly fluctuating climate. These changes culminated during the Quaternary period or Pleistocene epoch, the most recent interval of earth history, which began about 1.6 million years ago. This period is sometimes called the Age of Humanity, for it was during this epoch, the Great Ice Age, that humans first peopled most of the globe. The major climatic and environmental changes of the Ice Age form the backdrop for some of the most important stages of evolution.

The words Ice Age conjure up a vision of ice-bound landscapes and frigid, subzero temperatures that gripped the earth in a prolonged deep-freeze. In fact, the Pleistocene witnessed constant fluctuations between warm and intensely cold global climates. Deep-sea cores lifted from the depths of the world's oceans have produced a complex picture of Ice Age climate (Table 3.1). These cores have shown that climatic fluctuations between warm and cold were relatively minor until about 800,000 years ago. Since then, periods of intense cold have reoccurred about every 90,000 years, with minor oscillations about 20,000 and 40,000 years apart. Many scientists believe that these changes are triggered by long-term astronomical cycles, especially in the earth's orbit around the sun, which affect the seasonal and north–south variations of solar radiation received by the earth.

There were at least nine glacials that mantled northern Europe and North America with great ice sheets, the last one only retreating some 15,000 years ago. Interglacials, with climates as warm or warmer than that of today, occurred infrequently, and the constant changes displaced plants and animals, including humans, from their original habitats. During colder cycles, plants and animals generally fared better at lower altitudes and in warmer latitudes. Populations of animals spread slowly toward more hospitable areas, mixing with populations that already lived there and creating new communities with new combinations of organisms. This repeated mixing surely affected human evolution in many ways. For example, paleontologist Bjorn Kurten has estimated that no fewer than 113 of the mammal species living in Europe and adjacent Asia evolved during the past 3 million years.

The earliest chapter of human evolution unfolded during a period of relatively minor climatic change, indeed before the Pleistocene truly began. Between 4 and 2 million years ago, the world's climate was somewhat warmer and more stable than it was in later times. The African savanna, the probable cradle of humankind, contained many species of mammals large and small, including a great variety of the order of primates, of which we humans are a part.

Table 3.1 Major Climatic Events of the Ice Age

Temperature ← Lower Higher →	Dates (B.P.)	Periods	Epochs	Glacials	Human evolution	Prehistory
						Cities, agriculture
	10,000	Holocene	Holocene	Holocene	*Homo sapiens sapiens*	Settlement of New World
	118,000	Quaternary	B r u n h e s (Pleistocene)	Würm (Wisconsin in North America)		
	128,000			Saale		
	730,000		M a t u y a m a (Pleistocene)	Many cold episodes	*Homo sapiens*	Hunter-gatherers
					Homo erectus	
	1,600,000	Tertiary	Olduvai Event (Pliocene)		Early hominids and *Australopithecus*	

Uncertain climatic detail before 130,000 years ago

54

EARLY PRIMATE EVOLUTION AND ADAPTATION

The Order Primates

All of us are members of the order primates, which includes most tree-loving placental mammals. There are two suborders: *anthropoids* (apes, humans, and monkeys) and *prosimians* (lemurs, tarsiers, and other so-called pre-monkeys). The many similarities in behavior and physical characteristics between the *hominids* (primates of the family Hominidae, which includes modern humans, earlier human subspecies, and their direct ancestors) and the *pongids* (our closest living nonhuman primate relatives) can be explained by identical characteristics that each group inherited millions of years ago from a common ancestor. In other words, humans and our closest nonhuman primate relatives evolved along parallel lines from a common ancestor (Table 3.2).

When did humankind separate from the nonhuman primates? Experts disagree violently about the answer. It was in Africa that humans and apes diverged from monkeys, but no one knows when this divergence took place. Several species of apes were flourishing in Africa at the beginning

TABLE 3.2 A much-simplified version of how Old World monkeys, apes, and humans evolved.

Geological Epochs	Millions of Years B.C.	Old World Monkeys	Apes	Humans
Pleistocene				
	1.7			
Pliocene				
	5.2			
Miocene				
	23.5			
Oligocene				
	36			
Eocene				
	50			

of the Miocene epoch, some 24 million years ago. The basic anatomical pattern of the large hominids appears in the Middle Miocene, 18 to 12 million years ago. A second radiation began in the Late Miocene, between 8 and 5 million years ago. This radiation eventually produced four lineages, at least one of which, human beings, is known to have been considerably modified. It is interesting to note that a similar evolutionary pattern occurs among herbivores such as elephants. In both cases, the patterns reflect changing climates and habitats — from warmer, less seasonal, more forested regimens to colder, more seasonal, and less forested conditions. They also mirror changes in the configuration of continents, mountain systems, and antarctic ice.

For the hominids, the critical period was between 10 and 5 million years ago, when the segment of the African hominoid lineage radiated to produce gorillas, chimpanzees, and hominids. Unfortunately, this 5-million-year period is a black hole in our knowledge of early human evolution. We can only guess at the nature of the apelike animals that flourished in Africa during these millennia. Paleoanthropologist David Pilbeam theorizes that these animals were mostly tree-living, with long arms and legs and a broad chest. They would have used all four limbs in the trees, occasionally scrambling on the ground and even standing on their rear limbs at times. About 5 million years ago, Pilbeam believes, the hominoid lineage divided into western and eastern parts. The western segment, the proto-chimpanzee, remained dependent on fruit and other tree foods, scattered resources that required a flexible social organization.

Intense controversy surrounds the relationships between humans, chimpanzees, and gorillas, but many biologists agree that chimpanzees are humans' closest relatives. Using molecular time clocks, they calculate that these three primate forms last shared a common ancestor about 6 to 7 million years ago.

"Coming Down from the Trees"

A fall in world temperatures after 20 million years ago resulted in increasingly open environments in tropical latitudes. With this reduction in forested environments probably came a trend toward ground-adapted species. Many species of living and now extinct primates, including hominids, adapted to this kind of existence some time after 10 million years ago. In other words, "they came down from the trees."

About 5 million years ago, the African savanna, with its patches of forest and extensive grassland plains, was densely populated by many mammal species as well as specialized tree-dwellers and other primates. Some of these were flourishing in small bands, probably walking upright, and conceivably making tools.

Coming down from the trees created three immediate problems. First was the difficulty of getting around in open country. Hominids adopted a bipedal posture as a way of doing so at least 4 million years ago. Our ancestors became *bipedal* (walking on two feet) over a long period of time, perhaps as a result of spending more and more time feeding on food resources on the ground. Bipedalism is a posture that is configured for endurance rather than power or speed. An upright posture and bipedal gait are the most characteristic hominid physical features.

Upright posture is vital because it frees the hands for other actions, like toolmaking. It contrasts with *knuckle walking*, which provides an excellent power thrust for jumping into a tree or a short sprint (think of a football lineman). It is a specialized way of moving around in which the backs of the fingers are placed on the ground and act as main weight-bearing surfaces. Knuckle walking was adaptive in the forest because long arms and hands as well as grasping feet were still vital for climbing (Figure 3.1). Human arms are too short for us to be comfortable with this posture. Bipedalism favors endurance and the covering of long distances, important considerations in open country. It was a critical antecedent of hunting, gathering, and toolmaking.

Second, the savanna abounded in predators, making it hard for primates to sleep safely. Large hominids made home bases, where they sheltered from the hot sun and slept in safety. Quite what form these home bases took is a matter of great debate. Lastly, high-quality plant

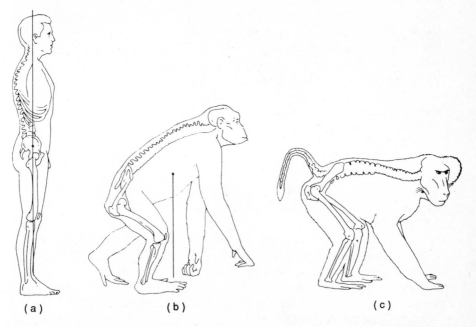

(a)   (b)   (c)

Figure 3.1 Knuckle walking and bipedalism. (a) Knuckle walking chimpanzee, with the center of gravity lying in the middle of the area bounded by arms and legs. (b) Human bipedal posture. The center of gravity of the body lies just behind the midpoint of the hipjoint and in front of the knee joint, so that both hip and knee are extended when standing, conserving energy. Also, walking is more efficient. (After Zihlman.)

foods, abundant in the forests, were widely dispersed over the savanna. It is striking that later hunter-gatherers subsisted off a broad range of game and plant foods. As part of human evolution, their hominid ancestors expanded their food range to include more meat, perhaps during long periods of plant scarcity. Among mammals, these characteristics are associated with a trend toward larger brain size. And, as brain size increased, so, gradually, the lifeways of evolving hominids became less apelike, and closer to that of human hunter-gatherers, a process that took hundreds of thousands of years to unfold.

Early hominids faced three major adaptive problems. They were large mammals, were terrestrial primates, and lived in an open, tropical savanna environment. Human beings are large and have additional food requirements due to higher metabolic rates. This means that each hominid has to range efficiently over a larger area to obtain food. Larger mammals are more mobile than their smaller relatives. They cover more ground, which enables them to subsist off resources that are unevenly distributed not only in space but also at different seasons. Mobility allows larger mammals like humans to incorporate unpredictable, often seasonal resources in their diets. They can tolerate extremes of heat and cold, a capacity that may have contributed to the spread of humans out of the tropics later in prehistory. Bipedal humans have sweat glands and are heavily dependent on water supplies. These glands are a direct adjunct to bipedalism, for they enhance endurance for long-distance foraging.

These and several other factors—such as increased longevity and brain enlargement—created adaptive problems for emerging humans. These problems resulted in a number of solutions, among them wider territorial ranges, the need to schedule food gathering, broadening of diet, a high degree of mobility, and much greater behavioral flexibility. This flexibility included enhanced intelligence and learning capacity, parental care, and new levels of social interaction.

THE FOSSIL EVIDENCE FOR HUMAN EVOLUTION
(4 million to 1.5 million years ago)

What we know of early human evolution and lifeways comes almost entirely from archaeological and fossil finds in tropical Africa (Figure 3.2).

Between 9 and 4 million years ago, the last common ancestral hominoid stock split into two main lineages, which evolved into apes and humans. The details of this split are still a complete mystery, largely because fossil beds dating to this critical period are very rare in Africa. The fossil record increases after about 5 million years ago, but is still very fragmentary and controversial.

Between 4 and 2 million years ago, the East African savanna was populated by a great variety of hominids. Palaeoanthropologists divide them into two broad groups: the Australopithecines and *Homo*.

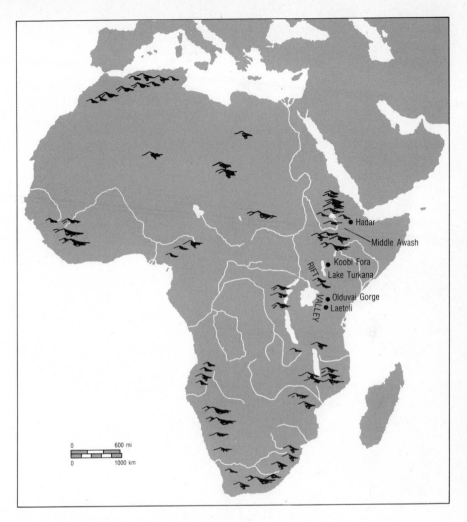

Figure 3.2 Map of archaeological sites described in Chapter 3.

Australopithecus (Before 5 million years ago to 1.0 million years ago)

Australopithecus (Latin for southern ape) was first identified by anatomist Raymond Dart in South Africa in 1925. He described a small, gracile primate that displayed both human and apelike features. Dart named his find *Australopithecus africanus*, a much lighter creature than another, more robust form of Australopithecine that subsequently turned up at other South African sites and, later, in East Africa (Figures 3.3 and 3.4). The latter is known as *Australopithecus robustus*, a squat, massively built primate with a crested skull.

For years, paleoanthropologists thought that *Australopithecus afri-*

Figure 3.3 *Australopithecus africanus.*

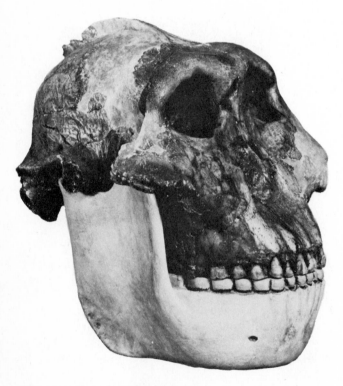

Figure 3.4 *Australopithecus robustus.*

canus was the direct ancestor of humankind, that human evolution had proceeded in a relatively linear way through time. More recent finds from East Africa have muddied the picture and shown that the process was much more complicated.

The earliest autralopithecines from East Africa come from the Middle Awash area of Ethiopia and have been potassium-argon dated to between .4.1 and 3.9 million years ago. At Hadar in northern Ethiopia, Maurice Taieb and Donald Johanson discovered a remarkably complete skeleton of a small primate (the famous Lucy) dating to about 3.75 million years ago, together with fragments of at least 13 males, females, and children. Lucy stood just under 4.0 feet (1.2 m) tall and was 19 to 21 years old (Figure 3.5). She, like other Hadar individuals, was a powerful, heavily muscled primate, fully bipedal, with arms slightly longer for their size than those of humans. Lucy and her contemporaries had humanlike hands and brains about the size of chimpanzees. There is no evidence they made tools.

The Hadar Australopithecines have generated great controversy. Johanson and some other experts believe that these fossils are a more primitive form they name *Australopithecus afarensis*, the common ancestor of all later gracile and robust Australopithecines. The Hadar fossils are of great importance. They show that bipedalism *predates* toolmaking and enlargement of the brain to a size greater than those in chimpanzees and

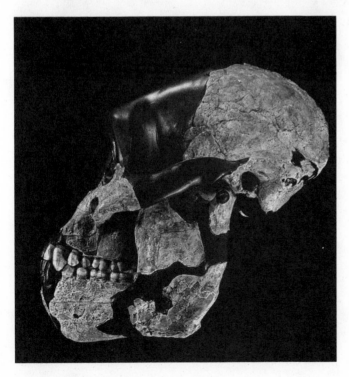

Figure 3.5 "Lucy," *Australopithecus afarensis.*

other nonhuman primates. In recent months, field research has resumed in Ethiopia, with the discovery of more *Australopithecus afarensis* teeth at Fejiji, 600 miles (965 km) southwest of Hadar. This find shows that this primitive Australopithecine ranged widely in East Africa between 3.7 and 4.5 million years ago.

Even more remarkable evidence of bipedalism comes from fossil-bearing beds at Laetoli in Tanzania, where Mary Leakey uncovered not only hominid fossils like those at Hadar, but the actual 3.59 million-year-old footprints of big game and some fairly large bipedal primates. The footsteps are those of an adult male and female, the latter carrying a child (Figure 3.6). "The tracks indicate a rolling and probably slow-moving gait, with the hips swiveling at each step, as opposed to the free-standing gait of modern man," Mary Leakey writes. Some scientists believe the

Figure 3.6 Hominid footprints from Laetoli, Tanzania.

Laetoli prints are from *Australopithecus afarensis*, flourishing 1,000 miles (1609 km) south of Hadar.

Homo habilis — The First Human (?2.5 million to 1.5 million years ago)

Further evidence of the great diversity of Australopithecine forms comes from Olduvai Gorge, made famous by the fossil discoveries of Louis and Mary Leakey (Figure 3.7). This spectacular rift in the Serengeti Plains of northern Tanzania cuts through deep lake beds of a long-dried up Pleistocene lake, frequented by early hominids. The Leakeys uncovered not only a robust *Australopithecus* potassium-argon dated to 1.75 million years ago, but the bones of a more gracile hominid, found in the same levels as crude stone choppers and flakes that were more primitive than any previously discovered in the world. Louis Leakey called this hominid *Homo habilis* (Handy Person), on the grounds that it was quite different from *Australopithecus*, even if it lived in the same general area.

At first, experts thought *Homo habilis* was perhaps a form of Australopithecine. But far north of Olduvai Gorge, in the East Turkana region of Kenya, Richard Leakey, son of Louis and Mary, and an international team of scientists, have recovered not only robust and gracile australopithecines, but more *Homo habilis* specimens (Figure 3.8).

These were hominids with unmistakably larger brains. Their brain

Figure 3.7 Olduvai Gorge, Tanzania.

Figure 3.8 Skull 1470 from East Turkana: *Homo habilis*.

capacities were between 650 and 800 cc, but otherwise they were about the same size as *Australopithecus*, weighing about 88 pounds (44 kg) and standing just over 4 feet, 3 inches (1.3 m) tall. Both were bipedal and predominantly fruit eaters, but *Homo habilis* would have looked less apelike around the face and skull. Their heads were higher and rounder, the face less protruding. Their hand bones were more curved and robust than those of modern humans. This was a powerful grasping hand, more like that of chimpanzees and gorillas than humans, a hand ideal for climbing trees. But an opposable thumb allowed both powerful gripping and precise manipulation of fine objects. This feature would have enabled *Homo habilis* to make tools.

A recent new *Homo habilis* find at Olduvai reinforces the impression that the earliest humans were closer to apes than to human beings. The newly discovered individual has upper arm bones that are almost as long as its thigh bone. This is a characteristic of chimpanzees and other apes, not of humans, whose arms are only about 70 percent of the length of the leg bones. Most likely, *Homo habilis* spent a great deal of time climbing trees, an adaptation that would make them much less human in their behavior, and presumably in their social structure.

AUSTRALOPITHECUS AND HOMO

Most experts agree that *Homo habilis* is the probable ancestor of the later human species *Homo erectus* and *Homo sapiens*. Much more controversial are the evolutionary relationships between *Australopithecus afarensis* and later Australopithecines on the one hand, and between *Homo habilis* and the Australopithecines on the other. The simple linear evolutionary schemes that passed from *Australopithecus* to *Homo* and then on to more modern forms have been replaced by branching models that stem from a realization that hominid evolution involved a far higher level of species diversity than was previously thought. Human evolution is more like a bush than the ladder that has been used for an analogy for so long (Figure 3.9).

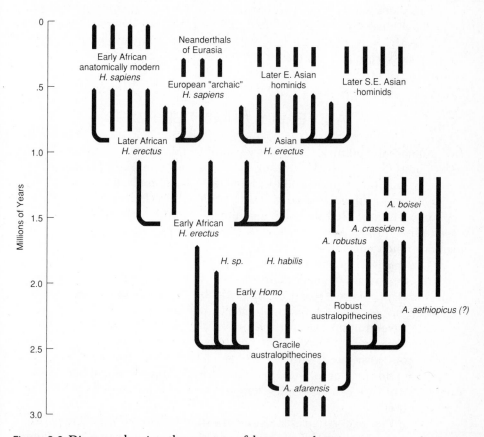

Figure 3.9 Diagram showing the process of human evolution as a series of adaptive radiations. The basis for each radiation was a mixture of adaptations to local conditions and geographic isolation. The result was the evolution of diverse behavioral and ecological strategies and different species and subspecies of hominids.

The current view of early human evolution accepts that the process began with the Australopithecines, followed by the emergence of *Homo habilis*, then later, by more modern forms. But there was considerable diversity at each stage, so much so that one cannot think of human evolution as merely a trend toward more modern forms. The Australopithecines were remarkably diverse, with the primitive *afarensis* form, the lightly built and later *A. africanus*, and the much more massive *A. robustus*. Between 5 and 1 million years ago, there was considerable adaptive radiation of australopithecines. The earliest members of the genus *Homo* were probably part of the radiation, *Australopithecus*-like forms with larger brains relative to body size. They are classified as *Homo habilis*, but it is certain that there was considerable variability. A more modern form, *Homo erectus* (Chapter 4), appeared about 1.6 million years ago and may also have been part of this adaptive radiation.

This same pattern of adaptive radiation may have continued much later in prehistory, during the long millennia when *Homo erectus* flourished in Africa, Asia, and Europe, with only a small part of this evolutionary process resulting in modern humans, *Homo sapiens*, probably in Africa.

TOOLMAKING AND EARLY HUMAN BEHAVIOR

We humans use culture as a primary way of adapting to our environments. The ability to make tools has long been cited as a uniquely human attribute. In fact, other animals like chimpanzees make tools, but only people manufacture artifacts regularly and habitually as well as in a much more complex fashion. We have gone much further in the toolmaking direction than other primates. One reason is that our brains allow us to plan our actions much more in advance.

The earliest human tools may well have been made of perishable wood, perhaps rudimentary clubs, digging sticks, or spears, but they have not survived. Simple stone tools, made by knocking one rock against another, appear in East Africa about 2.5 million years ago, the conventionally agreed upon date for the origin of human culture. These stone artifacts have been found in large numbers throughout East and southern Africa, and associated with broken animal bones in the East Turkana region at Olduvai Gorge. They were made from convenient pebbles, some perhaps converted into simple choppers by removing one or two flakes (Figure 3.10).

Stone tool expert Nicholas Toth has shown that the most important artifacts were not pebbles or even crude choppers, but the sharp-edged flakes removed from them. Angular flakes and lumps of lava made weapons, scrapers, and cutting tools, used to cut meat, butcher animals, and perhaps to shape wood. There are few formal tools, but Toth's controlled experiments show that the first toolmakers had a sophisticated

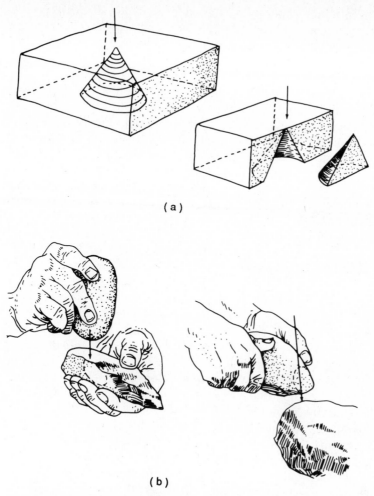

(a)

(b)

Figure 3.10 Early stone technology. Certain types of flinty rocks frac-
ture in a distinctive way, as illustrated in (a). When a blow is struck on
such rock, a cone of percussion is formed by shock waves rippling
through the stone (left). A flake is formed (right) when the block (or
core) is hit at the edge, and the stone fractures along the edge of the
ripple. (b) Early stoneworkers used a heavy hammerstone to remove
edge flakes or struck lumps of rock against boulders to produce the
same effect. Oldowan technology was simple, often consisting of little
more than a few flakes removed from lava cobbles.

understanding of the potential of stone as the basis for a simple, highly
effective technology that grew more complex over time. Eventually, the
simple choppers evolved into crude axelike tools, flaked on both surfaces
—the hand axe used widely over a million years ago. The earliest human
technology is called the *Oldowan*, after Olduvai Gorge, where it was first
described in detail.

Nicholas Toth has replicated thousands of Oldowan artifacts and shown by experiment that sharp-edged flakes are highly effective for slitting skin and butchering game animals. By studying the working edges of the tools under microscopes, he has detected wear from three possible uses: butchery and meat cutting, sawing and scraping wood, and cutting soft plant matter. Toth believes our earliest ancestors had a good sense of the mechanics of stone tool manufacture. They were able to find the correct acute angle for removing flakes by percussion (Figure 3.10). Not even modern beginners have this capacity; it takes several hours of intensive practice to acquire the skill. Unlike chimpanzees, who rarely tote the sticks and stones they use more than a few yards, *Homo habilis* carried flakes and pebbles over considerable distances, up to 8 miles (13 km). This behavior represents a simple form of *curation*, retaining tools for future use rather than just utilizing convenient stones, as chimpanzees do.

PROTOHUMAN CULTURE?

How did our earliest ancestors live and behave? Were they hunters and gatherers with a culture and lifeway that can be compared to those of modern hunter-gatherers? Or were they more apelike in their behavior? Modern researches that rely on many approaches to archaeological data make it clear that comparisons with modern hunting societies are of limited use. For a start, the early hominids belonged to a quite different species. Furthermore, their behaviors are not displayed by any living ape, or indeed by all early hominids.

After looking at Oldowan stone tools, the archaeologists of a generation ago claimed that the earliest humans were skillful hunters, who aimed and threw stone missiles, shared food, and so on. This overoptimistic view was deeply colored by analogies with modern hunter-gatherers like the San of the Kalahari Desert in southern Africa. At the other extreme are scholars who argue that the Oldowan hominids were at an apelike grade of behavior. They believe all the conceptual abilities and perceptions needed to manufacture Oldowan tools also appear in ape-manufactured tools like sticks used to fish for termites and sleeping platforms. Furthermore, not only Oldowan hominids but also chimpanzees scavenge and hunt for game, chasing down small animals, carrying meat over considerable distances, and using tools to break open animal bones and nuts. Chimpanzees, like early humans, use the same places again and again, pounding nuts at the same locations and carrying food to their favorite eating sites. There are, however, two behavioral differences between apes and early hominids: First, hominids were at an advantage in that they were bipedal, a posture that is far more efficient for carrying than walking on four limbs. Second, the Oldowan humans were adapted to both forest and savanna living, where they had to organize and cover far larger territories in open country than their primate relatives in the forest.

In the long term, these differences may have resulted in new concepts of space and spatial organization, concepts that were definitely reflected in more complex stone tool forms after a million years ago. It would be naive to claim that the behavior of early hominids was entirely apelike, for this means ignoring the importance of the evolution of enlarged primate brains. We can be certain that there were significant differences between nonhuman primates and hominids 2 million years ago, but the nature of these differences is still little understood. Certainly the opportunistic nature of primordial stone technology is in sharp contrast to the better designed, much more standardized artifacts of later humans.

ARCHAEOLOGICAL EVIDENCE FOR EARLY HUMAN BEHAVIOR

Two sources of information on very early human behavior survive in East Africa — the first is manufactured artifacts, the second scatters of tools and food remains found at a few locations like East Turkana and Olduvai Gorge.

Concentrations of broken animal bones and stone tools in these two regions and a few others have been excavated and studied with meticulous care. The concentrations are usually only some 20 to 30 feet (6.0 to 9.1 m) across, places that were visited and used by hominids either once or on several occasions. Later prehistoric hunter-gatherers made habitual use of *central places*, places where they returned to sleep, cook food, and engage in a wide variety of social activities. Are we, then, to assume that the Koobi Fora and Olduvai concentrations are evidence that our earliest ancestors also used central places like their successors did? Did they hunt and kill big-game animals, or did they merely scavenge flesh from abandoned predator kills?

At Koobi Fora in northern Kenya, a group of hominids found the carcass of a hippopotamus in a stream bed about 1.8 million years ago. They gathered around and removed bones and meat from the dead animal with small stone flakes. The sandy deposits in which the artifacts lay are so fine that we can be certain that every stone cobble was carried in to make tools at the carcass, some of them from as far as 9 miles (14 km) away. The site contains abundant evidence of butchering and of tool manufacture, but we do not know if the hominids actually killed the animal.

Site FxJj50, also at Koobi Fora, is also in an ancient watercourse, a place where the hominids could find shade from the blazing sun, located close to water and abundant toolmaking stone (Figure 3.11). The site is a cluster of stone artifacts and fragments, including sharp flakes, choppers, and scraping tools. More than 2000 bones from at least 17 mammal species, mostly antelope, are associated with the tools, some of which have been chewed by hyenas and other carnivores. There are clear signs the bones were smashed and cut by hominids, for reconstructed fragments

Figure 3.11 Excavation at site FxJj50, Koobi Fora, Kenya.

show traces of hammer blows and fine linear grooves that can have resulted only from cutting bone with stone flakes. Many of the FxJj50 bones
have their articular ends chewed off by carnivores, a characteristic of
bone accumulations resulting from carnivore kills. Perhaps the hominids
simply chased away lions and other predators, then moved in on a fresh
kill; we cannot be sure.

At Olduvai Gorge, Mary Leakey plotted artifact and bone scatters in
the lowest levels of the ancient lake bed. Many artifacts and bones were
concentrated in areas about 15 feet (4.6 m) across. At one site, a pile of
shattered bones and rocks lay a short distance away, the bones perhaps
piled in heaps as the marrow was extracted from them. Recent microscopic studies of the Olduvai scatters have shown that many of the bones
were heavily weathered. They had lain on the surface for considerable
periods of time, some for perhaps as long as a decade. The bones of many
different animals come from the scatters, parts of carcasses from a very
ecologically diverse set of animals. Limb bones predominate, as if these
body parts were repeatedly carried to the sites.

At both Koobi Fora and Olduvai, meat- and marrow-rich bones occur
concentrated in small areas with stone tools. The percentage of carnivore
bones is somewhat higher than the natural environment, as if there was
intense competition between hominids and other carnivores. Perhaps the
presence of such predators restricted the activities of hominids at Olduvai. They may have grabbed meat from fresh carnivore kills, then taken

their booty to a place where they had a collection of stone tools near water or other predictable food supplies. There they would hastily cut off meat and extract the marrow before abandoning the fresh bones to the carnivores hovering nearby. Without fire or domesticated animals, scientists believe that *Homo habilis* probably had to rely on opportunistic foraging for game meat, it being unsafe for them to camp in open water courses or on lake shores. It is worth noting that one hominid bone found at Olduvai Gorge had been gnawed by carnivores.

Most of the bones from the Olduvai accumulations are of smaller animals that could be run down and thrown to the ground with ease. This is more of an apelike form of behavior, although apes have been observed scavenging meat. Microscopic studies of the Olduvai bones show that the hominids rarely butchered and disarticulated large animals and carried their bones back to base. They seem to have obtained meat without cutting up too many carcasses, as if they scavenged it from already dismembered predators kills. In some cases, human cutting marks *overlay* predator tooth marks, as if the hominids had scavenged bones from carcasses that had already been killed by other animals. In others, predators have chewed bones abandoned by *Homo*.

Most paleoanthropologists believe that the earliest hominids hunted small- and medium-sized animals, but were expert scavengers when the opportunity arose. Opportunism has always been an important quality of humankind, from the earliest times. Undoubtedly, however, plants and all kinds of vegetable foods were an important, if not the most important, part of very early human diet.

THE EARLY ADAPTIVE PATTERN

The first phase of human evolution involved not only shifts in the basic patterns of subsistence and locomotion, but new ingredients — food sharing between individuals and toolmaking. These led to enhanced communication, better information exchange, and economic and social insight, as well as cunning and restraint. Human anatomy was augmented with tools. Culture became an inseparable part of humanity.

Cooperation, the ability to get together to solve problems of both subsistence and potential conflict, is a vital quality to human beings. We are unique in having a spoken, symbolic language that enables us to communicate our most intimate feelings to one another. Our closest living relatives, the chimpanzees, communicate with gestures and many voice sounds in the wild, whereas other apes use sounds only to convey territorial information. Controlled experiments with chimpanzees have shown that they can learn isolated symbols, but their learning ability is severely restricted. When, then, did humans abandon grunts for speech, opening up new vistas of cooperative behavior and unlimited potential for the enrichment of life?

Using sophisticated statistical analyses, anatomist Philip Laitman has shown that the australopithecines of 4 million years ago had flat skull bases and larynxes high in the neck, a position that limited the sounds they could make. Brain casts of the interiors of australopithecine skulls are also apelike. It was only much later, after about 300,000 years ago, that the skull base assumed its modern curvature, allowing for fully human speech. We may assume the first humans had more to communicate with than nonhuman primates, but modern articulate speech was a more recent stimulus to biological and cultural evolution.

Archaeologist Glyn Isaac believes that opportunism is a hallmark of humankind, a restless process like mutation and natural selection. The normal pressures of ecological competition were able to transform the versatile behavior of ancestral primates into the new and distinctive early hominid pattern. Weapons and tools made it possible to scavenge and butcher larger and larger animals. Vegetable foods were staples, protection against food shortages. Foraging provided stability, and it may have led to division of labor between men and women. The savanna was an ideal environment for hominids who lived on scavenging, hunting, and foraging combined.

By a million years ago, the hominid lines had been pruned to the extent that only one lineage, *Homo*, remained. The superior brain size and toolmaking skills enjoyed by *Homo habilis* gave these hominids an adaptive advantage over *Australopithecus* that resulted in the eventual extinction of these other hominid forms. The kind of systematic hunting and foraging that *Homo* engaged in required much larger territories and considerably lower population densities per square mile. Thus, *Homo habilis* may have lived in larger bands than nonhuman primates, and in a world where interactions with other individuals were far more complex and more demanding. The increased complexity of our social interactions may have been a powerful force in the evolution of the human brain. The brilliant technological, artistic, and expressive skills of humankind may well be a consequence of the fact that our early ancestors had to be more and more socially adept.

Chapter
4

Out of Africa

A.D. 1950 —

A.D. 1 —

15,000 B.P. —

50,000 B.P. —

100,000 B.P. —

500,000 B.P. —

1.0 Million —

2.5 Million —

*A*bout 1.6 million years ago, *Homo habilis* gave way to more advanced humans capable of far more complex and varied lifeways. These new human ancestors were the first to tame fire and the first to settle outside the tropical savannas of Africa. They did so at the beginning of the last geological epoch, the Pleistocene, sometimes called the Ice Age.

ICE AGE BACKGROUND

The Pleistocene began about 1.6 million years ago, after an intensification of glaciation worldwide after 2.5 million years ago. By this time great mountain chains had formed in the Alps, Himalayas, and elsewhere. Landmasses had been uplifted; connection between these latitudes and southern areas was reduced, lessening their heat exchange and causing greater temperature differences between them. Northern latitudes became progressively cooler after 3 million years ago, but climatic fluctuations between warmer and colder climatic regimens were still relatively minor during the first million years of the Ice Age. This was a critically important time when a new human form, *Homo erectus*, evolved in Africa and moved out of the tropics into Asia and Europe.

73

Perhaps the most important event during the entire Ice Age occurred about 730,000 years ago, when the earth's magnetic field reversed abruptly from a reversed state it had adopted about 2.5 million years ago to a normal one (Table 3.1). This Matuyama/Brunhes boundary, named after the geologists who first named it, marks the beginning of constant climatic change for the remainder of the Ice Age. Deep sea cores give us a record of changing sea temperatures. They tell us that ice sheets formed gradually, but deglaciation, global warming trends, took place with great rapidity. These corresponded with major sea level rises that flooded low-lying coastal areas. During glacial maxima, ice sheets covered a full third of the earth's surface, mantling Scandinavia and the Alps in Europe, as well as much of northern North America (Figure 5.2). Sea levels fell dramatically as a result, hundreds of feet below modern levels. The glaciers were about as extensive as today during warmer periods, the so-called interglacials, when sea levels were close to present shorelines. Much less is known about changes in tropical regions, although it is thought that the southern fringes of Africa's Sahara Desert expanded dramatically during cold periods.

Both *Homo erectus* and its successor, *Homo sapiens*, evolved during a long period of constant climatic transition between warmer and colder regimens in northern latitude. Experts believe that the world's climate has been in transition from one extreme to the other for over 75 percent of the past 730,000 years, with a predominance of colder climate over the period (Table 3.1). There were at least nine glacial episodes, a major one about 525,000 years ago, when there was ice as far south as Seattle, St. Louis, and New York in North America, and sea levels were about 650 feet (197 m) below modern levels. In contrast, there were periods of more temperate conditions between 515,000 and 315,000 years ago. This was the period when human settlement outside Africa expanded, as small bands of hunter-gatherers exploited the rich animal and plant resources of European and Asian river valleys and forests.

Another intensely cold cycle lasted from about 180,000 to 128,000 years ago, a cycle that coincided in general terms with the period when *Homo sapiens*, modern humans, were evolving in Africa. Between 100,000 and 15,000 years ago, the last Ice Age glaciation saw the spread of *Homo sapiens* throughout the Old World and into the Americas. These constant climatic changes played an important role in the spread of early human beings throughout temperate and tropical latitudes.

HOMO ERECTUS (c. 1.6 million to after 200,000 years ago)

Everyone agrees that the new forms of humans that appeared in Africa after 1.6 million years ago evolved from earlier *Homo habilis* populations. The earliest unquestioned specimen of this new form, *Homo erectus*,

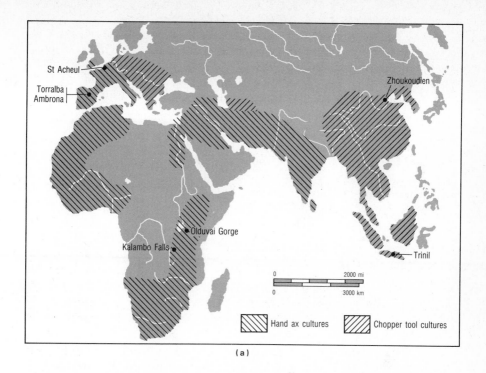

St Acheul

Torralba
Ambrona

Zhoukoudien

Olduvai Gorge

Kalambo Falls

Trinil

0   2000 mi

0   3000 km

▨ Hand ax cultures   ▩ Chopper tool cultures

(a)

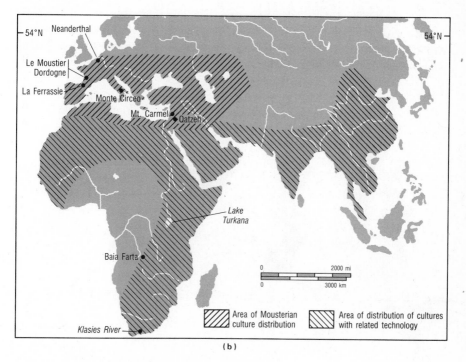

54°N   54°N

Neanderthal

Le Moustier
Dordogne

La Ferrassie

Monte Circeo

Mt. Carmel
Qatzeh

*Lake
Turkana*

Baia Farta

0   2000 mi

0   3000 km

Klasies River

▨ Area of Mousterian
culture distribution   ▩ Area of distribution of cultures
with related technology

(b)

Figure 4.1 Maps of sites mentioned in Chapter 4.

comes from East Turkana in Kenya, a skull with massive brow ridges and a larger brain than earlier *Homo*, dated to between 1.6 and 1.5 million years ago. Another fossil find, this time of a 12-year-old boy from the western side of Lake Turkana, dates to about the same time period. From the neck down, the boy's bones are remarkably modern looking. The skull and jawbone are more primitive, with brow ridges and a brain capacity perhaps as high as 700 to 800 cc, about half the modern size. The boy stood about 5 feet, 6 inches (1.8 m) tall, taller than most modern 12-year-olds. The Turkana boy seems to confirm the theory that different parts of the human body evolved at different rates, the body achieving fully modern form long before the head.

    Homo erectus is known to have lived over a wide area of the Old World, but occurs earliest in Africa (Figure 4.1). In addition to the Turkana finds, Louis Leakey found a million-year-old skullcap of *H. erectus* at Olduvai Gorge in Tanzania. *Homo erectus* fossils have come from Morocco and Algeria in North Africa, from Hungary and Germany. None of the European finds can be dated, but they probably belong to approximately 500,000 years ago.

    The classic *Homo erectus* finds come from Asia, from the Trinil area of Java where they date to between 900,000 and 600,000 years ago, and from northern China, dating to between 500,000 and 350,000 years ago (Figure 4.2). These well-preserved specimens show that these archaic humans had a brain capacity between 775 and 1300 cc, showing much variation. It is probable their vision was excellent and that they were capable of extensive thought. The *H. erectus* skull is more rounded than that of earlier hominids. It also has conspicuous brow ridges and a sloping

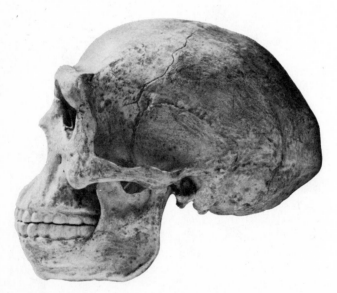

Figure 4.2 *Homo erectus* from Zhoukoudien, China.

forehead. *Homo erectus* had limbs and hips fully adapted to an upright posture. It stood over 5 feet, 6 inches (1.8 m) tall and had hands fully capable of precision gripping and many kinds of toolmaking.

During *Homo erectus'* long history, humanity adapted to a far wider range of environments, ranging from tropical savannas in East Africa to forested Javanese valleys, temperate climates in North Africa and Europe, and the harsh winters of northern China and central Europe. *Homo erectus* was certainly capable of a far more complex and varied lifeway than previous hominids. With such a wide distribution, it is hardly surprising that some variations in population occur. For example, Chinese scholars claim that the *Homo erectus* fossils from the famous Zhoukoudien cave near Beijing display a gradual increase in brain capacity from about 900 cc 600,000 years ago to about 1100 cc in 200,000-year-old individuals. In any case, *Homo erectus* was far more human than *Homo habilis*, a habitual biped, who had probably lost the thick hair covering that is characteristic of nonhuman primates.

THE RADIATION OF *HOMO ERECTUS*

As the climatic changes of the Ice Age became more frequent after a million years ago, and especially after the Matuyama/Brunhes reversal 730,000 years ago, African hominids had to adapt to cyclical alterations among savanna, forest, and desert. They could do so by migrating with the changing vegetational zones, as other mammals did, or they could adapt to new environments, changing their diets to accommodate different food resources. Finally, they could move out of tropical latitudes altogether, into habitats that human beings had never occupied before.

Paleoanthropologists now believe that *Homo erectus* adapted to changed circumstances in all these ways, with some hominids radiating out of Africa by way of the Sahara when the desert was capable of supporting human life. Climatologist Neil Roberts has likened the Sahara to a giant pump, sucking in animal populations during wetter climatic phases and forcing hunter-gatherers out toward the Mediterranean during drier cycles. In radiating out of Africa, *Homo erectus* behaved just like other mammals in its ecological community.

Hominids were carnivores and plant eaters, and thus linked ecologically with other predators. There was widespread interchange of mammals between Africa and more temperate latitudes before a million years ago. A major change in the mammalian populations of Europe took place about 700,000 years ago. Hippopotamuses, forest elephants, and other herbivores, also carnivores like the lion, leopard, and spotted hyena, seem to have migrated northward from Africa at about this time. Migrations by such predators as the lion and hyena, the animals with which hominids shared many ecological characteristics, were in the same direction as that taken by *Homo erectus*. That the first successful human settlement of

Europe and temperate Asia coincided with the radiation of a tropical mammalian community from Africa seems plausible.

Homo erectus may also have tamed fire, perhaps as early as 1.6 million years ago. Early humans would have been familiar with the great grass and brush fires that swept across the savanna during the dry months. Fire offered protection against predators and an easy way of hunting game, even insects and rodents fleeing from a line of flames. Perhaps *Homo erectus* developed the habit of conserving fire, taking advantage of long-smoldering tree stumps ignited by lightning strikes and other natural causes to kindle flames to light dry brush or simply to scare off predators.

It may be no coincidence that the radiation of *Homo erectus* out of tropical Africa into temperate environments in Asia and Europe occurred after the taming of fire and during a period of accelerated climatic change.

THE LIFEWAY OF *HOMO ERECTUS*

We still know little of the world of *Homo erectus*, beyond a certainty that humans had radiated far beyond their tropical African homeland. By 700,000 years ago, *Homo erectus* had settled in temperate Europe and the Near East, was probably living in India, and was certainly present in Southeast Asia and China (Figure 4.1). Nowhere were human beings abundant and the global population of archaic humans was undoubtedly minuscule. As far as is known *Homo erectus* did not settle in extreme arctic latitudes, in what is now Eurasia and Siberia, nor did these archaic humans cross into the Americas. Nor did they develop the watercraft needed to cross from island Southeast Asia to New Guinea and Australia, landmasses that remained isolated by the ocean until the late Ice Age.

Throughout this enormous area of the Old World, *Homo erectus* populations developed a great variety of lifeways and local toolkits that reflected different needs. The hominids were part of a vast animal community and their long-term success resulted from their ability to adapt to the cyclical changes in the Ice Age environment, from temperate to much colder, then to full glacial conditions and then, more rapidly, to warmer again. Many of these early human populations flourished in regions where dense, abundant, and predictable resources were to be found, isolated from other regions where similar conditions existed.

The climatic conditions of the Ice Age sometimes brought these isolated populations together, then separated them again, ensuring gene flow and genetic drift and continued biological and cultural evolution over the millennia. As it had been for *Homo habilis*, the key to adapting to temperate environments was mobility. Human bands could respond quickly to changes in resource distribution by moving into new areas. Theirs was a primarily opportunistic adaptation based on knowledge of where resources were to be found, rather than on deliberate planning, as was the case in much later times.

Separated as we are from *Homo erectus* by hundreds of thousands of years, it is difficult for us to obtain even a general impression of their simple but opportunistic lifeway. Almost invariably, the only signs of their existence are scatters of stone artifacts, most frequently discovered near lakes and in river valleys, where the most plentiful food resources were to be found. These myriad finds have enabled us to divide the world of *Homo erectus* into two broad and still ill-defined provinces: Africa, Europe, and some parts of Asia—more open country where hunting was important and multipurpose stone axes were commonly used, and a vast area of forested and wooded country in Asia where wood artifacts were all-important and stone technology far more conservative. This is almost certainly a gross simplification of a very complex picture, but it provides us with a general portrait of an archaic lifeway far removed from that of more modern humans.

Big-Game Hunting and Acheulian Technology

The simple Oldowan technology of *Homo habilis* remained in use for more than a million years before evolving slowly into a still simple, but more diverse, stone technology that itself remained in use for a further half-million years. Neither *Homo habilis* nor *Homo erectus* relied exclusively on stone, for we can say with confidence that our remote ancestors also made use of wood, one of the most versatile raw materials known to humanity. Although a 200,000-year-old wooden spear point has come to light in England, such finds are few and far between. Most insights into the technology of *Homo erectus* come from stone tools and the by-products associated with them.

In Africa, Europe, and some parts of Asia, *Homo erectus* is associated with a distinctive toolkit that includes not only a variety of flake tools and sometimes choppers, but also one of the most common exhibits in the world's museums—the hand axe (Figure 4.3). Unlike the crude flakes and choppers of the Oldowan, the Acheulian hand axe (named after the northern French town Saint Acheul) was an artifact with converging edges which met at a point. The maker had to envision the shape of the artifact, which was to be produced from a mere lump of stone, then fashion it not with opportunistic blows but with carefully directed hammer strokes.

Acheulian hand axes come in every size, from elegant oval types a few inches long to heavy axes more than a foot (0.3 m) long and weighing 5 pounds (2.3 kg) or more. They were multipurpose tools, used for grubbing up roots, woodworking, scraping skins, and especially skinning and butchering of animals. The hand axe and its near relative the cleaver (Figure 4.3) were ideal for butchery because the artifact could be sharpened again and again. When it became a useless lump of stone, it could be recycled into flake tools. But one can achieve effective butchery with simple flakes as well. A number of researchers have wondered whether the hand axe was not used for other purposes such as throwing at game or digging for roots.

Hand axes and related artifacts occur over an enormous area of the

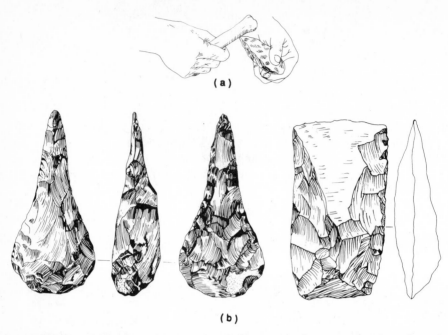

(a)

(b)

Figure 4.3 Acheulian technology. (a) Hand axes were multipurpose artifacts shaped symmetrically around a long axis. (b) Acheulian hand axe from Swanscombe, England and cleaver from Kalambo Falls, Zambia.

Old World and underwent considerable refinement during the million years or so they were in use. But what do we know of the behavior of their makers? Without question, *Homo erectus* hunted and foraged for food, probably in far more effective ways than *Homo habilis*. Time and time again, hand axes and other butchering artifacts have been found in association with the bones of large game animals. But did the hunters actually kill such formidable herbivores as the elephant and the rhinoceros? To do so would require social mechanisms to foster cooperation and communication abilities far beyond those of their predecessors.

Evidence for butchery and perhaps big-game hunting comes from two remarkable Acheulian sites at Torralba and Ambrona in central Spain. The Acheulians probably lived in this deep, swampy valley either 200,000 or 400,000 years ago (the date is controversial). Torralba has yielded most of the left side of an elephant, which had been cut into pieces, while Ambrona contained the remains of 30 to 35 dismembered elephants. Concentrations of broken bones lay all over the site and the skulls of the elephants had been broken open to get at the brains. In one place, elephant bones had been laid out in a line, perhaps to form stepping stones in the swamp, where the animals had been killed. Both sites were littered with crude hand axes, cleavers, scrapers, and cutting tools.

The original scenario for the sites had hunters watching the valley

Figure 4.4 Torralba, Spain. A remarkable linear arrangement of elephant tusks and leg bones that were probably laid out by those who butchered the animals.

floors, which may have lain astride an important game trail (Figure 4.4). At a strategic moment several bands would gather quietly, set brushfires, and drive the unsuspecting beasts into the swamps, where they would be killed and butchered at leisure. Other archaeologists challenge this scenario. They believe the hunters were actually scavenging meat from animals that had perished when enmired in the swamps.

Improvements in language and modes of communication are thought to have been a distinctive feature of *Homo erectus'* style of life. With enhanced language skills and more advanced technology, it was possible for people to cooperate in gathering activities and in the chase. Unlike the nonhuman primates, who strongly emphasize individual economic success, *Homo erectus* depended on cooperative activity by every individual in the band. The economic unit was the group; the secret of individual success was group success. People got along well as individuals, as families, and as entire groups. Judging from other finds of butchery sites in tropical Africa, *Homo erectus* was a much more skillful hunter-gatherer than earlier humans, one with the ability to kill even the largest and most formidable of big game.

Bamboo and Choppers

The eastern portions of the archaic prehistoric world lay in Asia, in an enormous region of woodland and forest with great environmental diversity. The tropical forests of Asia are rich in animal and plant foods, but these food resources are widely dispersed over the landscape. Thus,

Figure 4.5 Bamboo scaffolding in use in modern highrise construction.

Homo erectus bands were constantly on the move, carrying tools with them. Under these circumstances, it was logical for them to make use of bamboo, wood, and other fibrous materials — the most convenient materials at hand. There was no need for the specialized, often complicated artifacts used in the open country of the West, either for spear points or for the butchering tools used on large animals. As archaeologist Geoffrey Pope has pointed out, the distribution of the simple choppers and flakes used by eastern populations coincides very closely with the natural distribution of bamboo, one of the most versatile materials known to humankind. Bamboo was efficient, durable, and portable. It could be used to manufacture containers, sharp knives, spears, weapon tips, ropes, and dwellings. To this day, it is widely used in Asia as scaffolding for building skyscrapers (Figure 4.5). It is an ideal material for people subsisting not off large game but off smaller forest animals such as monkeys, rats, squirrels, lizards, and snakes, as well as plant foods. Simple stone flakes and jagged-edge choppers, the only artifacts to survive the millennia, would be ideal for working bamboo and may, indeed, have been used for this purpose for hundreds of thousands of years, long after *Homo erectus* had been superseded by more advanced human forms.

ARCHAIC *HOMO SAPIENS* (c. 400,000 to 130,000 years ago)

Homo erectus has long been considered the single human form to have lived on earth between about 1.5 million and 400,000 years ago. However, this all-embracing classification dates from the days when scholars thought of human evolution in more linear terms. They linked anatomically primitive features such as heavy brow ridges and bun-shaped skullcaps, which do indeed link the various *Homo erectus* fossils from Africa, Asia, and Europe. Derived features, such as the massive features found an Asian individuals, may in fact be evidence for geographically defined forms, only one of which evolved into *Homo sapiens*, anatomically modern humans. This branching view sees *Homo erectus* as an adaptive radiation of hominids by 700,000 years ago, with only a small part of this evolution resulting in the emergence of *Homo sapiens*.

Between about 400,000 and 130,000 years ago, *Homo erectus* was evolving toward more modern forms of human. Fossil fragments from Africa, Asia, and Europe display both *erectus*-like and *sapiens*-like traits, sufficient for them to be classified under the general label archaic *Homo sapiens*. These anatomical advances take several forms. Brain capacities are larger, the sides of the skull are wider, and the rear of the cranium is now more rounded. Human skeletons become less robust and molar teeth are smaller.

These general trends occur in African fossils, such as the well-known, massive Broken Hill skull from Kabwe, Zambia, in central Africa. They are found in China, too, where both primitive and *sapiens* traits appear, traits that Chinese anthropologists also claim appear in modern populations there. In Europe, too, fossil remains dating to this long period display a mosaic of *erectus* and *sapiens* features. But the fossils from each continent differ considerably, European fossils, for example, often appearing somewhat more robust than those from Asia. Everywhere, however, brain sizes increase gradually and skull shapes become rounder. In Asia and Africa, the changes seem to trend toward modern *sapiens*, whereas the European fossils are evolving toward a Neanderthal form (see below). This evolutionary trend toward more modern anatomy appears everywhere, but it was only on one continent, Africa, that *Homo erectus* gave rise to modern *Homo sapiens*. In other words, the pattern of human evolution based on the adaptive radiation seen with the australopithecines hundreds of thousands of years earlier persisted into much later prehistory.

TOOL TECHNOLOGY

Such branching theories of human evolution highlight a basic phenomenon of early prehistory. The stone artifacts of the archaic world are patterned in time and space in a general way that mirrors the pattern for early hominids. For example, the earliest Oldowan stone artifacts appear at the same time as the genus *Homo*. Bifacially worked hand axes become commonplace as *Homo erectus* emerges in Africa. Later, the world divides into two broad technological provinces, a western one with hand axes and an Asian one without. Everywhere except tropical Africa, the technological continuity is striking, with hand axes being used until as late as 100,000 years ago in Europe, and chopping tools lasting until late in prehistory in Asia. Only in tropical Africa did the technology of hand axes give way some 200,000 years ago to a new toolkit based on scrapers and crude projectile points mounted on wooden shafts (Figure 4.8). By 100,000 years later, some African populations were making much finer, parallel-sided flakes, which they fashioned into a wider range of more specialized artifacts. The new technology was far more varied and specialized than anything ever used before. It is not known whether this was associated with the evolution of fully modern humans south of the Sahara, for the emergence of modern humans is one of the most fiercely debated controversies of world prehistory.

THE ORIGINS OF *HOMO SAPIENS* (After 200,000 to 100,000 years ago)

Only one thing is certain in this controversy. Eventually *Homo erectus* evolved into *Homo sapiens*, but we do not even know when the gradual transition began or how or where it took place. Some researchers believe the change began as early as 400,000 years ago; others think it began much later, some time around, or after, 200,000 years ago.

First, what distinguishes us from archaic *Homo sapiens* and other earlier humans? *Homo sapiens sapiens* means the wise person. We are the clever people, the sage humans, animals capable of subtlety, of manipulation, of self-understanding. What is it that separates us from earlier humans, scientists wonder? First and foremost must be our ability to speak fluently and articulately. We communicate, we tell stories, we pass on knowledge and ideas, all through the medium of language. Consciousness, cognition, self-awareness, foresight, and the ability to express oneself and one's emotions—these are direct consequences of fluent speech. They can be linked with another attribute of the fully fledged human psyche: the capacity for symbolic and spiritual thought, concerned not only with subsistence and technology but also with the boundaries of existence and the relationships among the individual, the group, and the universe.

Fluent speech, the full flowering of human creativity expressed in art and religion, expert toolmaking—these are some of the hallmarks of *Homo sapiens sapiens*. With these abilities humankind eventually colonized not just temperate and tropical environments but the entire globe. With the appearance of modern humans we begin the study of people biologically identical to ourselves, people with the same intellectual qualities and potential as our own.

Candelabras and Noah's Arks

The controversies over the evolution of modern humans are bedeviled by a lack of fossil data from any part of the world. Thus, scientists have relied heavily both on theoretical argument and on minute anatomical traits found on fragmentary crania and jaws to argue their cases. In recent years, a new player has emerged, that of human genetics. Geneticists have added a new, and also controversial dimension to the debate by using DNA studies to trace the origin of *Homo sapiens sapiens* to tropical Africa.

The two major hypotheses for modern human origins are diametrically opposed to each other. The so-called *Regional Continuity Hypothesis* (sometimes called the Candelabra theory) theorizes that *Homo erectus* populations throughout the Old World evolved independently, first to archaic *Homo sapiens*, then to fully modern humans. This continuity model argues for multiple origins, of *Homo sapiens sapiens*. It assumes that modern geographic populations have been separated from one another for a long time, for perhaps as much as a million years.

The Single Origin Hypothesis (sometimes named the *Noah's Ark model*) takes the diametrically opposite view, that *Homo sapiens* evolved in one place, then spread to all other parts of the world (Figure 5.1). This replacement model implies that modern geographic populations have *shallow* roots in prehistory and were derived from a single source of relatively recent date.

These two models represent extremes, which pit advocates of anatomical continuity against those who favor rapid replacement of archaic populations. Until recently, most anthropologists favored the Regional Continuity model, as both human artifacts and fossil finds from Europe and the Near East appeared to document slow biological and culture change over long periods of time. Today, however, a torrent of new discoveries have shown that archaic human populations displayed great variation and were morphologically more different from anatomically modern humans than once suspected. Advocates of the Regional Continuity model rely heavily on anatomical traits from surviving fossils to argue their case, whereas Single Origin supporters make use not only of fossils but of genetics, an approach their opponents regard as highly controversial. The debate continues, despite a lack of new fossils, and is likely to continue for generations as both new discoveries and more refined genetic researches radically alter our knowledge of archaic *Homo sapiens* and its contemporaries and successors.

At the time of writing, many scholars appear to favor the Single Origin hypothesis, largely because findings by molecular biologists have hinted that Africa and Africa alone may have been the cradle of modern humans.

HOMO SAPIENS IN AFRICA

The molecular biologists have used mitochondrial DNA (mtDNA) to study mutation rates in humans and other animals. Mitochondrial DNA accumulates mutations much faster than nuclear DNA. Mitochondrial DNA is inherited only through the maternal line; it does not mix and become diluted with paternal DNA. Thus, it provides a potential genetic link with human populations deep in prehistory. When genetic researchers analyzed the mtDNA of 147 women from Africa, Asia, Europe, Australia, and New Guinea, they found that the differences between them were very small. Therefore, they argued, the five populations were all of comparatively recent origin. There were some differences, sufficient to separate a set of African individuals from all other groups, suggesting Africans were the earliest of these populations. Thus, some biologists concluded that all modern humans derive from a 200,000-year-old African population, from which populations migrated to the rest of the Old World with little or no interbreeding with existing, more archaic human groups.

The date of 200,000 years for the primeval population of African *Homo sapiens* was based on the assumption that there is a constant rate of mitochondrial DNA mutation of about 2 to 4 percent every million years in several vertebrate species. Biochemist Roberta Cann and others used similar calculations to estimate that there was a second split, which separated modern humans in Africa from those who moved out between 180,000 and 90,000 years ago, perhaps around 140,000 years ago.

The mtDNA research is at a very early stage and has been criticized on both methodological and chronological grounds. The research techniques being used are under constant refinement and it is difficult even for geneticists to know whether the reliability of the preliminary conclusions of some years ago will be proven. Fortunately, there is some archaeological and fossil evidence that tends to confirm an early appearance of anatomically modern humans in sub-Saharan Africa. According to German physical anthropologist Gunter Brauer, there were at least three grades of *Homo sapiens* in sub-Saharan Africa. An archaic *Homo sapiens* form was distributed from southern to northeast Africa some 200,000 years ago. These archaic populations had evolved from earlier *Homo erectus* populations and had higher cranial vaults and other anatomical features akin to those of anatomically modern humans. Between about 150,000 and 100,000 years ago, Brauer believes, late archaic *Homo sapiens* populations flourished throughout Africa, people displaying mosaics of both archaic and modern features. After 100,000 years ago, anatomically modern humans lived everywhere south of the Sahara.

Brauer believes that very early anatomically modern humans were widely distributed in eastern and southern Africa as early as 115,000 years ago, and perhaps earlier. He also believes that the biological developments that led to the appearance of modern humans had run their course as early as between 100,000 and 70,000 years ago, earlier than anywhere else in the world, where archaic human forms such as the Neanderthals (p. 89) still flourished.

WHY DID *HOMO SAPIENS* EVOLVE?

Ecological anthropologist Robert Foley points out that the savanna woodland of Africa 100,000 years ago was an ideal environment for promoting the speciation of modern humans. He has studied monkey evolution in Africa and found that the widely dispersed populations had diverged; they did not continue on a single evolutionary course. Africa experienced considerable habitat fragmentation and reformation during the constant cold and warm cycles of the Ice Age, fluctuations that enhanced the prospects of speciation among the continent's animals and plants. For example, says Foley, one monkey genus alone radiated into 16 species at about the same time as modern humans may have evolved in Africa.

Foley's monkey studies have convinced him that modern humans evolved in such a fragmented mosaic of tropical environments, developing distinctive characteristics that separated them from their archaic predecessors. There were areas where food resources were predictable and of high quality. In response to such regions, some human populations may have developed wide-ranging behavior, lived in larger social groups with considerable kin-based substructure, and been highly selective in their diet.

As part of these responses, some groups may have developed exceptional hunting skills, using a technology so effective that they could prey on animals from a distance with projectiles. With more efficient weapons, more advance planning, and better organization of both hunting and foraging, our ancestors could have reduced the unpredictability of the environment in dramatic ways. Few archaeologists would be so bold as to associate ancient technologies with specific fossil forms, but we do know that tens of thousands of years later, *Homo sapiens sapiens* relied on much more sophisticated tool technology than their predecessors. The new toolkits were based on antler, bone, wood, and parallel-sided, stone-blade manufacture. This technology was far more advanced than anything made by their predecessors and took many millennia to develop. There is no question but that it would have conferred a major advantage on its users, both in terms of hunting efficiency and energy expended in the chase.

Interestingly enough, there are signs of technological change throughout eastern and southern Africa between 200,000 and 130,000 years ago, as age-old hand axe technology gave way to lighter toolkits which combined sharp stone flakes with wooden spear shafts, and to other more specialized artifacts used for woodworking and butchery. Such simple artifacts, made on standard-sized flakes, could have been the archaic prototypes of far more efficient tools and weapons developed by anatomically modern humans after 100,000 years ago. But again, one must emphasize that the existence of such artifacts in Africa at the time when modern humans apparently first appeared there is not necessarily proof they were developed by *Homo sapiens sapiens*.

To summarize the controversy over modern human origins—the weight of such evidence as there is, and it is not much, tends to favor an African origin for *Homo sapiens sapiens*.

THE SPREAD OF *HOMO SAPIENS*

If tropical Africa was the cradle of modern humans, how and why did *Homo sapiens* spread into Europe and Asia? The critical period was between 100,000 and 45,000 years ago, the date by which *Homo sapiens* is known to have been living in the Near East.

The only barrier to population movement between tropical Africa and the Mediterranean region is the Sahara Desert. But the Sahara has not always been impassable desert. About 100,000 years ago, a cooler and wetter climate prevailed in the desert. For long periods, the country between East Africa and the Mediterranean was passable, supporting scattered game herds and open grassland. Thus, *Homo sapiens* may have hunted and foraged across the Sahara into the Nile Valley and the Near East as early as 100,000 years ago.

We know that anatomically modern people were living at Qafzeh Cave in Israel by at least 92,000 years ago, at almost as early a date as modern humans are known to have flourished in Africa. They lived there alongside more archaic, Neanderthal-like people for more than 45,000 years. Then, as the Near East became increasingly dry and less productive, the newcomers may have responded to population pressure and food shortages by moving across the wide land bridge that joined Turkey to southeastern Europe 45,000 years ago, spreading into the more productive steppe and tundra regions of Europe and western Asia (Figure 5.1).

We do not know when anatomically modern humans first appeared in Asia. Despite theories that they flourished in China as early as 70,000 years ago, there is a yawning gap in the fossil record after about 200,000 years ago. The earliest possible *Homo sapiens* fossils in China date to somewhere between 50,000 and 37,000 years ago. An intelligent guess for the first settlement of Asia by modern humans would perhaps be about 50,000 years ago, by which time *Homo sapiens sapiens* was well established in the Near East and Africa.

THE NEANDERTHALS (c. 150,000 to 32,000 years ago)

The lifeway of the many forms of archaic *Homo sapiens* ultimately replaced by our remote ancestors is still little known, except in central and western Europe, where the celebrated Neanderthals once flourished. We are all familiar with cartoons of the archetype cave people clad in rough skins, with brutish faces and wooden spears. These stereotypes are based on popular early twentieth-century images of the Neanderthals, the indigenous inhabitants of Europe and Eurasia encountered by modern humans as they spread out from the Near East after 45,000 years ago. In fact, the Neanderthals were strong, robustly built humans with some archaic features, like bun-shaped skulls and sometimes eyebrow ridges, when compared with modern people. There is every reason to believe they were expert hunters and beings capable of considerable intellectual reasoning (Figure 4.6).

There are, of course, striking anatomical differences between Neanderthals and modern humans, both in the robust postcranial skeleton and in the skull and forward-projecting face. These features are the reason this

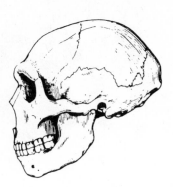

Figure 4.6 Neanderthal skull found at Mount Circeo, Italy.

extinct hominid form is classified as *Homo sapiens neanderthalensis*, and not as *Homo sapiens sapiens*, a fully modern human.

The Neanderthals flourished in Europe, Eurasia, and parts of the Near East from about 150,000 years ago until around 32,000 years ago. Their anatomical pattern evolved over about 50 millennia, then stabilized for another 50 millennia before changing rapidly to essentially modern human anatomy within a brief period of 5,000 years approximately 40,000 years ago. Neanderthal populations displayed great variation, but everywhere had the same posture and manual abilities as modern people. They differed from us in having massive limb bones, often somewhat bowed in the thigh and forearm, features that reflect their greater muscular power. For their height, the Neanderthals were bulky and heavily muscled, and their brain capacity was slightly larger than that of modern humans. Their antecedents are in the *Homo erectus* and earlier archaic *Homo sapiens* group, from which they inherited their heavy build, an adaptation so successful that it lasted for more than 100,000 years (Figure 4.7).

Neanderthal culture and technology was far more complex and sophisticated than that of their Acheulian predecessors. Many of their artifacts were not multipurpose tools, but were made for specific purposes, as stone spear points mounted on wooden spears, or curved scrapers for treating pegged-out hides. Like their predecessors, they occupied large

Figure 4.7 Reconstruction of Neanderthal lifeway in France during the early Würm glaciation.

territories, which they probably exploited on a seasonal round, returning to the same locations year after year when game migrated or plant foods came into season.

The Neanderthals were skilled hunters, especially when one realizes that they had to attack game at close quarters with spears and clubs rather than with the bow and arrow. They were not afraid to tackle such formidable animals as mammoth, reindeer, or wild horses. It appears that many western European bands lived in caves and rockshelters during much of the year as a protection against arctic cold. During the brief summer months they may have fanned out over the open plains, living in temporary tented encampments. There can be little doubt the Neanderthals knew their local environments intimately and that they planned their lives around migration seasons, and such factors as herd size and the predictability of animal movements. By this time, too, humans had learned how to store food for the lean months, maximizing the meat taken from seasonally migrating herds of reindeer and other animals. For this reason, there was much more cultural variability between different regions of the Neanderthal world.

This variability is reflected in the diverse Mousterian toolkits of Neanderthal groups (named after the village of Le Moustier in southwestern France). Unlike the hand axe makers, the Neanderthals made most of their artifacts on flakes, the most common being scraping tools and spear points. Some of their weapons were *composite tools*, artifacts made of more than one component — for example a point, a shaft, and the binding that secured the head to the shaft, making a spear. Their technology was simple, highly variable, and a logical development of earlier technologies developed over hundreds of thousands of years (Figure 4.8). Neanderthal sites in France have yielded a great diversity of toolkits. Some levels include hand axes; others notched flakes, perhaps used for stripping meat for drying or pressing fibrous plants. Such wide variation in Mousterian toolkits is found not only in France but at other Neanderthal sites

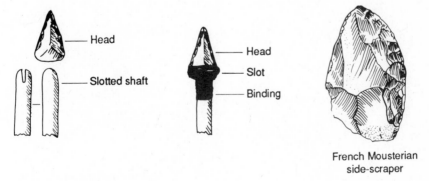

Head

Slotted shaft

Head

Slot

Binding

French Mousterian
side-scraper

Figure 4.8 Composite spear point and scraper made by European Neanderthals.

throughout Europe and the Near East and in North Africa, where other archaic *Homo sapiens* made similar tools. No one knows exactly what all these variations in toolkits mean, but they reflect the ability of the Neanderthals and other archaic *Homo sapiens* to develop tools for different, highly specific activities, perhaps at a time of rising human populations and slightly enhanced social complexity.

The Neanderthals and their archaic contemporaries elsewhere were hunter-gatherers and the world's population was still small, but life was gradually becoming more complex. We find the first signs of religious ideology, of a preoccupation with the life hereafter. Many Neanderthals were buried by their companions. Neanderthal burials have been recovered from caves and rockshelters, and from open campsites. One rockshelter, La Ferrassie near Les Eyzies in France, yielded the remains of two adult Neanderthals and four children buried close together in a campsite. Group sepulchers occur at other sites, too, signs that the Neanderthals, like most later hunter-gatherers, believed in life after death.

We find in the Neanderthals and their increasingly sophisticated culture the first roots of our own complicated beliefs, societies, and religious sense. But the Neanderthals, like other archaic *Homo sapiens* forms, gave way to fully modern humans, whose awesome intellectual and physical powers created a late Ice Age world unimaginably different from that of earlier prehistory. If the Noah's Ark hypothesis is correct, then *Homo sapiens sapiens* replaced the Neanderthals in Europe and the Near East after 45,000 years ago.

PART
Three

THE BIRTH OF THE MODERN WORLD

"Who among men and the creatures could live without the Sun-father? For his light brings day, warms and gladdens the Earth-mother with rain which flows forth in the water we drink and that causes the flesh of the Earth-mother to yield abundantly seed, while these—are they not cooked by the brand of fire which warms us in winter?"

Zuni priest quoted by Frank Cushing, "Zuni Breadstuff," The Millstone, 1884.

Chapter
5

Diaspora

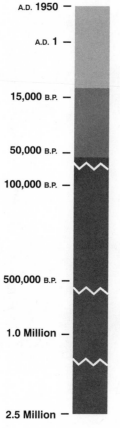

A.D. 1950 —

A.D. 1 —

15,000 B.P. —

50,000 B.P. —

100,000 B.P. —

500,000 B.P. —

1.0 Million —

2.5 Million —

*T*his chapter describes the late Ice Age world of about 50,000 to 15,000 years ago. We show how humans first adapted to extreme arctic climates and developed highly specialized hunter-gatherer cultures that subsisted off cold-loving animals such as the mammoth and steppe bison. We discuss, also, the radiation of *Homo sapiens* throughout the Old World, and then turn to one of the most controversial subjects in modern archaeology—the first settlement of the Americas (Figure 5.1).

THE LATE ICE AGE WORLD (50,000 to 15,000 years ago)

For most of the past 45,000 years, the world was very different from that of today. At the height of the last Ice Age glaciation, some 18,000 years ago, vast ice sheets mantled Scandinavia and the Alps, leaving a chilly corridor of open tundra between them. Sea levels were more than 300 feet (91.4 m) lower than today. Britain was joined to the European continent, the North Sea was under ice, and the Baltic Sea did not exist. One could walk from Turkey to Bulgaria dry-shod (Figure 5.2). Vast, treeless plains stretched north and east from central Europe to the frontiers

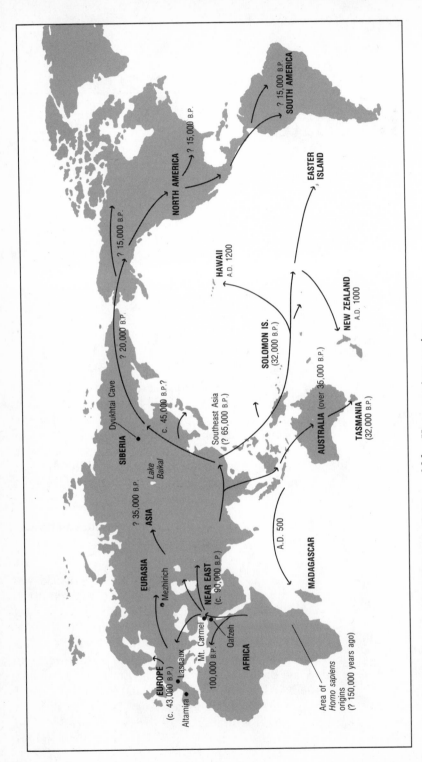

Figure 5.1 Map showing the settlement of the world by *Homo sapiens sapiens*.

EUROPE
(c. 43,000 B.P.)
Altamira
Lascaux
Mt. Carmel
Qafzeh
100,000 B.P.
NEAR EAST
(c. 90,000 B.P.)
AFRICA
Area of
Homo sapiens
origins
(? 150,000 years ago)
EURASIA
Mezhirich
ASIA
? 35,000 B.P.
Lake Baikal
SIBERIA
Dyukhtai Cave
c. 45,000 B.P.?
? 20,000 B.P.
? 15,000 B.P.
NORTH AMERICA
? 15,000 B.P.
SOUTH AMERICA
? 15,000 B.P.
Southeast Asia
(? 65,000 B.P.)
MADAGASCAR
A.D. 500
AUSTRALIA (over 36,000 B.P.)
TASMANIA
(32,000 B.P.)
SOLOMON IS.
(32,000 B.P.)
HAWAII
A.D. 1200
EASTER
ISLAND
NEW ZEALAND
A.D. 1000

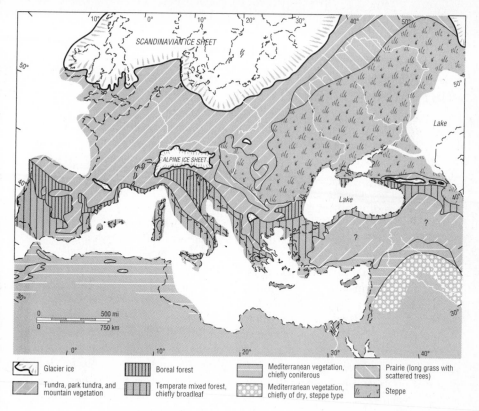

Figure 5.2 Generalized vegetation map of Europe during the late Würm glaciation.

of Siberia and beyond, a landscape of rolling scrub country dissected by occasional broad river valleys. The only signs of life were occasional herds of large big-game animals like the mammoth, bison, and reindeer, and they were often confined to river valleys. For humans to survive in these exposed landscapes required not only effective hunting methods and weaponry, but well-insulated winter dwellings and layered, tailored clothing that could keep people warm in subzero temperatures.

In more temperate and tropical latitudes, the effects of the last glaciation are harder to detect in geological strata. Tropical regions were often drier, many rainforests shrank, and there were more open grasslands and woodlands. In Africa, the Sahara Desert was as dry, if not drier, than today, as cold polar air flowed south of the Mediterranean. Much lower sea levels exposed enormous areas of continental shelf in Southeast Asia. Many offshore islands became part of the Asian mainland. Great rivers meandered over what were then exposed coastal plains, across another sunken Ice Age continent known to scholars as Sunda. Offshore lay two large land masses — Wallacea, made up of the present islands of Sulawesi and Timor, and Sahul, a combination of New Guinea, Australia, and the low-lying and now flooded shelf between them.

Let us now look at how late Ice Age humans peopled this diverse, often harsh, world.

THE PEOPLING OF SOUTHEAST ASIA AND AUSTRALIA (45,000 to 15,000 years ago)

Homo sapiens had appeared in Southeast Asia by at least 50,000 years ago. At the time, sea levels were much lower than today, so human settlement on Sunda, the exposed continental shelf, may have been concentrated in river valleys, along lake shores and on the coasts. If there were technological changes associated with *Homo sapiens*, they probably involved more efficient ways of exploiting the rich and highly varied environments of the mainland and offshore islands. The coastlines that faced offshore were relatively benign waters that probably offered a bounty of fish and shellfish to supplement game and wild plant foods. Perhaps coastal peoples constructed simple rafts for fishing in shallow or used rudimentary dugout canoes for bottom fishing. At some point, some of these people crossed open water to Wallacea and Sahul.

Sahul was a landscape of dramatic contrasts, of rugged mountain chains and highland valleys in the north, and rolling semi-arid lowlands over much of what is now Australia. Colonizing Sahul meant an open-water downwind passage of at least 62 miles (98 km), an entirely feasible proposition in simple watercraft in warm tropical waters and smooth seas.

The earliest documented human settlement of New Guinea comes from the Huon Peninsula in the southeastern corner of the island, where some 40,000-year-old ground stone axes came to light. The Huon Peninsula faces New Britain Island, 30 miles (48 km) offshore. Fishermen were living in caves on the island by at least 32,000 years ago. Some 4,000 years later, people had sailed between 81 and 112 miles (130 to 180 km) to settle on Buka Island in the northern Solomons to the south (Figure 5.3). From Buka it would have been an easy matter to colonize the remainder of the Solomon chain, for the islands are separated by but short distances. All of this data points to a rapid spread of late Ice Age hunter-gatherers through Sahul by at least 40,000 years ago, using some form of quite effective watercraft.

Human occupation in what is now Australia is well documented by 35,000 years ago, but may extend back 10,000 to 15,000 years earlier— the evidence is controversial. The Willandra Lakes region has yielded shell middens and campsites dating from perhaps as early as 37,000 to about 26,000 years ago. They include the skulls and limb bones of robustly built, anatomically modern people, the earliest human remains found in Australia. By 31,000 years ago, human beings had crossed the low-lying strait that joined the island of Tasmania to the Australian mainland in the far south, to colonize the most southerly region of the earth settled by Ice Age people. At the height of the glacial maximum, people

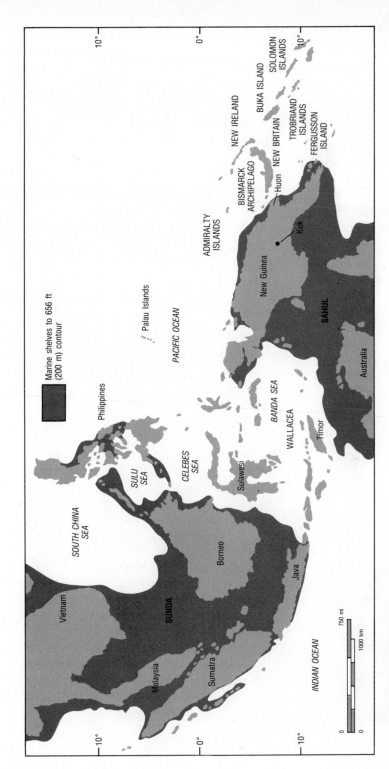

Figure 5.3 Sunda and Sahul.

Marine shelves to 656 ft (200 m) contour

SOUTH CHINA SEA

Vietnam

Malaysia

Sumatra

Borneo

Java

SUNDA

INDIAN OCEAN

Philippines

SULU SEA

CELEBES SEA

Sulawesi

BANDA SEA

WALLACEA

Timor

PACIFIC OCEAN

Palau Islands

ADMIRALTY ISLANDS

New Guinea

Kuk

Huon

BISMARCK ARCHIPELAGO

NEW IRELAND

NEW BRITAIN

BUKA ISLAND

SOLOMON ISLANDS

TROBRIAND ISLANDS

FERGUSSON ISLAND

SAHUL

Australia

10°

0°

10°

10°

0°

10°

0   750 mi
0   1000 km

lived in the rugged landscape of the Tasmanian interior, hunting red wallabies and ranging over a wide area for many centuries.

On the other side of the world, the inhabitants of Europe and Eurasia similarly adapted to extreme cold, a development that led ultimately to the colonization of Siberia and the Americas.

LATE ICE AGE EUROPE: THE CRO-MAGNONS (45,000 to 15,000 years ago)

The first fully modern Europeans are known to biological anthropologists as the Cro-Magnons, named after a rockshelter near the village of Les Eyzies in southwestern France. Anatomically, the Cro-Magnons are indistinguishable from ourselves (Figure 5.4), strongly built, large-headed people, whose appearance contrasts dramatically with that of their Neanderthal predecessors.

The Cro-Magnons had settled in southeast and central Europe by at least 40,000 years ago, apparently near Neanderthal groups. Some of them had penetrated into the sheltered, deep river valleys of southwestern France by 35,000 to 40,000 years ago. By 30,000 years ago, the Neanderthals had vanished and the density of Cro-Magnon settlement intensified considerably.

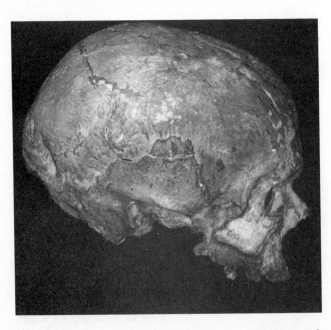

Figure 5.4 *Homo sapiens sapiens* from the Cro-Magnon rock shelter, Les Eyzies, France.

Subsistence

The Cro-Magnons entered Europe during a brief period of more temperate climate. Even then, climatic conditions and seasonal contrasts may have been such as to require new artifacts and much more sophisticated hunting and foraging skills. These adaptations developed rapidly, indeed spectacularly, after 30,000 years ago. It was during these millennia that *Homo sapiens* finally mastered winter, for it was in northern latitudes that human ingenuity and endurance were tested to the full. The Cro-Magnons of western and central Europe developed elaborate and sophisticated hunting cultures during this period. Their cultures were marked not only by many technological innovations, but by a flowering of religious and social life, reflected in one of the earliest art traditions in the world.

The center of these activities was away from the open plains, in the river valleys of southwestern France and northern Spain, and in parts of central Europe like the Danube Basin. Here, deep valleys supported lush summer meadows and a mix of open steppe and forest where cold-tolerant animals ranging in size from the mammoth and bison to the wild horse and boar flourished. High cliffs often provided caves and rockshelters warmed by the winter sun. The area lay astride reindeer migration routes in spring and fall, while salmon ran up the fast-running rivers. The Cro-Magnons may have migrated to open country during the short summer months, concentrating in more sheltered river valleys from fall through spring. They hunted not only big-game, but far smaller animals such as arctic fox, beaver, rabbits, wolves, and many birds as well as gathering plant foods. After about 16,000 years ago, they also fished for salmon, trout, perch, and eels from rivers and streams.

The Cro-Magnons survived in a harsh and unpredictable environment not only because they were expert hunters and foragers, but because they had effective ways of keeping warm outside in the depth of winter and the ability to store large amounts of meat and other foods to tide them over lean periods. Above all, anyone living in late Ice Age Europe had to be adaptable, capable of cooperating with others, and ready to grab opportunities to obtain food when they arose. Survival depended on diversification, on never concentrating on one or two animals to the exclusion of others.

For most of the year, the Cro-Magnons lived in small groups, subsisting off a wide range of game and stored foods. The times when they came together in larger groups may have been in spring, summer, and early fall, when reindeer, and in later times, salmon, were abundant. This period of coming together was an important annual occasion, when social life was at its most intense. It was then that people arranged marriages, conducted initiation rites, and bartered raw materials, artifacts, and other commodities with one another. Then, as winter closed in, the groups would disperse through the sheltered river valleys, returning to their stored foods and the small herds of game animals that also took refuge from the bitter winds.

Figure 5.5 Excavations at the Abri Pataud rock shelter, Les Eyzies, France.

Reindeer were vital to survival. At the Abri Pataud rockshelter near Les Eyzies in France's Dordogne, reindeer provided up to 30 percent of all prey for more than 10,000 years (Figure 5.5). The hunters located their camps close to shallow river crossings where they knew migrating reindeer were likely to pass. This complex rhythm of reindeer hunting was but a part of a constant pattern of group movements that persisted over many thousands of years. It survived for thousands of years from at least 32,000 years ago right up to the end of the Ice Age, when the glaciers finally melted and dense forest spread over the open plains and deep valleys of central and western Europe. Not that life stayed exactly the same through these many millennia, for climatic conditions changed constantly. The Cro-Magnons had an efficient and highly versatile toolkit and a wide range of food resources to choose from, so they could readily adjust to changing circumstances.

Cro-Magnon Technology

Cro-Magnon technology was versatile, yet fundamentally very simple. It depended on four interrelated foundations:

1. Careful selection of fine-grained rock such as chert, flint, or obsidian for blade cores;

2. The production of relatively standardized, parallel-sided artifact blanks from these cores that could be used to make more specialized cutting, piercing, and scraping tools;
3. The refinement of the burin (engraving tool), which enabled people to work antler and bone efficiently;
4. The use of the so-called "groove and splinter" technique for fabricating antler tools.

These technological innovations had a profound significance on the future course of human prehistory, for they were the material means by which humans adapted to the climatic extremes of Eurasia and Siberia.

Late Ice Age stoneworkers everywhere were highly selective in their use of flint and other fine-grained rock. Their primary objective was to produce long, parallel-sided artifact blanks, blades that could then be turned into a wide spectrum of specialized artifacts for hunting, for butchery and processing skins, for woodworking and clothing manufacture, and for the production of the raw materials needed to create specialized antler and bone tools in treeless environments. So great was Cro-Magnon concern for good toolmaking stone that they bartered it with neighbors over considerable distances.

Once procured, the precious raw materials were turned into carefully prepared blade cores that were carried around from one camp to the next. The cores were a kind of savings bank, an account of toolmaking stone used to produce tool blanks whenever they were needed. Thus, Cro-Magnon people were able to respond at a moment's notice to an opportunity to butcher an animal or to cut long slivers from fresh reindeer antlers.

The closest analogies in our own technology are the Leatherman and Swiss Army Knife. Both are multipurpose artifacts built on a strong chassis with a special spring system that enables the user to call on a wide variety of different tools, everything from a pair of scissors to pliers. The late Ice Age equivalents were the cores and the blades that came from them.

One important Cro-Magnon artifact was the burin, a delicate instrument for carving fine lines. The burin was used for woodworking, for cutting grooves in animal hides, for engraving designs on antler, bone, and cave walls, and, above all, for cutting the long antler blanks for making artifacts of antler, bone, and ivory (Figure 5.6). Many of these were specialized tools like barbed points, mounted with foreshafts which snapped off when the spear entered its quarry (Figure 5.6). Some were important innovations, especially the eyed needle, essential for making tailored winter clothes, and the spearthrower, a hooked and sometimes weighted device that extended the range and accuracy of hunting weapons (Figure 5.6). The same technology of fine-barbed antler head spears and stone-barbed weapons could be used for hunting big-game, as well as for taking salmon in shallow water, for dispatching rabbits, even for developing bows and arrows, which appeared some time during the late Ice Age.

The archaeological record reflects many refinements in Cro-Magnon technology over more than 15,000 years. In the early years of this century, French archaeologist Henri Breuil classified the late Ice Age cultures of southwestern France into four basic cultural traditions which culminated in the celebrated Magdalenian culture of about 18,000 to 12,000 years ago. The Magdalenian, named after the La Madeleine rockshelter on the Vezere River, was not only a technologically sophisticated culture, but one with a new concern for artistic expression and body ornament.

Cro-Magnon Art

The symbolic and ceremonial life of the Cro-Magnons was probably no more elaborate than that of their contemporaries known to have been painting in southern Africa and Australia at much the same time. Fortunately, much has survived, for Cro-Magnon artists used cave walls as their canvas, durable antler and ivory, not wood and skins, as palettes.

The first appearance of cave art coincides with a new concern with body ornamentation, especially perforated carnivore teeth and sea shells. This explosion in body ornamentation probably coincided with realizations that such adornments could define and communicate social roles — gender, group affiliation, and so on. Late Ice Age people mastered the ability to think in specific visual images, using them as well as chants, recitations, and songs to share and communicate images and ideas. They resulted in complex and diverse art traditions that lasted for more than 20,000 years.

The surviving Cro-Magnon art of Europe and Eurasia is but a minor proportion of their artistic output, for the artists almost certainly used many perishable materials — clay, wood, fiber, bark, hides, and bird feathers. Without question, too, they used red ocher and other pigments as body paint, for decoration. The surviving art occurs over a vast area from North Africa to Siberia, with major concentrations in northern Spain, southwestern France, also central and Eastern Europe. On cave walls, the artists engraved and painted animals and occasional humans, also schematic patterns: lines, elaborate panels, and complex shapes. The same artists engraved antler, bone, and ivory with consummate skill. They created animals in the round, engraved bison with delicate strokes that etched in every detail of eyes, manes, and hair. There are figurines of animals and humans in ivory, soft stone, and baked clay, such as the celebrated Venus figurines that depict women of all ages.

Upper Palaeolithic art is full of compelling images, many of them concentrated at major sites such as Lascaux and Trois Freres in southwestern France, and Altamira in northern Spain (Figure 5.7). These may have been places of unusual religious and symbolic importance. They were storehouses, meeting places, and ritual shrines, not only for local groups, but for people from far wider areas, too. Other locations were sacred

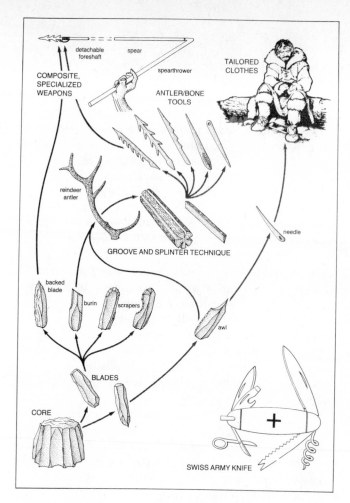

Figure 5.6 Blade core technology acts like a Swiss Army Knife, producing blanks for making many specialized artifacts for working bone and antler.

Figure 5.7 Wild bull from Lascaux, France.

places used occasionally for major ceremonies. These are illustrated dramatically by Le Tuc d'Audoubert Cave in the Ariege, France, where two carefully modeled clay bison lie in a remote, low-ceilinged chamber far from the entrance, placed against a rock. The bison are about one-sixth the full size, shaped with a skilled artist's fingers and a spatula, the eyes, nostrils, and other features marked with a pointed object. Ancient human heel marks can be seen around the figures in this remote and dark chamber. In many other caves, paintings and engravings are far from daylight. There are several instances in which the footprints of both adults and children are preserved in damp clay, perhaps left by small parties of initiates who attended ceremonies in remote subterranean chambers. Some caves may also have been chosen for their echoes and other resonant effects.

Upper Palaeolithic art defies easy interpretation, for the symbolic messages it communicates come from a world that is remote from our own. Yet the paintings and engravings still seem to come alive and appear larger than life when seen by modern candlelight flickering in the intense darkness. Did the artists paint art for art's sake, as some art historians and archaeologists allege? Or were they symbolically killing their prey before setting out on the chase? Such explanations are too simplistic, for we can be sure that the motivations for the art extended far beyond mere environmental and subsistence concerns.

Today, we know a great deal more about symbolic behavior and the art that goes with it, and much more about how hunter-gatherer societies function. In such societies, visual forms are manipulated to structure and give meaning to existence. For Cro-Magnon artists, there were clearly continuities between animal and human life and with their social world. Thus, their art was a symbolic depiction of these continuities.

Shamans, priests or spirit mediums, (the word comes from the Siberian Tungus word *saman*, meaning priest) are important members of hunter-gatherer and subsistence farming societies all over the world. They are individuals perceived as having unusual spiritual powers, the ability to cross over into the world of the gods and ancestors. Through trance and chant, they would intercede with the ancestors, define the order of the world and the creation, the relationship between the living and the forces of the environment. Perhaps, argue some experts, much of the cave art was involved with shamanistic rituals, the animal figures being images of spirit creatures or the life-force for the shamans.

Some of the art may also have been associated with initiation rites, the journey through dark passages adding to the disorienting ordeal of initiation. Almost certainly, the art was a way of transmitting environmental and other knowledge from one generation to the next. Australian Aborigines, for example, commit to memory vast quantities of information about their territory that is closely tied to the mythical and symbolic world of their ancestors. Much of this data is vital to survival, constantly imparted to the young in ceremonies and rituals.

THE MAMMOTH HUNTERS (35,000 to 15,000 years ago)

The open steppe-tundra plains that stretched from the Atlantic to Siberia were a far harsher environment than the sheltered valleys of southwestern Europe. To live there permanently, late Ice Age people had to find sheltered winter base camps, have the technology to make tailored, layered clothing with needle and thongs, and the ability to build substantial dwellings in a treeless environment. Only a handful of big-game hunting groups lived in the shallow valleys that dissected these plains before the glacial maximum 18,000 years ago. Thereafter, the human population rose comparatively rapidly, each group centered on a river valley where game was most plentiful, and where plant foods and fish could be found during the short summers. It was here that the most elaborate winter base camps lay.

One such base camp lay at Mezhirich on the Dnepr River, a complex of well-built, dome-shaped houses fashioned of intricate patterns of mammoth bones. The outer retaining walls were made of patterned mammoth skulls, jaws, and limb bones. The completed oval-shaped dwellings were about 16 feet across, roofed with hides and sod, entered through subterranean tunnels. The use of mammoth bone for houses was a logical strategy in a largely treeless environment. American archaeologist Olga Soffer has calculated that it would have taken some 15 workers about 10 days to build a Mezhirich dwelling, much more effort than would have gone into a simpler base camp or hunting settlement.

Soffer believes that these base camps were occupied by groups of about 30 to 60 people for about six months of the year. Mezhirich was but one of several important base camp locations in the Ukraine, sites that contain the bones of a greater variety of game animals than smaller, more specialized settlements (Figure 5.8). The mammoth bone dwellings also yielded many bones from fur-bearing animals like the beaver, also exotic materials and ornaments such as shiny amber from near Kiev and shells from the Black Sea, far to the south. The items from afar exchanged between neighboring communities were predominantly nonutilitarian, luxury goods that had social and political significance. Much of the trade may have been ceremonial, a means of validating important ideologies, of ensuring exchange of information and cooperation in daily life, just as it was elsewhere in the late Ice Age world at the time.

Late Ice Age groups settled much of the steppe-tundra as far east as Lake Baikal in Siberia, not through a deliberate process of migration, but as a result of the natural dynamics of hunter-gatherer life. The tundra hunters lived in small, highly flexible bands. As the generations passed, one band would coalesce into another, sons and their families would move away into a neighboring, and empty, valley. And, in time, a sparse human population would occupy thousands of square miles of steppe-tundra, concentrated for the most part in river valleys, at times venturing out onto

Figure 5.8 Artist's reconstruction of late Ice Age life on the Czechoslovakian Plains.

the broad plains, and always on the move. It was through these natural dynamics of constant movement, of extreme social flexibility and opportunism, that people first settled the outer reaches of Siberia and crossed into the Americas.

North and east of Lake Baikal, the steppe-tundra extends all the way to the Pacific, the home of more late Ice Age hunting groups that are known from a handful of settlements along lake shores and in river valleys. They are part of a widespread late Ice Age cultural tradition that reflects a varied adaptation by *Homo sapiens* to an enormous area of central Asia and southern Siberia from well west of Lake Baikal to the Pacific coast by 30,000 to 20,000 years ago. But where did these Siberian hunters come from? Did they originate in the west, or were their cultural roots in China to the south? These questions have a direct bearing on one of the most debated questions of world prehistory—the date of the first Americans.

THE FAR EAST (35,000 to 15,000 years ago)

We know enough about prehistoric Asia to realize that this was not a backward, peripheral region of the late Ice Age world. We cannot just argue that big-game hunters from the Ukraine and the western steppe-tundra migrated steadily northeastward into Siberia and then into the Americas. Rather, the spread of modern humans into central Asia, northern China, and the extreme northeast was a complex process that began at least 35,000 years ago.

Many biological anthropologists assume that *Homo erectus*, originally a tropical and subtropical animal, settled in the warmer southern parts of China first, then radiated northward into more temperate environments. But how far north? It is not until just before 35,000 years ago that a few signs of human settlement appear along the banks of the Huang Ho River in the arid grasslands of Mongolia. Open landscapes such as this and the neighboring steppe-tundra could support but the sparsest of hunter-gatherer populations, people who placed a high premium on mobility and portable toolkits. They were some of the first Ice Age people to develop diminutive microliths.

The *microlith* (a term derived from the Greek micros: small; lithos: stone) is a highly distinctive artifact, manufactured from carefully prepared wedge-shaped, conical, or cylindrical cores (Figure 5.9). By their very size, microliths were designed to be mounted in antler, bone, or wooden hafts to serve as spear barbs, arrow points, or as small knives and scraper blades. Such diminutive artifacts came into use almost everywhere in the post-Ice Age world, for they were highly adaptive when used with slender wooden arrow shafts or with stout wooden handles. They first appear in a crude form in northern China at least 30,000 years ago, were in widespread use by 25,000 to 20,000 years ago, and soon became popular in the arid open country of the steppe-tundra, an area where high mobility and portable toolkits were at a premium. A somewhat similar microblade technology developed in Siberia late in the Ice Age. We do not know, however, whether the first human inhabitants of northeast Asia were people with such diminutive toolkits, or whether they used a heavier weaponry that included stone-tipped spears with sharp projectile points.

Unfortunately, the archaeology of northern China, northeastern Siberia, and Alaska is little known because harsh environmental conditions make fieldwork possible for a mere two months or so a year in many places. We can only guess at a possible scenario for first settlement of this vast area, and of the Americas.

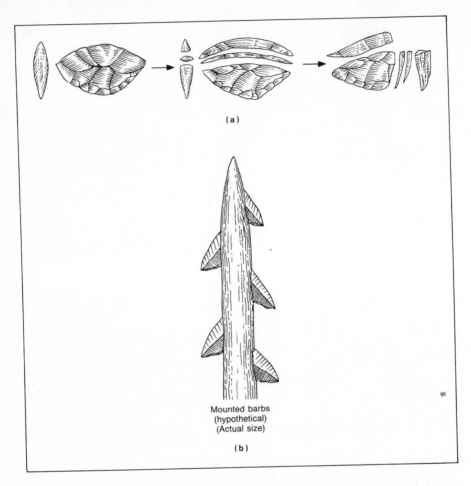

Figure 5.9 Microlith technology. (a) Siberian microblade artifacts were made by striking small blades off a wedge-shaped core, which produced fine, sharp artifacts that could be mounted on spears or in bone heads. (b) Later microliths used after the Ice Age were made by notching and snapping blades.

Sinodonty and Sundadonty

That the first Americans came from Siberia is unquestionable, but their ultimate ancestry is a matter of much debate. Christy Turner of Arizona State University has long studied the dental characteristics of native American populations and compared them to other groups in the Old World. He has shown that the crowns and roots of human teeth give clues to the degree of relationship between prehistoric populations. These tooth features are more stable than most evolutionary traits, with a high resistance to the effects of environmental differences, sexual distinctions, and age variations. In particular, he has focussed on a pattern of specialized tooth features he calls Sinodonty.

Sinodont hallmarks include incisor shoveling (the scooped-out shape on the inside of the tooth), double-shoveling (scooping out on both sides), single-rooted upper first premolars, and three-rooted lower first molars. Sinodonty is characteristic of all native Americans. They share this feature with northern Asians, including northern Chinese. The morphological difference between Sinodonts and the other populations, whom Turner labels Sundadonts, is so great that he believes Siberia and the Americas were settled by Sinodont populations from northern Asia. It was in China, he believes, that Sinodonty evolved, at least 40,000 years ago. The problem is to find the archaeological sites to confirm his theory.

Early Human Settlement of Siberia (? Before 20,000 to 15,000 years ago)

If the ancestry of the first Americans lies in Siberia, what, then, is the earliest evidence for human settlement in extreme northeast Asia? At present, there is no reliable evidence for late Ice Age occupation any earlier than about 20,000 years ago, although it is fair to say that field investigations have hardly begun.

Some of the earliest evidence of human settlement comes from Dyukhtai Cave in the Middle Aldan Valley. There Soviet archaeologist Yuri Mochanov found 14,000- to 12,000-year-old mammoth and musk ox bones associated with flaked-stone spear points, burins, microblades, and other Upper Palaeolithic tools. The earliest securely dated Dyukhtai-like site is Verkhene-Trotiskaya, also on the Aldan River, which has been radiocarbon dated to about 18,000 years ago. Subsequently, microblades and characteristic wedge-shaped cores have been found over a wide area of northeast Asia, across the Bering Straits in Alaska, and as far south as British Columbia.

With its microblades and wedge-shaped cores, the Dyukhtai culture has plausible links with widespread microblade cultures to the south, in China. A case can be made, then, for linking Dyukhtai cultural traditions with northern China, where Sinodonts have been found, as well as with microblade finds in Alaska and British Columbia. Were the Dyukhtai people thus the first Americans? Unfortunately, the dating of the earliest sites on both shores of the Bering Strait is too uncertain, for there is a strong possibility that the later Dyukhtai Culture of 14,000 to 12,000 years ago flourished *after* the first settlement of the New World.

When Dyukhtai people or even earlier settlers first crossed the windy, steppe-tundra covered land bridge that formed central Beringia remains a mystery (Figure 5.2). We do not even know how they subsisted, except for a likelihood that they preyed on all kinds of arctic game. They may also have hunted sea mammals and taken ocean fish. Unfortunately, their settlements are deep beneath the waters of the Bering Strait.

THE FIRST AMERICANS (? Before 15,000 ago to 9000 B.C.)

For all the last glaciation, the Bering land bridge joined extreme northeast Siberia and Alaska. During warmer intervals, it was little more than a narrow isthmus, during the glacial maximum a broad plain. Thus, it was theoretically possible for humans without canoes to cross into North America from the Old World dry-shod for all of the past 100,000 years. Therein lies one of the great questions of world prehistory. When and how did the first human beings settle the New World?

The controversies that surround the first Americans are still unresolved. Most authorities agree that the first Americans were anatomically modern humans, *Homo sapiens*. This is a strong argument in favor of first settlement during the last 45,000 years, but at this point the two sides of the controversy part company, for they disagree fundamentally on the date of first settlement. Some scientists argue passionately for a late Ice Age occupation before 30,000 years ago, perhaps as much as 15,000 years earlier. Their theories pit them against most American archaeologists, who believe humans first crossed into Alaska at the very end of the Ice Age, perhaps as the land bridge flooded, after 15,000 years ago. We must examine these two viewpoints more closely.

Settlement Before 30,000 Years Ago?

The case for early settlement rests on a handful of sites, most of them in South America, none of them yielding much more than a handful of alleged stone artifacts and sometimes animal bones. Therein lies the controversy, for what one archaeologist claims as a stone tool is rejected out of hand by another. Unfortunately, most of the claims for early settlement are based not on fine-grained, scientific examination of the artifacts and their context in the surrounding deposits, but on an individual archaeologist's subjective belief that a handful of chipped stones are humanly manufactured rather than of natural origin. For example, if one finds 35,000-year-old stone artifacts deep in a hypothetical Peruvian cave, it is not sufficient to state they are humanly manufactured. One must prove beyond all measure of reasonable scientific doubt that they were made by prehistoric people, and not formed, for example, by stones falling from a cliff face or by pebbles being knocked together in a stream that once ran through the cave. Such research is extremely time-consuming and very difficult and has not yet been carried out at most of the sites where early settlement has been claimed. Let us briefly examine some of the early sites.

The case for early occupation in North America is based on one recently discovered cave in New Mexico, where archaeologist Richard MacNeish claims to have found the bones of extinct big-game animals along with some crude stone stools and other traces of putative human occupation, dating to about 38,000 years ago. Few details of this find have been released, and one must suspend judgment pending more complete information. But it has been greeted with skepticism by many archaeologists.

In South America, French archaeologist Niede Guidon has reported evidence of hearths and stone artifacts dating back to as early as 47,000 years ago in the bottom layers of a rockshelter named Boqueirao da Pedra Furada in northeastern Brazil. To date, her claims are still poorly documented in the literature. Many experts have expressed doubt about how these early levels and the artifacts in them were formed. They are concerned that a stream once ran through the rockshelter and about the possibility that rockfalls from the surrounding cliffs manufactured tools. Again, the case is unproven pending further information.

Further south, in northern Chile, Tom Dillehay has uncovered a remarkable settlement on the edge of a stream. Monte Verde was occupied by hunter-gatherers living in simple wooden dwellings between 12,000 and 14,000 years ago. A 30,000-year-old lower level is said to contain a split pebble and wood fragments, but, to date, excavations in these levels have been relatively limited, insufficient to document the proven presence of human occupation at such an early date.

There is no *theoretical* reason why *Homo sapiens* could not have moved south from Beringia well before 25,000 years ago, but we still lack credible proof of such early human settlement in Siberia, let alone the Americas. Whether this is because the Americas were still uninhabited, or because the human population was so mobile and tiny that little or nothing material survived, continues to be hotly debated. As an outside observer, African archaeologist Nicholas Toth has made the important observation that it is pointless to place too much reliance on isolated finds. Rather, we should be searching for *patterns* of very early human settlement, characteristic distributions of artifacts and human activity that occur over wide areas, that indeed reflect widespread early occupation. Such patterns document the very earliest human occupation on earth. There is no theoretical reason why similar patterns should not turn up to chronicle the first Americans. So far, consistent distributions of human settlement in the New World date to after the Ice Age, to after 15,000 years ago. But we stress again that there is no reason why earlier settlement might not be found one day. So far, however, the evidence is unconvincing.

Settlement After 15,000 Years Ago?

Most American archaeologists prefer to consider first settlement a much later phenomenon. Under the late scenario, a few families may have moved into Alaska during the very late Ice Age, perhaps before 15,000 years ago. At that time, vast ice sheets mantled much of northern North America, effectively blocking access to the mid-continent. After 14,000 years ago, these ice sheets retreated rapidly, allowing a trickle of human settlers to move onto the plains and into a new continent.

This hypothesis is based on the earliest indisputable archaeological evidence for human settlement, which dates to between 14,000 and 12,000 years ago. In North America, a handful of sites, among them Meadowcroft Rockshelter in Pennsylvania, and Fort Rock Cave, Oregon, belong in this time frame. So do a scatter of sites from Central and South America, among them Valsequillo in Mexico, Taima Taima in Venezuela, and Monte Verde in northern Chile. All these sites have yielded small scatters of stone artifacts, occasionally a projectile point. After about 9500 B.C., the trickle of archaeological sites turns into a flood. There are now traces of *Paleo-Indian* (Greek paleos: old) settlement between the southern margins of the ice sheets in the north and the Straits of Magellan in the far south. The term Paleo-Indian is conventionally used to refer to the prehistoric inhabitants of the Americas from earliest settlement up to the beginning of the Archaic period, in about 6000 B.C.

How, then, did Paleo-Indians travel southward from the arctic to the heart of North America? Were they big-game hunters, who followed small herds of animals southward through a widening corridor between the two great North American ice sheets to the east of the Rockies as the ice sheets melted? Or were the first Americans expert sea-mammal hunters and fisherfolk, who crossed from Siberia along low-lying coasts in canoes, fishing and sea-mammal hunting? Did their successors then travel southward along the Pacific coast into more temperate waters? Again, fierce controversy surrounds what is virtually nonexistent archaeological evidence. Perhaps both coastal settlement and terrestrial occupation took hold in the rapidly changing world of the late Ice Age. We simply do not know, partly because the coastal sites of the day are buried hundreds of feet below modern sea levels.

At present, the consensus of archaeological opinion favors a relatively late human occupation of the Americas at the very end of the Ice Age, but it is entirely possible that this scenario will change dramatically as a result of future research.

THE CLOVIS PEOPLE (10,000 TO 9000 B.C.)

The earliest well-documented Paleo-Indian settlement is associated with the distinctive Clovis fluted point (Figure 5.10), which is found over much of North and Central America. The Clovis tradition, named after a town in New Mexico, once flourished in various forms over much of the Americas. It is best, and misleadingly, known from occasional mammoth and bison kills on the Northern American plains. These plains expanded at the end of the Ice Age, their short grasses providing ample feed for all kinds of big-game, including bison, mammoth, and other ruminants. Clovis bands on the plains preyed on these and many other game species,

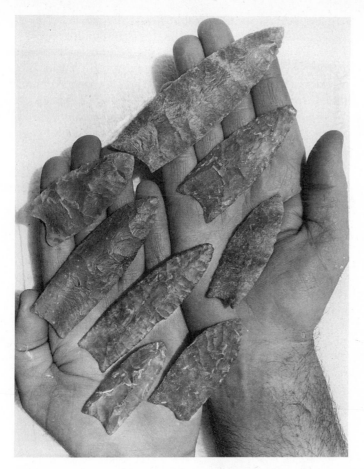

Figure 5.10 Clovis points found with a mammoth skeleton at Naco, Arizona.

large and small. They were constantly on the move, often camping along rivers and streams and close to permanent waterholes. Here they killed their prey, camping near the carcass where it lay.

It would be a mistake, however, to think of the Clovis people as purely big-game hunters. They settled not only on open grasslands, but in woodlands, tundra, deserts, and along sea coasts. In some areas, wild plant foods were probably as important, if not more important, than game. Fish and sea-mammal hunting may also have assumed great local importance, especially along rising coastlines. But wherever Clovis people and their contemporaries settled, large game was of significant importance, simply because it was a relatively abundant meat source.

Nowhere were Clovis populations large. Their toolkit was highly portable, based on an expert stone-flaking technology that produced fine, fluted-based points. The hunters mounted these on long wooden shafts, sometimes attaching the head to a detachable foreshaft that acted as a hinge. When the spear penetrated an animal, the foreshaft would snap off, ensuring that the lethally sharp point stayed in the wound. Like other later Paleo-Indian groups, and like Ice Age hunters in the Old World, the Clovis people hunted their prey on foot, relying on their stalking skill and the accuracy of their throwing sticks (atlatls) to dispatch their quarry.

The origins of the Clovis people remain a complete mystery. However, most experts believe their ultimate origins were among late Ice Age hunter-gatherer populations in Alaska and northeast Asia. If the first Americans crossed into the New World about 15,000 years ago, then the peopling of the uninhabited continent took place remarkably quickly. By 9000 B.C., Stone Age hunter-gatherers occupied every corner of the Americas. The overall human population probably numbered no more than a few tens of thousands, but they had adapted to every form of local environment imaginable.

By this time, the last glaciation was long over and the great ice sheets of the north were in rapid retreat. Climatic conditions were warming up rapidly and many species of Ice Age big-game vanished. The descendants of the first Americans adapted to these new circumstances in very diverse ways, along trajectories of cultural change that led, ultimately, to the brilliant array of native American societies encountered by Europeans in the late fifteenth century A.D. (Chapters 7, 8, 11, and 12).

With the first settlement of the Americas, the great radiation of *Homo sapiens*, the wise person, was nearly complete. This was the second great radiation of humanity, the climactic development of world prehistory. From it stemmed not only the brilliant biological and cultural diversity of modern humankind, but food production, village life, urban civilization, and the settlement of the Pacific Islands—the very roots of our own diverse and complex world.

Chapter
6

The First Farmers

A.D. 1950 —

A.D. 1 —

15,000 B.P. —

50,000 B.P. —

100,000 B.P. —

500,000 B.P. —

1.0 Million —

2.5 Million —

*A*bout 8000 B.C., as part of the process of adapting to radically different climates after the Ice Age, some hunter-gatherer groups in the Near East experimented with the deliberate growing of wild cereal grasses and taming small mammals as a means of expanding their food supply. The new food-producing economies proved dramatically successful. Ten thousand years ago, virtually everybody in the world lived by hunting or gathering. By 2,000 years ago, most people were farmers or herders. This chapter tells the story of the beginnings of food production throughout the world (Figure 6.1).

THE CHANGED WORLD OF THE HOLOCENE

Some 15,000 years ago, the great ice sheets began to retreat, at times very rapidly, ushering in postglacial *Holocene* times (Greek Holos: recent). At the same time, world sea levels rose dramatically, if irregularly, leading to major changes in world geography. The chilly waters of the Bering Sea separated Siberia and Alaska. Sunda in Southeast Asia became an enormous archipelago. Britain became an island and the North Sea and Baltic assumed their modern configu-

117

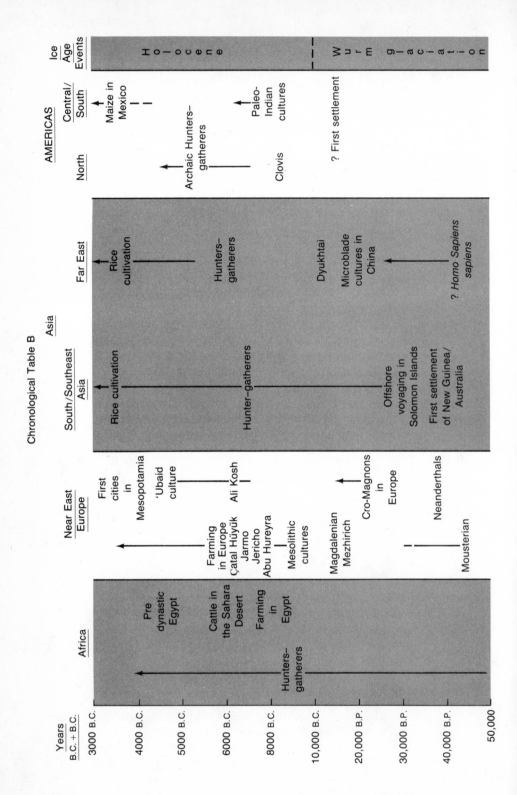

Chronological Table B

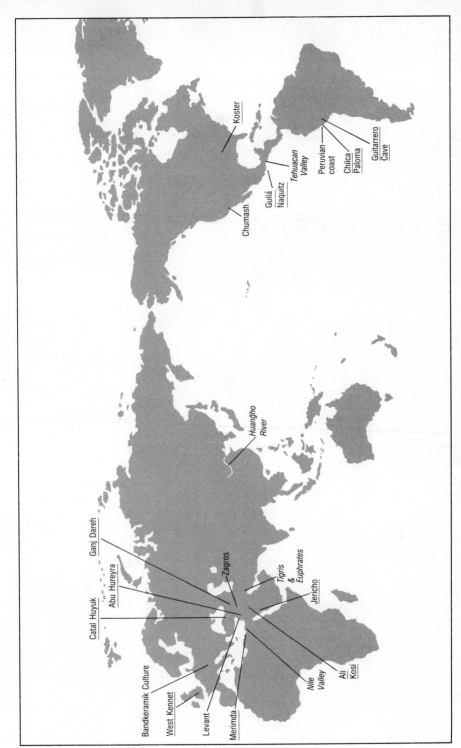

Figure 6.1 Map showing archaeological sites and major centers of early food production mentioned in this chapter.

rations. The most striking climatic and vegetational transformations took place in northern latitudes, in areas like western and central Europe and in regions of North America contiguous to the great ice sheets. Only 7,000 years after the Scandinavian ice sheet began retreating, forests covered much of Europe.

There were major vegetational changes in warmer latitudes, too. Rainfall patterns changed at the end of the Ice Age, bringing large, shallow lakes and short grasslands to the Sahara. As late as 6000 B.C., hunter-gatherer populations flourished in the desert, in areas that are now arid wilderness. In the Near East, warmer conditions saw the immigration of new plant species into highland areas such as the Zagros mountains in Iran, among them wild cereal grasses. Their distribution now expanded dramatically, to the point that wild wheat and barley became important staples for hunter-gatherers groups in the highlands and fertile river valleys like the Euphrates. Far away, in Mexico, rising temperatures brought a rich forest of cacti and legume trees to mountain valleys of the central highlands. This thorn-scrub-cactus forest included many wild ancestors of domesticated plants, among them the maguey; squash; bean; and teosinte, the wild grass that was probably the ancestor of wild maize, the crop that was to become one of the staples of American Indian life.

CHANGES IN HUNTER-GATHERER SOCIETY

These and other Holocene climatic changes had profound effects on hunter-gatherer societies throughout the world, especially on the intensity of the food quest and the complexity of their societies. So did natural population growth. By 15,000 years ago, the world's hunter-gatherer population was probably approaching about 10 million people. Except in the most favored areas, like southwestern France or the Nile Valley, late Ice Age environments were incapable of supporting anything but the sparsest of human population densities—well under one person per square mile. As a result, in early Holocene times still rising human populations began to match the ability of the world's environment to support them as hunter-gatherers. It was no longer possible to solve a subsistence problem by simply moving elsewhere. People began to exploit a wider range of food resources with greater efficiency, both to avert starvation and to protect themselves from food shortages caused by short-term droughts and other unpredictable changes. In time, hunter-gatherer societies underwent profound changes and in some areas acquired greater complexity.

The Intensification of Hunting and Gathering.

Nowhere can these changes be seen more clearly than in the Americas, settled by a handful of hunter-gatherer bands by 15,000 years ago. By 9000 B.C., the big game that formed a staple part of their diet was extinct.

The Paleo-Indians responded to changed circumstances by developing ever more intensive and specialized ways of exploiting local environments. The change is especially marked in areas of exceptional resource diversity like parts of the West Coast, the Peruvian coast, and the fertile river valleys of the southern Midwest and southeastern United States. In all these areas, hunter-gatherer populations became more sedentary, developed specialized technologies for hunting, foraging, and fishing, and in the process, developed some form of social ranking.

The famous Koster site in the Illinois River valley provides a chronicle of this process of intensification taking place over many thousands of years, from abut 7500 B.C. until A.D. 1200 (Figure 6.2). The first visitors were Paleo-Indian hunters who camped on the edge of the valley. About 6500 B.C., some later inhabitants founded a base camp that covered about 0.75 acre (0.1 ha). An extended family group of about 25 people returned repeatedly to the same location, perhaps to exploit the rich fall hickory nut harvests in the area. Between 5600 and 5000 B.C., there were substantial settlements of permanent mud and brush houses that were occupied for most, if not all, the year. During spring and summer the inhabitants took thousands of fish, gathering mussels and hickory nuts in fall and migratory birds in spring. Even when hunting deer on the nearby uplands, the people could find most of their food resources within 3 miles (4.8 km).

After 2500 B.C., Koster's population had risen to the point where the people were exploiting a much wider range of food resources, including acorns, which require much more preparation than hickory nuts. Eventu-

Figure 6.2 Excavations at Koster, Illinois.

ally, they experimented with the deliberate planting of wild native grasses like goosefoot, simply to increase supplies of wild plant foods.

The Koster excavations document several long-term trends in many Holocene hunter-gatherer societies; trends toward more sedentary settlement, intensive exploitation of locally abundant and predictable food resources such as salmon or nuts, and carefully organized mass processing and storage of staple foods. Such intensive exploitation, processing, and storage was adaptive in environments where seasonal phenomena such as salmon runs, caribou migrations, or hickory nut harvests required not only efficient harvesting of enormous quantities of food in a short time, but also their processing and storage for later use.

By using storage, and by careful seasonal exploitation of game, plant, and aquatic resources like fish and waterfowl, Holocene hunter-gatherers compensated for periodic food shortages caused by short-term climatic change and seasonal fluctuations. For example, native American societies developed a remarkable expertise with wild plant foods. They also evolved an array of simple pestles, grinders, and other tools to process seeds and other wild plant foods. Later, it was an easy matter to adapt these toolkits to new, specialized tasks such as farming.

More restricted territories, less mobility, rising population densities, and unpredictable environmental variations and seasonal flood fluctuations were problems common to Holocene hunter-gatherers throughout the world. A few of these societies, especially those in areas with rich and diverse food resources that included fish and sea mammals, achieved a greater complexity than any Ice Age society, with some signs of social ranking.

SOCIAL COMPLEXITY AMONG HUNTER-GATHERERS

Complex hunter-gatherer societies did not appear everywhere, but they developed in a remarkable variety of environments, from fertile river valleys to coastal deserts. Everywhere, however, certain general conditions were necessary. First, population movements had to be limited by either geography or the presence of neighbors. Second, resources had to be abundant and predictable in their seasonal appearance. Such resources included fish, shellfish, nuts, and seeds, species that are abundant and seldom exhausted. Third, population growth might reach a point at which food shortages occur and there is an imbalance between people and their food supply. Again, a solution was to intensify the food quest, an intensification that might result in a more complex society, or, as we shall see, in food production.

Social complexity was most common in areas where freshwater or marine fish, shellfish, or sea mammals were abundant. The full potential of marine and freshwater resources was realized only in a relatively few areas like northern Europe, Peru, and western North America. Here, higher than normal population densities were concentrated in restricted territories circumscribed by geography or neighbors. These populations acquired a more varied diet by using more specialized toolkits, also sophisticated food storage systems and preservation techniques. These groups often lived in sedentary, large base camps ruled by important kin leaders who monopolized trade with neighboring groups.

For example, the Chumash Indians of the southern California coast were skilled navigators, fishers, and sea-mammal hunters. Some Chumash communities numbered as many as 1,000 people, living under hereditary chiefs (*wots*). There was a small elite of ceremonial office holders, shamans, and such experts as canoe builders. Chumash culture was a maritime adaptation made possible by a specialized fishing technology that included planked canoes about 25 feet (7.6 m) long. Each community maintained exchange contacts with other coastal communities and with people living far in the interior. Chumash culture achieved a degree of social elaboration that represents about the limit of such complexity possible without adopting agriculture.

Why did such social complexity develop? Some scholars see the ocean as a kind of Garden of Eden, an environment sometimes so productive that hunter-gatherers could maintain permanent, sedentary settlements and maintain high population densities. Perhaps people turned to fish, shellfish, and sea mammals in a period of rapid environmental change, like that at the end of the Ice Age. Unfortunately, however, we do not know how decisive marine or riverain resources were in allowing dense populations and sedentary living, both essential prerequisites for social complexity.

Away from coasts, rivers, and lake shores, and especially among groups living at the edges of several ecological zones, people living in more or less permanent settlements in rich inland environments turned to another strategy. They experimented with the planting of wild plant staples to supplement food resources in short supply. The cultural changes forced upon them by Holocene climate change made it easier for their descendants to adopt radically new economic strategies such as full-time food production.

THE ORIGINS OF FOOD PRODUCTION

Food production began at different times in various parts of the world, being established in the Near East by about 7500 B.C., in Mesoamerica by 3500 B.C., but in tropical Africa only by about 1000 B.C. and then only in some locations. Why did agriculture and animal domestication appear in some areas much earlier than in others? At the end of the Ice Age, hunter-gatherers in subtropical zones such as the Near East and highland Mesoamerica were exploiting potentially domesticable wild grasses and root plants with increased intensity (Figure 6.3). Dependence on such foods probably came earlier in these regions, where there were only a few

Figure 6.3 Guila Naquitz, Valley of Oaxaca, Mexico, a site where hunter-gatherers exploited potentially domesticable plants.

forageable plant foods. Such dependence was essential to long-term survival and led almost inevitably to experimentation with deliberate planting of wild cereals and ultimately to cultivation. In contrast, populations in more humid, plant-rich tropical regions, like the African and Amazonian rainforests, probably did little more than plant a few wild species to minimize risk of starvation in lean years long after farming appeared in more temperate regions.

Theories of Origin

V. Gordon Childe's "Neolithic Revolution" hypothesis mentioned earlier is now universally regarded as simplistic. Recent theorizing about the origins of food production revolves around complex models that combine many factors. Today's theories fall into two broad categories, those dealing with what might roughly be called risk management and ecological models.

Risk Management: Population and Resources   All of us take risks in our lives and try and protect ourselves against the dangers of a sudden catastrophe. This is why wise investors diversify their holdings, and why parents with young families carry life insurance policies. This is known as *risk management*. In the case of prehistoric people, it meant minimizing anything that would threaten long-term survival.

All environments, however favorable, involve some form of risk for hunter-gather societies — drought cycles, long, cold winters, and unpredictable floods, to mention only a few. Often people respond to these risks by moving away or by developing new storage and food preservation technologies. One logical and straightforward solution to rising populations, resulting food shortages, or risk factors may be to go one step further, to cultivate familiar plants and domesticate common prey so that people can draw on familiar stored prey during scarce periods. In other words, food production arose as a result of risk management, as a way of increasing food supplies.

Ecological Models Proponents of ecological models talk of so-called opportunities for the introduction of food production, of people turning to superior local resources when the moment arrived. Under this kind of scenario, some resources, say wild wheat or barley, or wild goats, are seen as attractive. People use them more and more, to the point that they are eventually domesticated.

Ecological theories are strongly based on the notion that human societies are cultural systems operating within much larger environmental systems. The classic exposition of this point-of-view is that of University of Michigan archaeologist Kent Flannery, who works in Mexico's southern highlands and who discovered that between 10,000 and 6,000 years ago the local people relied on five basic food sources — deer, rabbits, maguey, tree legumes, and prickly pears — for their sustenance. By careful prediction of the seasons of each food, they could schedule their hunting and gathering at periods of abundance and before animals gained access to the ripe plants. Flannery assumed that the southern highlands and their inhabitants were part of a large, open environmental system consisting of many subsystems — economic, botanical, social, and so on — that interacted with one another. Then something happened to jolt the food procurement system toward the deliberate growing of wild grasses. Flannery's excavations at dry caves dating to between 7,000 and 4,000 years ago showed wild maize cobs slowly increasing in size as well as other signs of genetic change. Thus, he suggested that the people began to experiment with the deliberate planting of maize and other crops, intentionally expanding the areas where they would grow. After a long period of time, these intentional deviations in the food procurement system caused the importance of wild grass-collecting to increase at the expense of other collecting activities until it became the dominant one. Eventually, the people created a self-perpetuating food procurement system, with its own vital scheduling demands of planting and harvesting that competed with earlier systems and won out because it was more durable. By 4,000 years ago, the highly nutritious bean and corn diet of the highland people was well established.

The crux of all these theoretical approaches is to identify the processes that caused people to shift over to deliberate cultivation and domestication. For example, were there new cost-benefit realities that favored farming? What about such factors as the nutritive value and seasonal availability of different foods? Did genetic changes in plants and animals play a role? Unfortunately, it is difficult to link complex theoretical models with actual field data, largely because the factors involved in such profound cultural change, the reasons *why* people make the changeover, do not lend themselves to easy documentation.

We must now survey the archaeological evidence for the origins of food production in Old World and New.

EARLY FOOD PRODUCTION IN THE NEAR EAST (9000 to 5000 B.C.)

Between 15,000 and 10,000 years ago, the Near Eastern climate warmed up considerably. Forests expanded rapidly at the end of the Ice Age, for the climate was still cooler and considerably wetter than today. Many areas were richer in animal and plant species than they are now, making them highly favorable for human occupation.

About 9000 B.C., most human settlements lay in the Levant (the area along the Mediterranean coast) and in the Zagros mountains of Iran and their foothills (Figure 6.4). Some local areas, like the Jordan River valley, the Middle Euphrates valley, and some Zagros valleys, were most densely populated than elsewhere. Here more sedentary and more complex societies flourished. These people exploited the landscape intensively, foraging on hill slopes for wild cereal grasses and nuts, while hunting gazelle (a small desert antelope) and other game on grassy lowlands and in river valleys. Their settlements contain exotic objects such as sea shells, stone bowls, and artifacts made of obsidian (volcanic glass), all traded from afar. This considerable volume of intercommunity exchange brought a degree of social complexity in its train.

About 500 years later, much drier and unpredictable environmental conditions led to dramatic changes in human life, well documented at the Abu Hureyra mound in Syria (Figure 6.5). Abu Hureyra was founded about 9500 B.C., a small village settlement of cramped pit dwellings (houses dug partially in the soil) with reed roofs supported by wooden uprights. For the next 1,500 years, its inhabitants enjoyed a somewhat warmer and damper climate than today, living in a well-wooded steppe area where wild cereal grasses were abundant. They subsisted off spring migrations of Persian gazelles from the south. With such a favorable location, about 300 to 400 people lived in a sizable, permanent settlement. They were no longer a series of small bands, but lived in a large community with more elaborate social organization, probably grouped into clans of people of common descent. In 8200 B.C., as climatic conditions deteriorated, the ancient village was abandoned.

Five centuries later, about 7700 B.C., a new village rose on the mound. At first, the inhabitants still hunted gazelle intensively. Then, about 7000 B.C., within the space of a few generations, they switched abruptly to herding domesticated goats and sheep and to growing einkorn, pulses, and

Figure 6.4 Abu Hureyra, Syria. Excavations in the earlier settlement, showing interconnecting pits that were roofed with poles, branches, and reeds to form small huts. Part of a later rectangular hut can be seen at a higher level (top right).

other cereal grasses. Abu Hureyra grew rapidly until it covered nearly 30 acres (12 ha). It was a close-knit community of rectangular, one-story mud-brick houses, joined by narrow lanes and courtyards, finally abandoned about 5000 B.C.

Many complex factors led to the adoption of the new economies, not only at Abu Hureyra, but at many other locations. Most lay on low ground, near well-watered, easily cultivatable land. Their inhabitants usually lived in small, densely clustered villages of circular or oval one-room houses. The most famous of these many settlements is at the base of the Biblical city of Jericho, famous for the siege in which Joshua collapsed the city walls with the blast of trumpets. A small camp flourished at the bubbling Jericho spring by at least 8500 B.C., but a more permanent farming settlement quickly followed. Soon the inhabitants built massive stone walls

Figure 6.5 Stone tower, part of early farming settlement at Jericho.

complete with towers and a rock-cut ditch more than 9 feet (2.7 m) deep and 10 feet (3 m) wide around their settlement (Figure 6.5). Their bee-hive-shaped huts clustered inside the defenses. The communal labor of wall and ditch building required both political and economic resources on a scale unheard of a few thousand years earlier. Why the walls were needed remains a mystery, but they may have been for defense, resulting from competition from neighboring groups for scarce food resources.

The population of the Levant increased considerably between 7600 and 6000 B.C., scattered in permanent villages as far east as the more arid Syrian plateau. Emmer wheat, barley, lentils, and peas were grown in small fields, crops rotated with pulses to sustain soil fertility. Some commitments like Jericho became important trading centers. The farmers were using obsidian from Turkey, turquoise from Sinai, and sea shell ornaments from the Mediterranean and the Red Sea. The volume of trade was such that many villages used small clay spheres, cones, and disks to keep track of commodities traded. These tokens are thought to represent a simple recording system that later evolved into written script (Chapter 9).

In the Zagros highlands of Iran, the herding of goats and sheep probably began somewhat earlier than in the lowlands. Here, open steppe was ideal country both for intensive hunting of wild goats and sheep, and, after about 8000 B.C., for herding them as well. At the village of Ganj Dareh near Kermanshah in Iran, hunter-gatherers occupied a seasonal hunting camp in about 8500 B.C. About 1,500 years later, a small farming village of rectangular mud-brick houses stood on the same spot, a settlement based on goat and sheep herding and cereal horticulture. One of the best known prehistoric farming villages in the Zagros is Jarmo, little more than a cluster of 25 mud houses, forming an irregular huddle separated by small alleyways and courtyards. Jarmo was in its heyday in about 5000 B.C., by which time more than 80 percent of the villagers' food came from their fields or herds.

Below, on the lowlands, farming began along the eastern edge of the flat Mesopotamian plain as early as it did in the Levant. The village of Ali Kosh on the plains of Khuzistan, north of where the Tigris and Euphrates become one river, started off life as a small settlement of rectangular mud-brick houses as early as 8000 B.C. As time went on, the houses became larger, separated one from another by lanes or courtyards. The people drove their herds of goats and sheep to the highlands during the hot summer months, bringing them back to lush lowland pastures in fall. These same seasonal herding practices continue to this day. Ali Kosh documents more than 2,000 years of farming and herding on the lowlands, a period that saw the development of improved cereal strains and the development of irrigation as a means of intensifying agricultural production. Only 5,000 years after food production first appeared, people in the Levant and Mesopotamia were living in cities with thousands of inhabitants.

EGYPTIAN FARMERS (8000 B.C. to 4000 B.C.)

What about early food production in other parts of the Near East, one might legitimately ask. The same dynamics of growing populations crowded into restricted territories developed in other regions as a result of Holocene climatic change. During the late Ice Age, the Nile valley was a rich, diverse habitat, abounding in game, fish, and wild plant foods. The river's banks were home to many hunter-gatherer groups, who lived on the banks of lagoons and flood channels of the Nile, seeking game in the riverside woodlands and fishing for catfish and perch in the swamps.

Here, too, wild cereal grasses were important in the diet from at least 15,000 years ago.

The Nile valley is unusual in that its water supplies depend not on local rains but on floods from rainfall gathered far upstream in Ethiopia. The fluctuations in these yearly inundations had a profound effect on the pattern of human settlement downstream. The irregular cycles of higher and lower rainfall may have caused major, sudden changes in distributions of animals and plants. These shifts in the Saharan environment caused people who lived off grasslands to manage wild food resources very carefully, especially the small herds of wild cattle, who needed regular water supplies to survive. It may be that they began some small-scale herding, while at the same time extending the distribution of wild cereal grasses by

Figure 6.6 Ancient Egyptian estate workers cultivating the soil. The roots of ancient Egyptian agriculture date back to at least 6000 B.C.

cultivating them. Cattle may have been domesticated in the Sahara as early as 8000 B.C.

By 6000 B.C., dozens of farming villages flourished in the Nile valley, settlements that are now buried beneath deep layers of sand and gravel laid down by thousands of years of river floods. Only 1,500 years later, the inhabitants of the valley were subsisting almost entirely off agriculture, living in small villages like Merimda Beni Salama near the Nile valley. Merimda was a cluster of oval houses and shelters, built half underground and roofed with mud and sticks. The farmers planted barley and wheat as the annual floods receded, while their animals grazed in flat river grasslands. Population densities were still low, so the average Nile flood allowed early Egyptian farmers to harvest grain over perhaps two-thirds of the river floodplain (Figure 6.6). Thus there was no need for irrigation works, which first appear in about 3000 B.C., when Egypt became a unified state (Chapter 9).

Before 6000 B.C., cattle herders ranged widely over the semi-arid grasslands of what is now the Sahara Desert. These nomads left superb wall paintings of their beasts in the caves and rockshelters of the Saharan massifs, grazing their herds along the shores of shallow lakes like a much larger Lake Chad on the southern edge of the desert. The Sahara dried up rapidly after 6000 B.C., forcing its cattle-herding population into permanent oases or to the fringes of the desert. But it was not until much later, around 1000 B.C., that herders moved into sub-Saharan Africa, and that West Africans domesticated such tropical cereals as sorghum and millet (Chapter 10).

THE SPREAD OF FARMING INTO EUROPE (7500 B.C. to 3000 B.C.)

The new economies were so successful that they spread rapidly from the Near East into contiguous areas, especially as hunter-gatherer populations rose and natural food supplies were no longer sufficient to support increasingly sedentary hunter-gatherer groups. Many of them turned to food production to supplement their age-old game, plant, and fish diet. By using a mosaic of key sites and radiocarbon dates, we can trace the spread of farming over wide areas of Europe and southern Asia.

Agriculture and animal domestication spread rapidly north from the Near East into Turkey after 8000 B.C., and from there into Greece, the Balkans, and temperate Europe. Between 7500 and 5000 B.C., long-distance exchange, especially of obsidian, became a major factor in daily life. Obsidian was prized for making tools and ornaments. From Turkey's Lake Van it traveled to the Levant and as far afield as the Persian Gulf. A few Turkish settlements like Catal Huyuk became small, prosperous towns by controlling the trade. At the height of its prosperity between 6000 and 5000 B.C., Catal Huyuk covered 32 acres (12.9 ha). It was a town of numerous small mud-brick houses backed onto one another, the outside

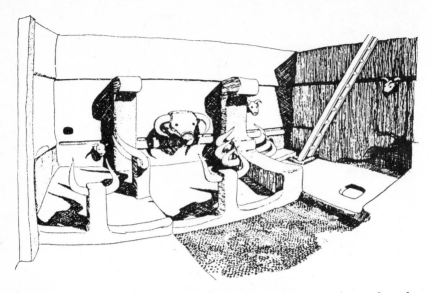

Figure 6.7 Reconstruction of a shrine at Catal Huyuk, Anatolia, with sculptured ox heads, horns, benches, and relief models of bulls and rams. The shrine was entered by the ladder at right.

walls serving as a convenient defense wall. Catal Huyuk is remarkable for its enclosed shrines, entered from the roof and adorned with sculptured ox heads, horns, and relief models of bulls and rams (Figure 6.7). But the town never became a full-fledged city. There were no powerful leaders who monopolized trade and production. It was a community of individual households and families that lacked the elaborate, centralized organization of a city.

Temperate Europe (6000 B.C. to 3000 B.C.)

At the time Catal Huyuk was a bustling small town, farming was already well established on the Aegean Islands, in Greece, and in parts of southeastern Europe. Since the end of the Ice Age, Europe had been the home of numerous, scattered hunter-gatherer groups who lived off forest game, plant foods, and sea and freshwater fish and mollusks. As in the Near East, these populations were preadapted to cultivation and animal domestication, especially in areas where short-term population shifts and local environmental change may have required new subsistence strategies.

Domesticated animals and grains were probably introduced into southeast Europe from the Near East by local bartering. The plants were Near Eastern cereals like emmer and bread wheat, which were demanding crops that extracted large quantities of nutrients from the soil. The farmers had to husband their land carefully, rotating cereals with nitro-gen-fixing legumes and revitalizing their fields with animal manure. Thus was born the European farming system that carefully integrated cultiva-tion and animal rearing into a close-knit subsistence strategy based on individual households supplying their own food needs.

Temperate Europe has year-round rainfall and marked contrasts be-tween summer and winter seasons. With plentiful wood and cooler tem-peratures, timber and thatch therefore replaced the mud-brick architec-ture of the Near East. The expansion of farming society into central and western Europe coincided with a cycle of higher rainfall and warmer winters around 5500 B.C. Within a thousand years, farming based on cattle herding combined with spring-sown crops developed over an enormous area of continental Europe. As farming groups spread across lighter soils, clearing forest for fields and grazing their animals in once-forested lands, many indigenous hunter-gatherer bands adopted the new economies.

The best-known early European farming culture is named the *Band-keramik complex* after its distinctive, line-decorated pottery. It first ap-peared in the Middle Danube valley in about 5300 B.C., then spread rapidly along sheltered river valleys far west to southern Holland and east into parts of the Ukraine. Bandkeramik communities were well spaced, each with territories of some 500 acres (202 ha). The people lived in long, rectangular timber and thatch houses, from 18 to 46 feet (5.4 to 14.0 m) long, presumably sheltering families, their grain, and their animals (Fig-ure 6.8). Between 40 and 60 people lived in Bandkeramik villages. As the centuries passed, the population rose rapidly and the gaps between indi-vidual settlements filled in.

In time, village territories became more circumscribed, their settle-ments protected by earthen enclosures. This was a time when communal tombs came into fashion, among them the celebrated megaliths (Greek mega-lithos: big stone). These were sepulchers fashioned from large boulders and buried under earthen mounds (Figure 6.9). Such corporate burial places may have been locations where revered kin leaders were buried; people with genealogical ties with the ancestors were of para-mount importance to a group of farming communities with strong attach-ments to their fertile lands. Judging from modern analogies, the ancestors are often seen as the guardians of the land, the links between the living and the forces of the spiritual world that control human destiny. Some-what later, between about 2800 and 2300 B.C., individual graves as well as communal sepulchers appeared. These may have been the burial sites of individual leaders, prominent men who were laid to rest with their elabo-rate regalia of rank. They may have been the sole male ancestor of the group, the source of authority over land ownership. Inheritance of land and wealth was now legitimized, as the character of European agriculture changed rapidly, partly as a result of the introduction of the plow by about 2800 B.C.

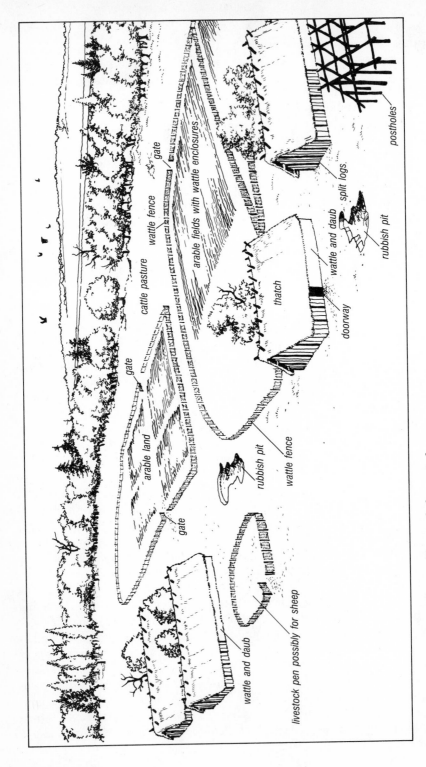

Figure 6.8 Reconstruction of a Bandkeramik farmer's house.

134

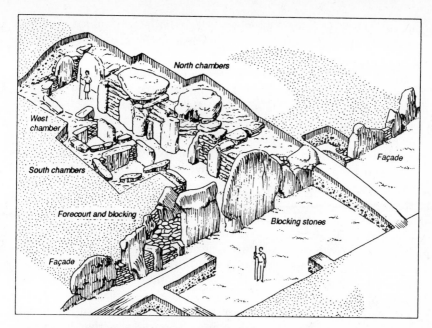

Figure 6.9 Megalithic tomb: West Kennet long barrow, Wiltshire, England. A stone burial chamber of massive boulders was buried under an earthen mound, the side chambers filled with burials.

EARLY CHINESE FARMERS (BEFORE 7000 B.C. to 2000 B.C.)

Food production developed in several parts of the world quite independently with cultivation based on entirely different groups of potentially domesticable plants. One major center of plant domestication was in Asia, where food production developed locally for much the same reasons as it did in the Near East and the Americas. Early food production was based on both root crops like taro and yams and on indigenous cereals like foxtail millet in China. It was not until rice was domesticated that cereal agriculture became a major factor in Asian life.

Rice is one of the world's staple crops and was first domesticated somewhere between northeast India, northern Southeast Asia, and Southern China. The initial cultivation of wild rice probably took place in an alluvial swamp area, where there was plenty of water to stimulate cereal growth. Perhaps this cultivation occurred under conditions in which seasonal flooding made field preparation an easy task. Such conditions existed on the Ganges Plain in India, in northern Thailand, and in China's middle Yangtze valley, where domesticated rice grains date to earlier than 7000 B.C. Chinese archaeologists have excavated several rice-growing communities in southern China which date to at least 5000 B.C. The lush lower Yangtze valley was home to sophisticated rice farming settlements of fine timber houses by this time.

Another set of farming traditions emerged in the Huang-Ho River valley of northern China at about the same time. Here soft-textured soils could be tilled with wooden digging sticks and planted with various species of wild millet, sorghum, hemp, and the mulberry. Either there was a long period of experimentation with local crops or agricultural techniques were introduced from the south, but by 5000 B.C. the Yangshao village farming culture was flourishing over an area as large as the early centers of agriculture in Egypt or Mesopotamia. Each Yangshao community was self-contained, usually built on a ridge overlooking fertile river valleys, situated to avoid flooding or to allow maximal use of floodplain soils (Figure 6.10). By 3000 B.C. Yangshao had developed a distinctively Chinese culture, with its own naturalistic art style and cooking vessels that reflect the importance of steaming foods in Chinese cuisine.

As in Egypt and Mesopotamia, the foundations of later Chinese and Southeast Asian civilization lay in densely populated village communities in fertile river valleys where ranked societies and new social institutions appeared. Over many centuries they evolved into distinctive, indigenous state-organized societies, described in Chapter 10.

Figure 6.10 Reconstruction of Yangshao huts, northern China.

EARLY FARMERS OF THE AMERICAS (Before 7000 B.C. to 2000 B.C.)

Food production developed independently, also, in the Americas. For thousands of years after first settlement, the native Americans subsisted off hunting and gathering, developing an increasing expertise with wild plant foods of all kinds. In some regions, they exploited such resources intensively, especially in the Midwest and Southeast, where some groups were able to occupy more or less permanent settlements for many generations. In time, however, they also started planting wild grasses as a means of supplementing wild plant resources. In time, too, this led to agriculture, especially in areas where wild grasses were plentiful. By the time of Columbus, the prehistoric Americans had developed a truly remarkable expertise with all kinds of native plants, using them not only for food but for medicinal and many other purposes.

The most important staple crop was maize, the only significant wild grass in the New World to be fully domesticated. It remains the most important food crop in the Americas, used in more than 150 varieties as both food and cattle fodder. Root crops formed another substantial food source, especially in South America, and included manioc, sweet potatoes, and many varieties of the potato. Chili peppers were grown as hot seasoning. Amaranth, sunflowers, cacao, peanuts, and several types of beans were also significant crops. In contrast to Old World farmers, the Indians had few domesticated animals. Among them were the llama of the Andes and alpacas, which provided wool. The dog, the guinea pig, the raucous turkey, and the muscovy duck were also tamed.

Most archaeologists now agree there were two major centers of plant domestication in the Americas: Mesoamerica for maize, beans, squash, and sweet potatoes, and the highlands of the central Andes for root crops like potatoes and manioc. There were also four areas of later cultivation activity: tropical (northern) South America, the Andrean area, Mesoamerica, and southwestern and eastern North America.

The Origins of Maize

Most botanists believe that the wild ancestor of maize was a perennial grass named teosinte. The process of domestication may have started as an unintentional by-product of gathering wild teosinte. What may have happened was that the foragers favored the most harvestable of teosinte grasses, those whose seeds scattered less easily when ripe. In time, this favored type of teosinte would become established near campsites and in abandoned rubbish dumps. In time, too, people would remove weeds from these teosinte stands, then start deliberately planting the more useful types. Eventually, the grass became dependent on human intervention. A genetic revolution followed, which led to maize.

There is no archaeological evidence for transitional forms of teosinte, perhaps because the domestication process was very rapid. Traces of experimentation with the deliberate cultivation of crops like maize and squash have come from several regions of highland Mexico, notably the dry Tehuacan Valley in the South. Here Richard MacNeish has excavated a series of caves and open sites that document human occupation over a period of more than 10,000 years (Figure 6.11). MacNeish found that the earliest Tehuacan people lived by hunting and foraging, with wild plant foods assuming ever more importance in human diet. By at least 4500 B.C., about 90 percent of the Tehuacano diet consisted of tropical grasses and plants such as cacti.

After 4000 B.C., the Tehuacanos grew amaranth, beans, gourds, and maize in considerable quantities, foods that could be stored to tide them over the hungry months. The earliest maize cobs were smaller than modern forms. The primitive form of domesticated eight-rowed maize (*Maiz de ocho*) represented at Tehuacan was the common ancestral corn that spread thousands of miles from its original homeland. Subsequent derivatives of this basic maize developed elsewhere throughout the Americas.

Figure 6.11 Excavations at Coxcatlan Cave, Tehuacan Valley, Mexico.

How and Why Did Maize Agriculture Begin?

Some of the most intensive debates in American archaeology surround the origins of corn. Archaeologist Kent Flannery bases his arguments on the systems/ecological hypothesis we outlined above (p. 125). He also believes maize cultivation began as a result of strategies designed to cope with continuous short-term climatic fluctuations and constant population shifts. He bases his arguments on his own excavations at the Guila Naquitz rockshelter in the Valley of Oaxaca (Figure 6.3). Guila Naquitz was occupied about six times over a 2000-year period between 8750 and 6670 B.C. The tiny hunter-gatherer groups who visited the cave faced unpredictable climatic fluctuations due to periodic droughts in an area that could support very few people per square mile indeed.

The Guila Naquitz people foraged 11 different edible plant species over the year. In wet years, they experimented with deliberate planting of beans. Bean cultivation near the cave allowed people to collect more food and travel less. At first the experiments were confined to wet years, but as time went on and they gained more confidence, plant yields rose and they relied more heavily on their own cultivation as opposed to foraging. In time, the Guila Naquitz people simply added gourds, beans, and a simple form of maize to a much earlier foraging adaptation. Flannery believes that this kind of changeover occurred in many areas of Mesoamerica.

Early Food Production in the Andes (Before 5000 B.C. to 2000 B.C.)

If Flannery is correct, plant domestication in Mexico was not so much an invention in one small area as a shift in ecological adaptation deliberately chosen by people living where economic strategies necessitated extensive exploitation of plant foods. The same shift occurred high in the South American Andes. In the Andes, with its high altitude plateaux, mountain valleys, and steep slopes, environmental zones are stacked one above the other, instead of being distributed horizontally.

By 10,000 years ago, the inhabitants of Guitarrero Cave 1.5 miles (2.4 km) above sea level in the Peruvian Andes were not only collecting wild plants but were perhaps tending wild beans (Figure 6.12). This same pattern of plant tending persisted for many centuries in the Andes, one that had people growing not only beans, but gourds, potatoes, and ulluco as well. All these casual crops served as supplementary foods, as a means of expanding into hitherto marginal areas, often at higher altitudes.

After 5000 B.C., vegetable diets assumed even greater importance. A millennium later, the potato was cultivated on a much larger scale as were other crops. Both llamas and guinea pigs had been tamed. At this time, too, contacts with the coastal lowlands increased and a pattern of interdependency between coast and mountains developed that was to assume paramount importance in later millennia. This brought fish meal, iodine-

Figure 6.12 Guitarrero Cave, highland Peru.

rich seaweed to combat endemic goiter, and, later, cotton textiles to the highlands in exchange for potatoes and other highland products that went to the coast.

The Peruvian coast forms a narrow shelf at the foot of the Andes, an arid desert strip dissected by river valleys with deep, rich soils and plentiful water for some of the year. For thousands of years, coastal communities lived off the incredible bounty of the Pacific and gathered wild plants in summer. Fishing may have assumed greater importance after 5000 B.C., when the climate was warmer and drier than today. By this time the people were also cultivating some plant species like squash, peppers, and tuberous begonias.

At large, more or less permanent coastal settlements like Chilca and Paloma, fish and mollusks were staples, but the inhabitants also ground up wild grass seeds into flour and grew squashes. By 3800 B.C., the Chilca people were growing several types of beans including the ubiquitous lima, also squashes. They lived in circular matting and reed huts erected on frameworks of canes or occasionally whale bones.

The succeeding millennia saw many permanent settlements established near the Pacific, the people combining agriculture with fishing and mollusk gathering. But fish and sea mammals were so abundant that agriculture remained a secondary activity much later than it did in Mesoamerica.

The adoption of food production in many areas of the world led to major biological, cultural, and social changes in human society. We must now examine the consequences of food production on human society and some of the cultural developments in village societies that resulted.

Chapter
7

Ocean Voyagers, Pueblos, and Moundbuilders

A.D. 1950 —

A.D. 1 —

15,000 B.P. —

50,000 B.P. —

100,000 B.P. —

500,000 B.P. —

1.0 Million —

2.5 Million —

*T*he spread of food production throughout the entire world took only about 8,000 years. Food production spread to all corners of the world except where an environment with extreme aridity or heat or cold rendered agriculture or herding impossible or where people chose to remain hunters and gatherers. The new economies brought dramatic changes in human life in their train—sedentary village settlements, new agricultural technologies based on the axe, the hoe, and the digging stick, and greater political and social complexity. They also enabled humans to settle the offshore islands of the Pacific.

RECIPROCITY AND BIG MEN

Perhaps the most profound changes in the new farming societies were social and political rather than economic. They stemmed in large part from the necessity for farmers to live in compact, permanent settlements, to adopt sedentary lifeways. Early agricultural villages like Abu Hureyra or Merimda in the Near East or permanent farming settlements in Mexico's Tehuacan Valley brought households into much closer juxtaposition than ever before. The members of a hunter-gatherer band could always move away

142

when factional disputes threatened to disrupt the band. Farmers, anchored to their land, did not have such a luxury. As a result, kinship ties,
not only of immediate family, but of more distant kin, assumed much
greater importance in daily life. Subsistence farming households produce
their own food needs, but their survival depends both on cultivating a
diversity of soil types and on reciprocal obligations with fellow kin. Reci-
procity was vital to survival, for it created networks of obligation between
near and more distant kin. These allowed people to ask for help when
their crops failed, knowing that one day their kin would need help in turn,
assistance given without question.

The ties of kinship, of membership in hereditary clans and lineages,
provided not only institutions that allowed for the settlement of domestic
disputes, but also mechanisms for the ownership and inheritance of farming and grazing land. The ownership of land was vested not in individual
hands, but in a clan or lineage founded by a powerful ancestor. Thus, the
relationship between people and their land was closely related to their
links to their ancestors, who were the guardians of the soil. It is probably
for this reason that early farmers in the Levant and Turkey maintained
figurines or the plastered skulls of their forebears (Figure 7.1).

Everywhere where the new economies developed, farmers relied
increasingly on their neighbors. While late Ice Age hunters traded fine-
grained rock and exotic objects over long distances, the more sedentary
agriculturalist was forced to obtain many more commodities from elsewhere. These could include foodstuffs, game meat and hides, hut poles,
obsidian, and other vital materials, to say nothing of ornaments and other
rare objects from afar. Myriad exchange networks connected village with
village, household with household, narrow trails that carried visitors from
one community to the next, brought objects bartered from hand to hand
over enormous distances. It was such networks that brought Gulf Coast
seashells deep into the North American Midwest and glass beads from
India far into the African interior. In time, the same exchange networks
became more formal long-distance trade routes wherever state-organized
societies appeared, linking widely separated cultures and communities
into much larger economic systems. Thus, in time, were born the regional,
and later global, economic systems of later history.

Everything points to the earliest farming villages having been egalitarian communities, for signs of social ranking do not appear in burials
until long after food production took hold. In time, however, this egalitarian form of village life often gave way to new, more complex agricultural
societies headed by powerful kin leaders. These were individuals, important religious leaders linked to their followers by close kin ties and by
their ability to reward loyalty with gifts of food and exotic commodities
and goods obtained from afar. Anthropologist Marshall Sahlins, who has
studied modern-day Pacific Island societies, calls such people Big Men.
They are clever entrepreneurs, whose power is based strictly on their
above-average abilities and the loyalty which they command from their

Figure 7.1 Plastered skull from Jericho.

followers. This loyalty is but transitory, for it does not pass from one generation to the next. This makes for volatile, ever-changing political, economic, and social orders.

In time, some Big Men acquired such power that they were able to create hereditary dynasties, which passed chiefly authority from one generation to the next. Prestate societies of this greater complexity developed in almost every part of the prehistoric world, in late prehistoric Europe, in sub-Saharan Africa, Polynesia, and parts of North America. Everywhere chieftainships of this type evolved, they were exceptionally volatile, as the reins of political and economic power passed from one chiefly family to another, from one center to the next. None of these elaborate prestate societies was able to maintain tight political, economic, and social control over little more than a local area. It was state-organized societies that achieved such larger-scale integration, which often transcended local ecological zones.

Some complex prestate societies, notably those in western Europe, eventually came under the sway of expanding civilizations like that of Rome. Others, like those of Africa, Polynesia, and North America, survived into historic times, until the arrival of European explorers during the Age of Discovery, which began in the 15th century A.D. We cannot hope to describe all the more complex prestate farming societies that developed throughout the world, so we shall confine our discussion to the first settlement of the Pacific and to the emergence of elaborate chiefdoms in North America.

THE NAVIGATORS: POLYNESIAN CHIEFDOMS

By the end of the Ice Age some 15,000 years ago, *Homo sapiens* had settled in every corner of the Old World and New. Only two areas remained uncolonized by human beings. One was Antarctica, not even visited until the eighteenth century A.D., the other the remote islands of Melanesia and Polynesia in the Pacific (Figure 7.2). In Chapter 5, we saw how late Ice Age hunter-gatherers voyaged across open straits to colonize

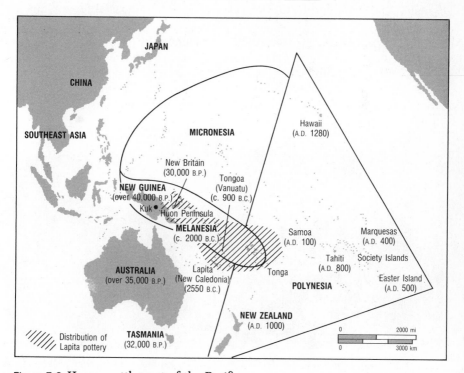

Figure 7.2 Human settlement of the Pacific.

Sahul and the Solomon Islands. Small groups of them had settled on the islands close to New Guinea, in the Bismarck Archipelago of the southwestern Pacific, by at least 31,000 years ago. Here colonization paused for many thousands of years. The successful settlement of islands even further offshore depended on the development of large offshore sailing craft and the ability to navigate far out of sight of land. It also hinged on the successful cultivation of root crops like taro and yam, also on small, portable animals like chickens and pigs that could be penned and transported in canoes. These conditions were met by 2000 B.C.

The first settlement of offshore Melanesia and Polynesia was closely connected to the cultivation of yams and taro, which enabled people to live on islands far from the mainland, land masses too isolated for animals or plants to migrate to. The maritime expansion to the more distant Melanesian islands took place between about 1600 and 1000 B.C. and covered 3,100 miles (4,988 km) of island chains and open ocean during a period of six centuries. The voyages took place in ocean-going double-hulled canoes capable of carrying heavy loads (Figure 7.3). They are associated with the so-called Lapita culture, named after a site on New Caledonia Island. The Lapita people originated in the Bismarck Archipelago region of western Melanesia some millennia earlier. Their canoes carried obsidian, foodstuffs, and other commodities from island to island over long distances. Lapita trade networks were part of a chain of such contacts that extended from Malaysia in the east to coastal New Guinea and offshore.

The rapid expansion offshore occurred among people who lived in an island environment where short interisland passages were an integral part of daily life. But the journeys to offlying islands like Fiji and Tonga involved much longer passages, some as many as 600 miles (966 km). Here, one-way journeys may have been rare and trade was at best spo-

Figure 7.3 Double-hulled canoe from Tahiti by the eighteenth-century artist Sydney Parkinson.

radic. Navigation out of sight of land required expert skills. Canoe navigators became a respected and close-knit group, who passed their knowledge down from generation to generation by word of mouth. Young
apprentices acquired their skills over many years of sailing under expert
supervision. They learned the angles of rising and setting stars, the trends
of ocean swells, the telltale and often inconspicuous phenomena that
indicate the general direction and distance of islands.

From Melanesia, canoes voyaged from island to island through western Polynesia, taking the plants and domesticated animals of their home-
lands with them. Melanesians voyaged to Micronesia and Polynesia about
2,000 years ago. After a lengthy period of adaptation in western Polynesia, small groups began to settle the more remote islands. The Marquesas
were colonized by A.D. 400 and the Society Islands and Tahiti by A.D. 800.
The first canoes arrived in Hawaii some 1,350 years ago and on Easter
Island by A.D. 500. New Zealand, the largest and among the most remote
of all Pacific islands, has a temperate climate, not the tropical warmth of
Polynesia. Despite this ecological difference, New Zealand was first settled by Polynesian ancestors of the Maori people, who voyaged southward, perhaps as early as A.D. 1000. New Zealand's temperate North
Island made the cultivation of yams and other tropical island crops difficult, so the early settlers relied heavily on hunting, fishing, and foraging.

Technologically, Micronesia and Polynesia were still in the Stone Age.
They relied heavily on stone axes and an elaborate array of bone and
shellfish hooks. The crops people planted varied from island to island, but
breadfruit, taro, coconut, yams, and bananas were the staples. By combining fish with simple agriculture, the islanders were able to accumulate
significant food surpluses that were the basis of powerful chiefdoms.

In Polynesia, as elsewhere in the world, agricultural surpluses generated on the larger islands were used as a form of wealth. This wealth, in
turn, concentrated political power in the hands of a relatively few people.
When European explorers visited Tahiti in the mid-eighteenth century,
they chanced on a center of a vigorous eastern Polynesian society (Figure
7.4). The islands were ruled by a powerful hierarchy of warlike chiefs and
nobles, many of them descendants of the canoe crews who had first settled
the archipelago. The chiefs acquired prestige by controlling and redistributing wealth and food supplies just as they did in Europe, North America, and elsewhere in the prehistoric world. Their formidable religious
and social powers led, inevitably, to intense competition, to warfare, and
to ever more ambitious agricultural projects.

Tahitian society was riddled with factionalism and vicious infighting,
as were the chiefdoms that developed far to the north, in the Hawaiian
Islands, at about the same time. Polynesian chiefdoms were highly volatile
and politically unstable. This volatility is well documented in New Zealand, where the introduction of the sweet potato in about A.D. 1400 made
a dramatic difference to Maori life. The population of North Island grew
rapidly as agricultural surpluses created new wealth and greater social

Figure 7.4 Tahitian *marae* (temple). (By William Watson.)

complexity. Soon overcrowding on the best sweet potato lands led to intense competition between neighboring chieftains. When Europeans arrived in 1769, they found the Maori living in fortified villages and engaged in constant warfare (Figure 7.5). Their military campaigns on land and sea were short and violent, often launched from elaborately carved war canoes up to 80 feet (24.3 km) in length. By this time, warfare was a key element in Maori society, to the extent that it was institutionalized and an important factor in maintaining cohesion and leadership.

The chiefdoms of Polynesia were fully as elaborate and hierarchical as those elsewhere in the prehistoric world. But they were still based on kin ties and on communal ownership of land. These were societies where leadership, even when inherited, depended heavily on the personal qualities of leaders and on their ability to retain the loyalty of their followers. Their chieftains were not despotic monarchs, exercising supreme political, religious, and economic authority, but people who ruled because of their inborn abilities and because of their close ties to their people. As we shall see in the case of North America, some of these prestate societies achieved remarkable levels of elaboration, but they were very different from the tightly controlled, socially stratified states of the Near East, China, or the Americas, described later in this book.

The transformation in Maori society that resulted from the introduction of the sweet potato can be mirrored by the history of maize in North

Figure 7.5 Maori *pa*, a fortified village. (By Augustus Earle.)

America. Both in the Southwest and in the South and Southeast, the arrival of corn led to major changes in indigenous society, but changes that varied greatly from one region to the next. In each area, highly variable ecological factors and social realities led to the development of complex farming societies.

PUEBLO FARMERS IN THE SOUTHWEST (1500 B.C. to A.D. 1600)

Maize originated in Mexico and was in common use by 2500 B.C. The new staple did not, however, spread northward across the Rio Grande until much later, perhaps around 1500 B.C., when maize is first recorded in the Southwest. From there, corn reached the southern Plains and then eastern North America, coming into widespread use by A.D. 800. We begin our story, then, in the Southwest.

The Arrival of Maize (1500 B.C.)

Approximately 11,000 years ago the southwest United States was populated by hunter-gatherers whose culture was adapted to desert living. For thousands of years, these southwesterners gathered many plant foods, including yucca seeds, cacti, and sunflower seeds. They developed an expertise with all kinds of plant foods, which preadapted them for farming after 2000 B.C. Maize, beans, and squash agriculture came to North America from Mexico, after generations of sporadic contacts between desert hunter-gatherers and settled farmers. Knowledge of domesticated plants, even gifts of seeds or seedlings, passed from south to north.

Climatic data from tree rings tells us that between about 2500 and 100 B.C., the southwestern climate was relatively stable, perhaps somewhat wetter than today. However, it was a semi-arid environment where hunting and gathering were high-risk occupations, mainly because rainfall was always unpredictable.

Domesticated plants like maize and beans might have low yields in these dry environments, but they had one major advantage: they were predictable food sources. Cultivators of the new crops could control their location and their availability at different seasons by storing them carefully. The people living in the southern deserts of the Southwest may have adopted maize and beans as supplementary foods not because they wanted to become farmers, but so they could become more effective foragers and maximize the potential of their environment.

Maize first entered the Southwest during a period of higher rainfall between 1500 and 1000 B.C. It spread rapidly through the region, especially when combined with beans after 500 B.C. Beans helped return vital nitrogen to the soil, maintaining fertility for longer periods of time. Maize farming in the dry Southwest was never easy, for the farmers were working close to the limits of corn's range. They selected moisture-retaining soils very carefully, used north- and east-facing slopes that received little direct sun, planted near canyon mouths and diverted water from streams and springs. They did everything they could to minimize risk, dispersing their gardens to reduce the danger of local drought or flood.

The appearance of maize did not trigger a dramatic revolution in southwestern life. The earlier corns were not that productive, but more bountiful local forms soon became a vital staple to many Southwestern groups who were now living in permanent hamlets and much smaller territories. They also led to more complex Southwestern societies that adjusted to changing climatic conditions with remarkable flexibility.

Hohokam, Mogollon, and Anasazi (300 B.C. to A.D. 1600)

By 300 B.C., many centuries of experimentation had produced much more productive domestic crops and a greater dependence on farming. The cultural changes of these centuries culminated in the great southwestern cultural traditions: Hohokam, Mogollon, and Anasazi.

Hohokam people occupied much of what is now lower Arizona. They were desert farmers, who grew not only maize and beans, but cotton, which flourishes in hot environments. Where they could, they practiced irrigation from flowing streams; otherwise they cultivated floodplains and caught runoff from local storms with dams, terraces, and other devices. For centuries, much Hohokam life and trading activity centered around Snaketown, a large settlement and ceremonial center near the Gila River (Figure 7.6). The inhabitants maintained trading relationships not only with other parts of the Southwest and with the Pacific coast to the west, but also with Mexico. The Hohokam obtained tropical bird feathers, copper artifacts and other exotic objects from the South, but scholars are sharply divided on the amount of Mexican influence or Hohokam culture and religious beliefs. The Hohokam vanished after A.D. 1500, its cultural heirs the Papago and Pima Indians of today.

Mogollon was a more highland cultural tradition, which flourished mainly in what is now New Mexico from about 300 B.C. to between A.D. 850 and 1150. Mogollon farmers relied on direct rainfall and used little irrigation, living in small villages of pit dwellings with timber frames and mat or brush roofs. In only a few areas did more elaborate settlements develop, but by this time Mogollon was becoming part of the western pueblo Anasazi tradition.

Figure 7.6 The earthen ball court at the Hohokam site of Snaketown, Arizona. It is not known what games or ceremonies were conducted here.

Anasazi developed out of indigenous hunter-gatherer roots and was centered on the Four Corners area, where Utah, Arizona, Colorado, and New Mexico meet. Anasazi people made heavy use of wild plant foods, even after they took up serious maize farming after A.D. 400. Most of their farming depended on seasonal rainfall, although they used irrigation where practicable.

At first the Anasazi lived in small pithouse villages, but after A.D. 900 much of the population congregated in above-ground settlements of adjoining rooms. These became the famous pueblos, often clustered in small arcs to make them equidistant from the subterranean ceremonial rooms, the kivas, in the middle of the settlement. The largest and most spectacular pueblos were located in densely populated areas like Chaco Canyon in New Mexico and Mesa Verde in Arizona. It was in areas like these that Pueblo society sometimes achieved a higher degree of complexity, with larger, densely populated towns that controlled large exchange networks.

Chaco Canyon with its dramatic cliffs was the center of a remarkable flowering of Anasazi culture that lasted for two centuries after A.D. 900. During this time, the Chaco Phenomenon, as it is called, expanded from its canyon homeland to encompass an area of 25,000 square miles of the San Juan Basin and adjacent uplands. The people constructed large, well-planned towns, extensive road and water control systems, and outlying sites linked to the canyon by roadways and visual communication systems (Figure 7.7). The thirteen large towns and kivas of Chaco Canyon con-

Figure 7.7 Pueblo Bonito, Chaco Canyon, New Mexico.

tained many luxury items, including turquoise from near Santa Fe, sea-shells, copper bells, even the skeletons of macaws, colorful birds from the lowland rainforests of Mesoamerica much prized for their bright feathers. When Chaco was in its heyday between A.D. 1075 and 1115, the canyon was not only a focus for turquoise ornament manufacture, but an impor-tant ceremonial center for dozens of outlying settlements.

Chaco flourished during a period of uncertain rainfall and the local farming land could never have supported more than about 2,000 people, although population estimates for the pueblos rise as high as 5,600. Thus, archaeologists argue, Chaco may have had a relatively small permanent population and been a place where much food was stored, and where large crowds of Anasazi congregated for major ceremonial observances.

What, then, was Chaco? Was it a highly centralized chieftainship, controlled by a small, but powerful elite of chiefs and nobles, who had a monopoly over trade and important spiritual powers? Or was it what archaeologist Gwinn Vivian calls an egalitarian enterprise, a cooperative mechanism developed by dozens of communities living in a harsh and unpredictable environment? We do not know, but elaborately decorated burials were discovered in Chaco by early archaeologists. The Anasazi lived in a society where kin ties were all important, where everyone had complex obligations to fulfill both to his own community and to the clan. Without such obligations, it would have been impossible to carry large quantities of food to Chaco's storerooms, or to transport the more than 200,000 wooden beams needed to build its large pueblos and kivas. Perhaps the Chaco Phenomenon was an adaptive mechanism whereby local kin leaders regulated and maintained long-distance exchange net-works and ceremonial life as a means of supporting far more people than the environment would normally carry. They used economic, social, and ritual ties among a scattered rural population to encourage cooperation between isolated communities in times of need.

The Chaco Phenomenon reached its peak between A.D. 1100 and 1130, when a prolonged drought caused the system to collapse. The Anasazi moved away into more dispersed settlements, maintained alli-ances with one another, or flourished in scattered, independent pueblos.

Perhaps the most famous of all Anasazi cultural developments is that centered on the Mesa Verde canyon system in the northern San Juan Basin. By 1100, as many as 30,000 people lived in the nearby Montezuma Valley, mainly concentrated in villages of 1,000 people or more. Only about 2,500 of them lived in Mesa Verde. Between 1200 and 1300, people moved from open locations into crowded pueblos. Cliff Palace, which was the largest settlement, had 220 rooms and 23 kivas (Figure 7.8).

Both in Mesa Verde itself and in the surrounding countryside, large villages, almost towns, were homes for between 1,000 and 2,500 people, living in room clusters associated with kivas and other ceremonial build-ings. Everywhere in Mesa Verde, the emphasis was on individual commu-

Figure 7.8 Cliff Palace, Mesa Verde, Colorado.

nities. Judging from the numerous kivas, there was considerable cooperative and ritual activity, and there were numerous occasions when
inhabitants of different communities organized large labor parties to carry
out sophisticated water control works and other communal projects. This
Anasazi tradition was very different from Chaco Canyon, with its intricate
mechanisms for integrating dispersed communities, or the chiefdoms of
the South and Southeast with their large centers and satellite villages.

The twelfth and thirteenth centuries saw the culmination of four
centuries of rapid social and political development in the Mesa Verde
region. About 1300, however, the entire San Juan drainage, including
Mesa Verde, was abandoned by Pueblan peoples. They moved in scattered groups south and southeastward into the lands of the historic Hopi,
Zuni, and Rio Grande pueblos, where their ultimate descendants live to
this day.

Following the abandonment of large areas of the Southwest in the late
thirteenth and early fourteenth centuries, large settlements formed in
previously sparsely inhabited areas. Some of these pueblos are recognized
as those of direct ancestors of modern communities. Southwestern pueblo
society never achieved the cultural complexity found in eastern North
America or among the Hawaiians or Tahitians, but it achieved the limits of
regional integration possible for a region where rainfall was irregular and

the climate harsh. Perhaps the best way to describe much southwestern organization is as a theocracy, a government that regulated religious and secular affairs through both individuals like chiefs and king groups or associations (societies) that cut across kin lines. The basic social and economic unit was the extended family, but for hundreds of years southwestern peoples fostered a sense of community and undertook communal labors like irrigation works using wider social institutions that worked for the common good.

Maize farming was a relatively late development throughout North America, not only in the Southwest, but also in the Midwest and southeastern United States. Here, distinctive and quite complex hunter-gatherer societies turned to the cultivation of native plants, then maize and beans as population densities rose and food shortages became more common.

THE MOUNDBUILDERS OF EASTERN NORTH AMERICA (2000 B.C. to A.D. 1500)

In eastern North America, the densest hunter-gatherer populations flourished in the Mississippi River valley and other fertile river floodplain areas. By 2000 B.C., local populations had increased to the point that group mobility was restricted and there were periodic food shortages. Under these circumstances, it was almost inevitable that some groups turned to the deliberate cultivation of native food plants like goosefoot and marsh elder to supplement wild cereal grass yields.

At the same time, the first signs of social ranking appear in local burials. We find, also, an increasing preoccupation with burial and life after death. For the first time, individual communities and groups maintained cemeteries on the edges of their territories, which may have served to validate territorial boundaries. As the centuries passed, the funeral rites associated with death and the passage from the world of the living to that of the ancestors became ever more elaborate and important. This elaboration was associated not only with increasing social complexity and an explosion in long-distance exchange, but with the building of ceremonial earthworks as well.

In this vast, and highly diverse region flourished the Adena and Hopewell cultures and other local traditions that culminated in the powerful chiefdoms of the Mississippian culture that survived until European contact and beyond.

Adena and Hopewell (500 B.C. to A.D. 500)

Thousands of years of long-distance exchange between neighboring communities had given certain raw materials and exotic artifacts high prestige value in eastern North American society. Such imports were scarce and hard to come by, important gifts exchanged between kin leaders and chiefs. They assumed great social value and significance in societies that placed a high premium on prestige. Hammered copper artifacts, conch shells from the Atlantic and Gulf coasts, certain types of stone axes — these became status symbols, buried with their powerful owners at death. By 500 B.C., the individuals who controlled these exchange networks were influential not only in life, but in death, for they were buried under large burial mounds.

The Adena culture, which flourished in the Ohio Valley between 500 B.C. and about A.D. 400, was one of the first to build extensive earthworks. Adena earthworks follow the contours of flat-topped hills and form circles, squares, and other shapes, enclosing areas as much as 350 feet (107 m) across. There were ceremonial enclosures rather than defensive works, sometimes built to surround burial mounds, other times standing alone. Adena burial mounds were usually communal rather than individual graves. The most important people were buried in log-lined tombs, their corpses smeared with red ocher or graphite. Nearby lie soapstone pipes and tablets engraved with curving designs or birds of prey. Some prestigious kin leaders were buried inside enclosures or death huts that were burned down as part of the funeral ceremony. Occasionally the burial chamber was left open so that other bodies could be added later.

The building of these mounds was invariably a communal effort, probably involving fellow kin from several settlements who piled up basketfuls of earth. The earthworks grew slowly as generations of new bodies were added. Apparently, only the most important people were interred in the mounds. Most Adena folk were cremated and their ashes placed in the communal burial place.

Between 200 B.C. and A.D. 400, the Hopewell tradition, an elaboration of Adena, appeared in Illinois. Its religious cults were such a success that they spread rapidly from their heartland as far afield as upper Wisconsin and Louisiana and deep into Ohio and New York State. The Midwest experienced a dramatic flowering of artistic traditions and of long-distance trade that brought copper from the Great Lakes region, obsidian from Yellowstone, and mica from southern Appalachia. The Hopewell people themselves dwelt in relatively small settlements and using only the simplest of artifacts in daily life. They wore leather and woven clothes of pliable fabrics. All the wealth and creative skill of society was lavished on a few individuals and their life after death. At first glance, Hopewell exotic artifacts and ritual traditions seem completely alien to the simple indigenous culture of the area, but they are deeply rooted in local life.

The cult objects buried with the dead tell us something of the rank and social roles of their owners. Some of the exotic grave goods, such as pipe bowls or ceremonial axes, were buried as gifts from living clan members to a dead leader. Others were personal possessions, cherished weapons or sometimes symbols of status or wealth. Hopewell graves contain soapstone pipe bowls in the form of beavers, frogs, birds, bears,

Figure 7.9 Hopewell sheet mica ornament in the form of a claw of a bird of prey.

and even humans. Skilled artisans fashioned thin copper and mica sheets into head and breast ornaments that bear elaborate animal and human motifs (Figure 7.9). There were copper axes and arrowheads, trinkets and beads.

Most of these artifacts were manufactured by a few specialists, perhaps produced in workshops within large earthwork complexes, themselves close to major sources of raw materials. Ceremonial objects of all kinds were traded from hand to hand throughout Hopewell territory along the same trade routes that carried foodstuffs and everyday objects from hamlet to hamlet. However, the prized manufactures may have passed from one person to another in a vast network of gift-giving transactions that linked different kin leaders with lasting, important obligations to one another. The closest modern analogy to such an arrangement is the famous *kula* ring exchange system of the Trobriand Islands of the southwestern Pacific. There, distinctive types of shell ornaments pass in perennial circles between individuals, linking them in lasting ritual and trading partnerships, in ties of reciprocal obligation. This kind of environment encourages individual initiative and competition, as kin leaders and their followers vie with one another for prestige and social status that is as transitory as life itself. Perhaps somewhat similar practices were commonplace in Hopewell times. Once dead and buried with their prized possessions, the deceased were no longer political players, for their mantles did not necessarily pass to their children or relatives.

Hopewell burial mounds are much more elaborate than their Adena forebears (Figure 7.10). Some Hopewell mounds rise 40 feet (12 m) high and are more than 100 feet (30.5 m) across. Often, the builders would deposit a large number of bodies on an earthen platform, burying them over a period of years before erecting a large mound over the dead. Hopewell burial complexes reached imposing sizes. The 24 burial mounds at Mound City, Ohio, lie inside an earthen enclosure covering 13 acres (5.26 ha).

Figure 7.10 Great Serpent Mound, Ohio. The serpent's jaws encompass a burial mound.

The Mississippian Culture (A.D. 600 to 1500)

The center of religious and political power shifted southward after A.D. 400, as the Hopewell tradition declined. It was then that the people of the densely populated and lush Mississippi floodplain may have realized the great potential of maize as a high-yielding food staple. Maize reached the Mississippi and southeastern North America from the Southwest sometime before A.D. 1000. But its full potential was not realized for some centuries, until the arrival of domesticated beans. Beans had the advantage of a high protein value but also the asset of compensating for the nutritional deficiencies of corn. The new crops arrived as rising populations, and, perhaps, the insatiable demands of a small but powerful elite, were causing considerable economic and social stress.

Maize and beans may have been planted initially as supplementary foods, but they differ from native plants such as goosefoot in that they demand more start-up labor to clear land. Within a short time, the river valley landscape was transformed in such a way that hunting and fishing provided less food for energy expended than farming. Major social and political changes and an entirely new economic pattern followed, changing eastern North American society beyond recognition.

Thus was born the Mississippian culture, the most elaborate prehistoric cultural tradition to flourish in North America. Regional Mississippian societies developed in river valleys over much of the Midwest and Southeast and interacted with one another for centuries. Many Mississippian populations lived in fertile river valleys with lakes and swamps. They lived by hunting, fishing, and exploiting migrating waterfowl. Every family harvested nuts and grew maize, beans, squashes, and other crops. The cultivation of native plants like goosefoot and marsh elder, as well as sunflowers, was of vital importance—to mention only a few species. Theirs was a complex adaptation to highly varied local environments. Some groups flourished in small, dispersed homesteads, while others lived in compact villages, some so large they might be called small towns; in locations like Cahokia, on the banks of the Mississippi opposite the modern city of St. Louis, thousands of people lived.

By A.D. 900, some larger Mississippian communities housed thousands of people and were fortified with defensive palisades. Cahokia had a population of at least 30,000 to 35,000 people in its heyday. It was a great ceremonial center; its mounds and plazas dominated the countryside for miles. Monk's Mound at the center of Cahokia rises 102 feet (31 m) above the Mississippi floodplain and covers 16 acres (6.5 ha) (Figure 7.11). On the summit stood a thatched temple at the east end of an enormous plaza.

Figure 7.11 Reconstruction of Cahokia, Illinois.

Around the plaza rose other mounds, temples, warehouses, administrative buildings, and the homes of the elite. The entire ceremonial complex of mounds and plazas covered more than 200 acres (81 ha) and was fortified by a log fence with gates and watchtowers. Cahokia was planned and controlled by a powerful elite of leaders and priests and was home to many craft specialists.

Cahokia was by no means unique. It lay in the north of Mississippian territory. A major center lay to the south, at Moundville in Alabama. Dozens of small centers and towns sprang up between the two. More than just sacred places for annual planting and harvest ceremonies, the centers were markets and focal points of powerful chiefdoms. Cahokia owed some of its importance to the manufacture and trading of local salt, and chert, a fine-grained rock used to make hoes and other tools.

We know little about how Mississippian society functioned, but each major population center was probably ruled as a series of powerful chiefdoms by an elite group of priests and rulers who lived somewhat separated from the rest of the population. Unlike their recent predecessors, these individuals may have inherited political and economic power, also social position, as the hereditary offices of the elite were passed from one generation to the next. The chieftains controlled long-distance trade and were the intermediaries between the living, the ancestors, and the gods.

As in the Hopewell culture, high-ranking individuals went to the next world in richly decorated graves, with clusters of ritual objects of different styles that symbolized various clans and tribes. Excavations at one burial mound revealed at least six different burial events that involved 261 people, including 4 mutilated men and 118 women, who were probably retainers sacrificed to accompany a chief in the afterlife. One such chief lay on a layer of thousands of shell beads, accompanied by grave offerings from as far afield as Wisconsin and Tennessee.

Cahokia and most other larger Mississippian communities had more or less standardized layouts. The inhabitants built platform-like mounds and capped them with temples and the houses of important individuals. These mounds were grouped around an open plaza, while most people lived in thatched dwellings clustered nearby. As we shall see in Chapter 19, somewhat similar architectural groupings are typical of Mesoamerican ceremonial centers and cities, tempting many scholars to claim that Mississippian chiefs were under strong cultural influence from Mexico.

Mississippian graves and mound centers contain finely made pottery and other artifacts that bear elaborate designs and distinctive artistic motifs. These artifacts include stone axes with handle and head carved from a single piece of stone, copper pendants adorned with circles and weeping eyes, shell disks carved with woodpeckers and rattlesnakes, elaborately decorated clay pots, and engraved shell cups adorned with male figures in ceremonial dress. The themes and motifs on these objects have many common features throughout the South and Southeast and as far afield as the borders of the Ohio Valley.

At first, experts thought that these ceremonial artifacts represented a Southern Cult, that its ideology and motifs like a weeping eye had arrived in North America in the hands of Mexican artisans and priests. But a closer look at indigenous art traditions show that such motifs were commonly used by many North American groups. Many Mississippian ceremonial artifacts served as badges of rank and status, and as clan symbols. They were traded from hand to hand over long distances as symbolic gifts between widely separated chieftains who shared many common religious beliefs. The Mississippian was an entirely indigenous cultural tradition, the climax of millennia of steady cultural evolution in eastern North America.

Cahokia, Moundville, and other great Mississippian centers were past the height of their powers by the time European explorers reached the Mississippi Valley in the sixteenth century. But numerous chiefdoms still flourished in the mid-South and Southeast right up to European contact and beyond. It is interesting to speculate what trajectory the successors of Mississippian society would have taken if Europeans had not arrived. Would they have evolved into a full-fledged, state-organized society, to rival that of the Maya and Aztec to the south? Experts believe they would not have, simply because of the growing seasons for maize and beans in North America are too short and the climate too harsh to support either speculated agriculture or high urban population densities under preindustrial conditions. It would have been difficult for any chieftain to accumulate the food surpluses necessary to maintain authority over more than a relatively limited area.

In sum, the most important cultural consequences of food production were a long-term trend toward greater political elaboration, a degree of social ranking, and greater interdependency in a wide range of village farming societies. The trends toward complexity that developed in eastern North America and the Pacific also unfolded in temperate Europe and in sub-Saharan Africa (Chapter 10). In Europe, the most able of village kin leaders eventually became warrior chieftains and even hereditary leaders ruling from small towns. One catalyst for such development was an explosion in long-distance exchange that coincided with the widespread use of bronze, and later, iron, metallurgy that linked even isolated communities together in larger economic, and later political, units. Julius Caesar's legions found the Iron Age people of western Europe a tough enemy to conquer. Centuries later, the descendants of these people were to shatter Rome's reputation as an invincible power.

But the most momentous consequences of food production were those that led to the emergence of the state-organized society, the urban civilizations that developed in many parts of the world after 3000 B.C.

PART
Four

EARLY CIVILIZATIONS

When Enlil, lord of all the lands, had given the kingship of the Land to Lugalzagezi, had directed to him the eyes [of all the people] of the Land from east to west, had prostrated [all the people] for him . . . from the lower sea, along the Tigris [and] Euphrates to the upper sea . . . from east to west, Enlil gave him no rival . . . the Land rejoiced under his rule; all the chieftains of Sumer [and] lords of foreign lands bowed down before him. . . .

Sumerian vase inscription commemorating King Lugalzagezi of Mesopotamia's rule over the ancient world.

Samuel Kramer

The Sumerians (Chicago: University of Chicago Press, 1963, p. 323).

Chapter
8

State-Organized Societies

*A*bout 3250 B.C., the first state-organized societies appeared in Egypt and Mesopotamia, ushering in a new chapter in human history. The emergence of the world's first states was a complex process that took many centuries. This chapter defines a state-organized society in more detail, discusses some of the factors that contributed to the development of early civilization, and examines the major theories surrounding their origins.[1]

WHAT IS A STATE-ORGANIZED SOCIETY?

Like food production, state-organized societies developed in many parts of the world. States first appeared between the Euphrates and Tigris Rivers and in the Nile valley by 3250 B.C. They flourished in the Indus valley of Pakistan by 2000 B.C., on Crete and in Greece during the second millennium B.C., and in the Huang-Ho River valley of northern China at about the same time. Preindustrial states developed rapidly in Mesoamerica and the Andean region in the first millennium B.C. and survived in highly developed forms until Europeans arrived in the 15th century A.D. (Figure 8.1). Each of these many civilizations evolved its own culture and distinctive civilization, to the point where it is almost impossible to develop a precise definition of a state-organized society. Each shares, how-

---

[1]For the purposes of this book, for convenience and to avoid confusion, the terms "state-organized society," "civilization," "pre-industrial civilization," and "state" are used interchangeably.

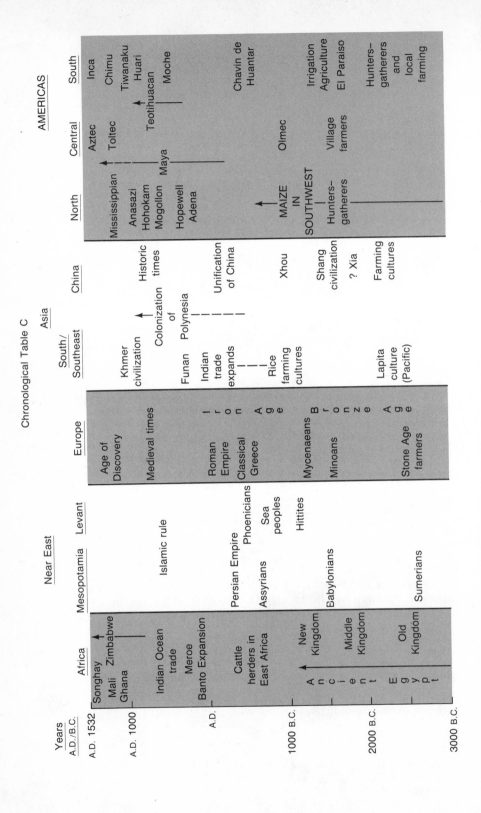

Chronological Table C

ever, some generally agreed upon special attributes that distinguish them from prestate cultures. These attributes are as follows:

1. They were based on a specific regional territory such as the Nile Valley or the Valley of Mexico, as opposed to the much smaller areas controlled by individual kin groups in prestate societies.
2. They were dependent on intensified agricultural production that enabled them to support high population densities, usually in urban settings. This intensification usually involved some form of water control or irrigation.
3. They had economies that were based on the *centralized* accumulation of capital and social status through tribute and taxation. This type of economy allowed the support of hundreds, often thousands, of nonfood producers such as artisans and priests.
4. They were socially stratified into distinct social classes, with a tiny elite and large groups of artisans, officials, priests, and other classes. Most people were commoners, with slaves and prisoners at the lowest level of the social pyramid. Their rulers maintained their power not only through personal ability, but by a combination of religious authority, economic monopoly, and force.

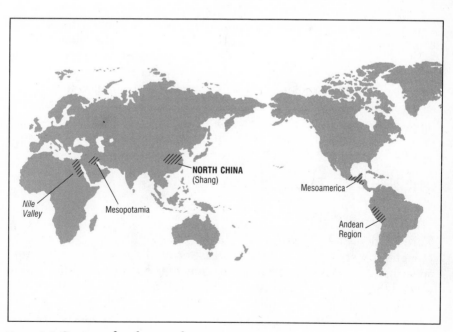

Figure 8.1 Centers of early state formation.

5. They built imposing public buildings and distinctive monumental architecture, usually in the form of temples, palaces or storehouses.
6. They used some form of record-keeping system, usually a written script.

State-organized societies are the first in which cities appear. The earliest cities took many forms, from the compact, walled settlement of Mesopotamia to the Maya ceremonial center with a core population in the central precinct and a dense rural population in the hinterland. In contrast, the cities of the Harappan civilization of the Indus Valley were carefully planned communities with regular streets and assigned quarters for every social class. Mycenaean and Minoan states in Greece and the Aegean were centered not on cities, but on palaces that served as both shrines and trading centers, with most of the population living in the surrounding countryside. Because of these differences it is difficult to define a city in terms of population, but a lower limit of about 5,000 people is commonly used.

What distinguishes a city from prehistoric villages and towns is its economic and organizational complexity: its great temples, markets, palaces, and artisans' quarters, and the large number of nonfarmers who live and work within city limits. The city itself did not function in isolation: it was part and parcel of a complex system of different settlements that relied on its many services and facilities.

In the final analysis, the preindustrial state is distinguished from smaller-scale, prestate societies by its inherent complexity, and by its built-in component of social inequality. The preindustrial civilization was run for the benefit of a tiny minority, who controlled the labor of thousands of commoners by a mixture of religious coercion, economic monopoly, and force. For example, the ancient Egyptian Pharaohs ruled over a complex, stratified society. The royal family and nobility formed the ruling class. Under them were distinct, hierarchical classes of artisans, bureaucrats, priests, soldiers, and other functionaries. And, at the bottom of the social pyramid, were thousands of commoners and slaves.

THEORIES OF THE ORIGIN OF STATES

An Urban Revolution?

Vere Gordon Childe's *Urban Revolution* (Chapter 2) discussed the development of metallurgy, an invention that created a new class of full-time specialists and changed the rules of human social organization. Childe argued that the new specialists were supported by food surpluses resulting from intensive agriculture. The products of the artisans had to be distributed, and raw materials had to be obtained from outside sources.

Both needs reduced the self-reliance of subsistence farming societies. Irrigation increased productivity, leading to centralized control of food supplies, production, and distribution. A new class-stratified society, based on economic classes rather than kin, came into being. Writing was essential for keeping records and for developing the sciences. Finally, a unifying religious force dominated urban life as priest-kings and despots rose to power in Egypt and Mesopotamia and built great temples and public buildings as symbols of their authority.

Childe's notion of an Urban Revolution is appealing, but it does not reflect historical reality. We know today that there were many different forms of state-organized societies, and many ways in which they developed in different parts of the world. It is true that some degree of craft specialization and centralized religious beliefs are common to all preindustrial states, but to speak of an urban revolution is to ignore the great diversity of early civilizations that developed in the prehistoric world.

Contributing Factors to State Formation

Today's theories take many factors into account, for wherever preindustrial civilizations appeared, it was during a period of major economic and social change. In Egypt, for example, the unification of the Nile valley under a single state was the consequence of major political upheaval, intercommunity rivalries, growing contacts resulting from long-distance trade, a need to intensify agricultural production, and new, universal religious beliefs — to mention only a few underlying factors. These many factors include ecology, population growth, technology, irrigation, trade, religious beliefs, and warfare.

Environmental factors undoubtedly played a major role in the emergence of civilization, for it is no coincidence that some of the world's earliest states appear in areas of unusual agricultural potential, often on the edges of several closely juxtaposed ecological zones. For example, the Minoans and Myceneans of the Aegean and Greece cultivated both olives and vines, which grew in quite different, neighboring environments. A combination of olive oil and wine provided both these civilizations with a useful economic base, achieved by integrating the yields from two crops. It was this process of integration, of control of different food staples, that provided a hedge against famine essential for managing large food surpluses and feeding large numbers of nonfarmers.

Population growth has been considered a factor in human culture change ever since Thomas Henry Malthus argued in 1798 that human reproductive capacity far exceeds the available food supply. Thus, say many scholars, more intensive agricultural methods created new food surpluses. These in turn led to more population growth and to new social, political, and religious institutions along the way. Economist Ester Boserup and others have argued to the contrary, that population growth caused irrigation and intensive agriculture, and the social evolution that went along with it. Neither in Egypt and Mesopotamia, nor in other areas of early state formation, is there any evidence for rapid population increase in the centuries immediately preceding civilization. In many areas, it was more productive field agriculture, such as swamp farming or using regular river floods, that allowed *denser*, but not necessarily larger, populations to congregate in larger settlements. In Mesopotamia, for example, growing villages became towns and later cities during centuries when exploitation of the local ecosystem became more ordered and more systematic. There is thus no reason to believe that a critical population density was the only prerequisite for urban life.

Irrigation and Intensive Land Use   While many factors contributed to the development or state-organized societies, three elements appear to have been of great importance. The first was the creation of large food surpluses, used to support new economic classes of nonfarmers. Such surpluses require long-term storage far above the capacity of individual households. Thus, not only greater agricultural efficiency, but social and cultural changes such as centralized storage systems were needed to manage the new food supplies.

Second, major agricultural production focused on the most productive crops. But it was still diversified, both to protect people against famine, and also to stimulate the development of trade and exchange of foodstuffs. This deliberate diversification and exchange encouraged the emergence of centralized political authority.

Third, intensive land use increased agricultural output, through the use of simple irrigation works, specialized swamp agriculture, or other means. The earliest irrigation works involved just the construction and maintenance of small-scale canals that watered fields close to rivers, a logical extension of natural flood conditions.

Archaeologist Robert Adams has studied large-scale irrigation works in Mesopotamia and shown that the Sumerians took maximum advantage of the natural hydrology of local rivers. Each small community organized its own canals, as they did in early Egypt. It was only long after the establishment of despotic rule that the central government organized irrigation works on a large scale. Such systems extended over entire river valleys and landscapes, requiring constant administration and maintenance.

Technology   Agricultural technology changed very slowly in the centuries before state-organized societies emerged anywhere. The implements used to clear and cultivate fields were simple axes, digging sticks, and hoes, artifacts used for thousands of years in areas like Mesopotamia, Mesoamerica, or the Andes, long after powerful rulers were adorned with brightly shining copper ornaments and gold regalia. In fact, the major technological innovations resulting from early civilization were such items

Figure 8.2 Ancient Egyptian boat from pharaoh Tutankhamun's tomb. This is a ceremonial vessel, but simpler sailing
vessels were vital to the state's commerce.

as the wheel and the sailing vessel, of more benefit to trade and transportation than to agriculture.

Trade   Prehistoric peoples have exchanged goods and raw materials with
one another for tens of thousands of years. The volume of long-distance
exchange picked up considerably with the appearance of farming in the
Near East around 7500 B.C. The trade in obsidian, for example, reached
impressive proportions, linking dozens of farming villages in exchange
networks that were to persist for thousands of years.[2] The long-term
consequence was to make societies living in different ecological zones
more dependent upon one another, to the point that this interdependency
eventually became critical to survival.

It is significant, for example, that most early Egyptian and Mesopotamian trade was based on large rivers, where bulk transportation by boat
was easy (Figure 8.2). This ease of communication fostered connections
between the Mesopotamian lowlands and highlands, between upper and
lower Egypt. In the Andes, there were many centuries of sporadic ex-

---

[2]Archaeologists often distinguish between *exchange*, the bartering of objects and commodities between individuals, and *trade*, more organized commerce: for convenience, the two
terms are used interchangeably here.

change between communities on the arid Pacific coast and those in the highlands. As maize became a staple in the highlands, the interdependency between mountains and lowlands became crucial. Farmers living on predominantly carbohydrate diets needed protein to combat goiter and other diseases. Fish meal from the distant Pacific provided such essential nutrients for upland farmers, while root crops and other products from high in the Andes became an integral part of coastal life.

Long-distance trade expanded greatly in state-organized societies, trade that flowed toward the capital city for the benefit of the elite. Small village trade networks became part of vast overland caravan routes that linked the Tigris and Euphrates to the Mediterranean, the Nile valley to the Sinai Peninsula and the Levant, and eventually North and sub-Saharan Africa. Caravan routes criss-crossed the Mediterranean world for many centuries, a form of organized trading that kept to carefully defined routes set up and controlled by state authorities for their own use. Black asses and mules carried not only metals and fine ornaments to wealthy merchants, they were the means whereby rulers collected tribute from subject peoples year after year. Animal transport enabled powerful leaders to control the commerce that was the lifeblood of the state. Whatever city-state was in power, whatever king all-powerful, the caravans kept moving, for they were the lifeblood of civilization.

Markets were an essential part of such large-scale trading, networks of central places where people could gather to buy and sell all manner of artifacts and commodities. They were places where people traded all manner of goods at relatively stable, almost fixed prices. Prehistoric Mesoamerican states developed the market to a high degree of sophistication. The great market at Aztec Tenochtitlan covered several acres. The Spanish conquistadors said it was as large as that in Seville or Constantinople. They estimated that between 20,000 and 25,000 people a day visited it daily, and 50,000 on scheduled market days. There were special sections for "dealers in gold, silver, and precious stones, feathers, cloaks, and embroidered goods, and male and female slaves were sold there," wrote conquistador Bernal Diaz. Items from every corner of the Aztec world could be bought here, under the watchful eyes of government inspectors. "The murmur and hum of . . . voices and the words that [people] used could be heard more than a league off," Diaz remembered.[3]

The Tenochtitlan market had its equivalents, usually on a much more modest scale, in every major town in Mesoamerica. Markets were a complex form of trading found in every preindustrial civilization, but all long-distance trade, and the interdependencies that went with it, changed constantly in response to fluctuating demands and availabilities of commodities and goods. For example, the entire pattern of trade between India and East Africa was affected by changing fashions in glass bead colors in the far interior of Africa.

---

[3]Bernal Diaz, *The Conquest of New Spain*, Pelican, Baltimore, 1963.

In sum, the massive expansion of long-distance trade came in the centuries following the emergence of states, and the imposition of the centralized controls of economic life that went with them. And it was this centralization and burgeoning linkages with others that gave rise eventually to the regional economic systems, and then the expanding world systems, that have dominated the history of recent centuries. Today, we are all interconnected by a global economy. The emergence of state-organized societies saw this process not begin, but accelerate.

Warfare has often been cited as a factor in state formation. Anthropologist Robert Carneiro has developed what he calls a *coercive theory* of state origins. He used data from Peruvian coastal valleys to argue that in some areas the amount or agricultural land is very limited and circumscribed by desert. As the population rises, neighboring villages start competing for each others' lands. Soon some village leaders emerge as successful warlords, become chieftains, and preside over larger tribal groups. The valley population continues to grow and warfare intensifies until the entire region falls under the sway of one warrior-ruler. The leader now presides over a single state, which eventually expands through more conquest into neighboring valleys, creating a much larger civilization.

There is an attractive simplicity to the notion that the early town or city was a mighty fortress to which surrounding groups flocked in times of stress. Thus, goes the argument, the people who congregated within the walls come to depend upon one another and their city as a fundamental part of society. In fact, the archaeological evidence both from the Near East and the Americas strongly suggests that large-scale warfare, the emergence of warrior classes in society, and the appearance of standing armies, were consequences of states rather than the cause of them. Earlier warfare was confined to highly localized, and often transitory, tribal conflicts. It was not until absolute monarchs came to power that raiding and sustained military campaigns became instruments for achieving large-scale political and diplomatic ends. Institutionalized warfare is a product of civilization.

Ceremonial Centers and Organized Religion   The great Mesopotamian temples (*ziggurats*) were built atop artificial, mud-brick mountains. Ancient Egyptian temples with their many columns have been likened to forests in stone. The precincts of Mesoamerican cities and Andean pyramids like Teotihuacan, Tikal, or Sechin Alto were carefully laid out to symbolize overwhelming supernatural power (Figure 8.3). These imposing structures, built at enormous cost in manual labor, helped validate the political and religious authority of the tiny elites who ruled preindustrial civilizations.

The rulers of all preindustrial civilizations relied on the anonymous labors of thousands of commoners. They attracted their loyalty through redistributing wealth and foodstuffs, through force, and by careful manipulation of powerful religious beliefs. And the great temples and shrines of the centers of major cities were important symbols of cosmic certainty. As

Figure 8.3 Aerial view of the Maya city of Tikal, Guatemala.

historian Paul Wheatley remarks, the ceremonial center in all its diversity
was "the sanctified terrain where [the common people were] guaranteed
the season renewal of cyclic time, and where the splendor, potency, and
wealth of their rulers symbolized the well-being of the whole community."

Nowhere is this more dramatically illustrated than in Mesoamerica.
The Mayan lords who ruled from Copan, Palenque, Tikal, and other
lowland Mesoamerican cities in the mid-first millennium A.D. laid out their
plazas, pyramids, and temples in a symbolic representation of their mythic
world, complete with sacred mountains and forests. The lord himself used
his spiritual powers to communicate with the ancestors, to cross the
threshold between the worlds of the living and the ancestors, appearing
before the people in dramatic shamanistic trances. Such ceremonies were
living proof of the role of the ruler as intermediary with ancestors and
gods, with the forces that governed Mayan life.

The ceremonial center, and the monumental architecture that went
with it, developed as the relationships between people and their land
changed dramatically. In village life, the relationships between the living
and the ancestors played a major role in ceremonies that interceded with
the spiritual world for fertile soils and good crops. There were shrines and
sacred places at Jericho, at Çatal Hüyük in Anatolia, and at Las Haldas in
Peru long before states developed. These modest shrines were the fore-
runners of the great ceremonial centers of Egypt, Mesopotamia, Mesoamerica, and the Andes. In each part of the world where civilization

appeared, ceremonial centers were preceded by inconspicuous proto-types tended by priests or cult leaders. These people must have been the first to be freed of the burden of having to produce food, and to be supported by the communities they served. In time, the growing ceremonial center was the initial focus of power, exchange, and authority, an authority vested in religious symbolism and organized priesthood.

It was no coincidence that Mesopotamia's first recorded gods were those of harvest and fertility, or that in Mexico Tlaloc was the god of rain and life itself. Those who served the deities of fertility had always been people of authority, the individuals who controlled economic surpluses, offerings, and the redistribution of goods. As their authority became more formalized, and more centralized, the humble village shrine became a new device for organizing fresh political, social, and religious structures. The temple turned into an instrument for disseminating new beliefs, a means for ever-more powerful rulers to justify their acts and develop coherent policies. In a real sense, ceremonial centers *were* the essence of their civilizations, material expressions of the beliefs that caused everyone to accept social inequality, to conform to common beliefs and goals.

As the power of kingship grew, the political influence of the ceremonial center tended to decline, although its religious functions were faithfully retained. This process of secularization was especially marked in Mesopotamia where *lugals*, kings or warlords, assumed militaristic direction of the state after 3000 B.C. This may have been the point when government and organized religion took divergent paths, as political leadership now fell to secular (nonreligious) rulers. The power of the religious leader, or *en*, was restricted to spiritual matters.

If none of these factors individually caused the rise of states, what combination of them were significant? Current theories bring both ecological and social perspectives to the problem.

ENVIRONMENTAL AND SOCIAL THEORIES OF STATE FORMATION

The Environmental Approach

Both environmental and social theories for the origins of state-organized societies share a common concern: to develop a sophisticated explanation for highly complex developments that unfolded over several centuries, and in many areas.

The environmental approach assumes that population growth and pressure were the dynamics in cultural systems that fueled the process of state formation. However, it was centralized management of resources that was the key. When population densities grew, there were obvious benefits in centralizing the storage of food surpluses from nearby fields, as well as trade and exchange. Powerful authority figures, be they priests or

important kin leaders, have the information about communally-held resources at their disposal. They also have the ability to command peoples'
labor and to collect and redistribute the results of that labor. Such centralization allowed economies to grow beyond the household level. States
therefore arose in social and environmental contexts in which centralized
management solves problems effectively.

This approach argues that effective leadership gave emerging states
the ability to deal with a great diversity of ecological and population
problems. For example, Barbara Price and William Sanders argue that
rapid population growth in the Valley of Mexico after 1000 B.C. caused
major problems for small-scale village societies, accustomed to egalitarian
political organization. States emerged because they were beneficial as a
way of organizing increased food supplies through intensified agriculture,
as well as through trade and relations with neighboring populations. Thus,
states would appear only in certain environmental settings, those with
especially severe population problems or shortages of agricultural land.
Effective, centralized management of food production, through state-
organized irrigation systems and other means, and management of trade,
would bring ecological imbalance under control within a short time.

The environmental approach has problems. How, for example, does
one tell which environments would foster state formation? Fertile river
floodplains like Mesopotamia? Coastal river valleys like those in Peru? Or
areas where agricultural land is in short supply, as it is in parts of highland
Mexico? States have arisen in regions where there are few geographical
constraints, like the Mayan lowlands of Mesoamerica, and in the Nile
valley. Furthermore, civilizations have arisen without any sign of rapid
population growth, in Iran and other parts of the Near East. Although
agricultural intensification often accompanied state formation, it occurred
in many forms — in the adoption of swamp garden agriculture (Mayan
lowlands), in the diversion of river water into floodbasins (Egypt), and by
exploitation of different ecological zones (the Aegean). There may be
many kernels of truth in environmental models, but they are very difficult
to document with actual archaeological data.

The Social Approach

Social approaches argue that the social structure of a society ultimately
determines its transformation over time. The classic social theories are
those of Karl Marx and Friedreich Engels, who argued more than a century ago that metallurgy led to new economic institutions like slavery that
divided society into ranked classes. The state, with its special mechanisms
for maintaining law and order, came into being as a means of reducing
social conflict. While Engels was obviously wrong in invoking metallurgy
as the cause of civilization, anthropologist Elman Service argues that
social ranking developed as a result of the intensification of social institu-

tions like tribute and taxation of goods and labor that were commonplace in more elaborate prestate societies.

Service believes that there were political reasons for state formation. Many early chieftains, even if they were perceived as having divine powers, were in insecure positions. Their power depended on the loyalty of their followers, which evaporated when they made mistakes or poor judgments. Thus, he argues, such Big Men achieved permanent dominance by developing new political structures to bolster their authority. States, then, arose as a result of conflicts resulting from political, rather than economic, considerations. Under this argument, the process of state formation might be considered a series of effective strategies designed and implemented by tribal chieftains trying to survive challenges to their authority.

At first, the strategies might be nothing more than well-timed political marriages or carefully crafted alliances between neighbors. In many cases, as happened in Hawaii and Tahiti, environmental limitations such as steep mountains or limited carrying capacity of agricultural land might limit the prospects for state formation. In others, such as the Nile valley, ambitious leaders' options might widen as they became less constrained by local conditions. As they achieved monopolies over key resources like potting clay or fleets of river boats, they could expand their political and economic influence over far wider areas, reinforcing their new economic clout with force, if necessary. Environmental factors play an important role in social theories, for ecological variables could present serious obstacles or opportunities to people pursuing political and economic goals.

Archaeologist Elizabeth Brumfiel believes that the Aztec civilization of Mexico provides a good example of how social factors played a major role in state formation. She believes the Aztec state came into being as a result of several complex developments. First, competition over land and trade intensified between small chiefdoms in the Basin of Mexico in the fourteenth century A.D. This intensified competition crystallized in a powerful alliance in 1434, the celebrated Triple Alliance between three cities: Aztec Tenochtitlan, Texcoco, and Tlacopan. The emerging rulers now centralized their power by means of deliberate political reform that consolidated power in their hands and reduced the influence of local leaders and nobles. The Triple Alliance then consolidated its power even further by undertaking ambitious military campaigns and major public works in the Basin, not only temple and road building, but massive swamp agriculture. By the late fifteenth century, a complex bureaucracy oversaw the affairs of state, and power was firmly consolidated in the hands of a tiny minority. When Hernan Cortes arrived at Tenochtitlan a half century later, the Aztec state was performing many of the functions of environmental manipulation that one might expect of powerful bureaucratic and political systems.

These kinds of social approaches divert attention away from purely ecological factors to other, perhaps more fundamental, questions: What were the goals of the political actors of the day, who were pursuing their individual goals while states were coming into being? Which ecological variables were obstacles? Which were opportunities? Until we have the answers to these questions on an area-by-area basis, it will be difficult to develop any general theories of state formation.

THE COLLAPSE OF CIVILIZATIONS

Even a casual glance at the history of civilization reveals a complex and ever-changing landscape of fluctuating political fortunes. States rise suddenly from obscurity, enjoy a brief period of prosperity, then sink rapidly into historical oblivion. What was true of later states was equally so of earlier civilizations, which were remarkable as much for their volatility as for their durability. Few early states stayed the course or endured as long as ancient Egyptian civilization did, for more then 2,500 years. What caused this volatility? Why did early civilizations collapse?

In Mesopotamia, for example, King Sargon of Akkad used military force and shrewd trading to establish his iron-fisted rule over Mesopotamia in about 2350 B.C. His empire lasted a mere two centuries before it collapsed in the face of widespread rebellion. Half a century later the kings of Ur and their efficient bureaucrats created an enormous empire that extended far north and northwest from what is now southern Iraq. It, too, collapsed rapidly as Babylon rose to prominence. The same chronic political volatility persisted into Roman times and beyond.

A similar history of remarkable volatility can be found in Mesoamerica and Peru. In the Basin of Mexico, for example, the great city of Teotihuacan flourished between about 200 B.C. and A.D. 700. In A.D. 600, more than 125,000 people lived within its precincts. Teotihuacan was then the sixth largest city in the world. About 85 percent of the population of the eastern and central Basin of Mexico lived in, or close to, Teotihuacan. Just over a century later, the civilization suddenly collapsed. Within half a century, the population declined to one-fourth of its former size.

Why did early civilizations collapse with such suddenness? Within a few decades, perhaps even a generation, a complex urban state suddenly became smaller, simpler, and often more egalitarian. Population densities fell; trade and economic activity dried up; information flow declined. Were such collapses the result of food shortages, a catastrophic event such as a major earthquake, of social conflict or warfare?

To understand the mechanisms of collapse, we must look back at the ways in which states came into being. As archaeologist Joseph Tainter has pointed out, an initial investment by a society in growing complexity is a rational way of trying to solve the needs of the moment, to cope with food shortages, rising population densities, and so on. At first the strategy works well. Agricultural production increases through more intensive farming methods; an emerging bureaucracy operates efficiently; expanding trade networks being wealth to the new elite, who use their authority and economic clout to undertake great public works, such as pyramids and temples. These imposing structures validate their spiritual authority and divine associations. Mayan civilization in Mesoamerica prospered in this way for some centuries—until a point of diminishing return was reached.

This point comes when the least costly solutions to society's needs are exhausted. It is now imperative that new organizational and economic answers be found, even if these have lower yields and cost a great deal more. For instance, the Inca rulers expanded food production by resorting to labor-intensive, unproductive efforts to expand cultivation up marginal hillsides. As efforts like these developed, argues Tainter, states like those of the Inca and May become increasingly vulnerable to collapse. There are few reserves to carry the people through famines, floods, or other natural disasters. Eventually, important segments of society, especially commoners and those who cultivate the soil, perceive that centralization and social complexity simply do not work well and that they are better off on their own. Under these circumstances, there are compelling pressures toward collapse, which is not necessarily a long-term catastrophe, except for those at the pinnacle of political power.

Collapse is, in a sense, a rational process that occurs when increasing stress requires some organizational change. The population declines and other catastrophic effects that either just preceded, accompanied, or followed collapse may have been traumatic at the time, but in the context of history they can be thought of as a natural scaling-down process when cultures break down.

There is, of course, more to collapse than merely a scaling-down process. Complete collapse can occur only in circumstances in which there is a power vacuum. In many cases, there may be a powerful neighbor waiting in the wings. For example, in Mesopotamia, many small Sumerian city-states and kingdoms traded and competed with one another within a tiny area between the Euphrates and Tigris Rivers. The same was true in Greece and the Aegean, in early China, and in the Mayan lowlands. These competitive situations were driven by constant diplomacy, by trade and warfare. Under such circumstances, to collapse is an invitation to be dominated by one's competitors, so political power and the fabric of the state are preserved at almost any cost.

In the Mayan lowlands, for example, dozens of small states flourished for centuries, their influence waxing and waning at each others' expense. At the same time, the elite warred and competed, commemorating their deeds in grandiloquent inscriptions. When the collapse finally came, it affected all the southern lowland states within a brief period of time. For centuries, the notion of the Mayan state had been legitimized in the eyes of its citizens by the existence of other states that functioned in the same way. When such states began to disappear and the commoners realized they were better off on their own, the entire system came apart and the Maya dispersed into small village settlements.

The collapse of early civilizations may, then, be closely connected to declining returns from social complexity. At first, the state expanded rapidly, agricultural production kept pace with growing nonfarming populations, and the elite assumed ever tighter control over economic, social, and political life. The state reached the height of its power and prosperity. Then the economic and political pack of cards began to collapse, as the productive capacity of the land, and the commoners, came under increasing stress. Eventually there came a point where the state literally collapsed under the weight of its overburden of social complexity.

Having examined some of the factors which contributed to the rise (and fall) of state-organized societies, we can now take a journey through the world of the early civilizations.

Chapter 9

The Mediterranean World

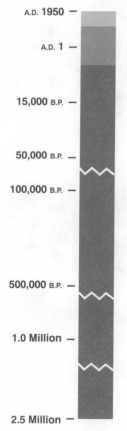

A.D. 1950 —

A.D. 1 —

15,000 B.P. —

50,000 B.P. —

100,000 B.P. —

500,000 B.P. —

1.0 Million —

2.5 Million —

*T*he world's first state-organized societies developed almost simultaneously in the Near East in about 3250 B.C. The flat, intensely hot plains between the Euphrates and Tigris Rivers in southern Mesopotamia nurtured the Sumerian civilization. An entirely different state, that of the ancient Egyptians, developed along the banks of the Nile in extreme northeast Africa. This chapter explores these two remarkable societies, then traces the subsequent development of state-organized societies in Greece, the Aegean, and the eastern Mediterranean (Figure 9.1).

THE SUMERIANS OF MESOPOTAMIA (c. 3200 B.C. to 2300 B.C.)

Village Farmers—'Ubaid (c. 5000 B.C.)

By 5500 B.C., hundreds of small farming villages dotted the rolling plains of northern Mesopotamia, settlements connected by long-distance trade routes that carried obsidian, finely painted pottery, and other goods over hundreds of miles, from Turkey as far as southern Iraq. By this time, much of the trade,

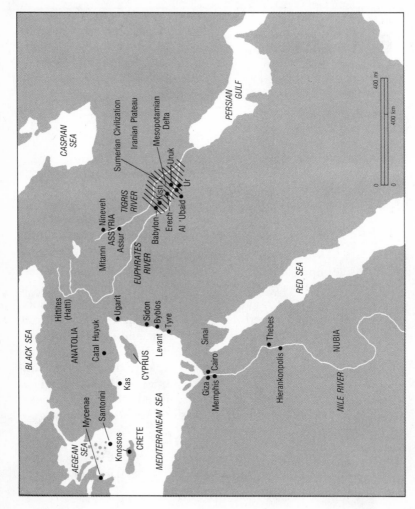

Figure 9.1 Map showing sites in Chapter 9.

especially in pottery, was concentrated in the hands of a small elite, living in key centers along water routes.

The first farmers to move onto the southern lowlands located their villages in clusters along natural channels of the Euphrates. Any form of agriculture that depended on rainfall alone was impracticable in this challenging environment. However, once watered, the soils of Mesopotamia proved both fertile and potentially highly productive. As early as 5000 B.C., a few farming communities were diverting floodwaters from the Euphrate and Tigris onto their fields, then draining them away to prevent salt buildup in the soil. The largest of these clusters consisted of small rural communities located around a larger town that covered about 28 acres (11.3 ha) and housed between 2,500 and 4,000 people. Some of their small irrigation canals extended out about 3 miles (4.8 km) from the river. From the very beginning some of these 'Ubaid culture settlements boasted of substantial buildings, alleyways, and courtyards. Others consisted of little more than humble mud-brick and reed huts. Each cluster was a group of villages linked by kin ties, with a clan leader living in one larger settlement overseeing village affairs and, probably, the irrigation schemes that connected them.

As Mesopotamian society grew rapidly in complexity in the centuries that followed, so did the need for social, political, and religious institutions that would provide some form of centralized authority. Some settlements assumed great importance after 4500 B.C., among them Uruk, the world's first city.

The First Cities—Uruk (4500 B.C. to 3250 B.C.)

Uruk began life as a small town and soon became a growing city, quickly absorbing the populations of nearby villages. During the fourth millennium B.C., Uruk grew to cover an estimated 617 acres (250 ha). Satellite villages extended out at least 6 miles (9.7 km), each with their own irrigation systems. All provided grain, fish, or meat for the growing urban population. The city itself was a densely packed agglomeration of houses, narrow alleyways and courtyards, probably divided into distinct quarters where different kin groups, or artisans, such as potters, sculptors, and painters lived. Everything was overshadowed by the stepped temple pyramid, the *ziggurat*, that towered over the lowlands for miles around. The ziggurat complex and its satellite temples were the center of Uruk life, not only places of worship, but storehouses, workshops, and centers of government (Figure 9.2).

The ruler of Uruk and the keeper of the temple was the *en*. He was both a secular and spiritual ruler. His wishes were carried out by his priests and by a complex hierarchy of minor officials, wealthy landowners, and merchants. Tradespeople and artisans were a more lowly segment of society. Under them were thousands of fisherfolk, farmers, sailors, and slaves that formed the bulk of Uruk, and other cities' burgeoning popula-

Figure **9.2** Reconstruction of a *ziggurat* at Eridu, Mesopotamia.

tions. By 3500 B.C., the Mesopotamian city had developed an elaborate system of management. This system organized and regulated society, meted out reward and punishment, and made policy decisions for the thousands of people who lived under it.

Writing and Metallurgy

Two innovations appeared as Uruk and other Sumerian cities grew rapidly. The first was writing, the second metallurgy. The origins of written records go back thousands of years before the Sumerians, to a time soon after the adoption of food production when the volume of intervillage trade demanded some means of tracking shipments. As early as 8000 B.C., villagers were using carefully shaped clay tokens, which they carried around on strings. By 5000 B.C. commercial transactions of all kinds were so complex that there were endless possibilities for thievery and accounting errors. Some clever officials made small clay tablets and scratched them with incised signs that depicted familiar objects such as pots or animals. From there it was a short step to simplified, more conventionalized, cuneiform signs (Figure 9.3).

At first, specially trained scribes dealt almost entirely with administrative matters, compiling lists and inventories. Eventually, the more creative among them explored the limitless opportunities afforded by the ability to express themselves in writing. Kings used tablets to trumpet their victories. Fathers chided their errant sons, lawyers recorded com-

Figure 9.3 Cuneiform tablet.

plicated transactions. Sumerian literature includes great epics, love stories, hymns to the gods, and tragic laments.

The Sumerians' homeland was without metals, so they imported copper, gold, and other ores from the Iranian highlands and elsewhere as early as 3500 B.C. At first, these shiny metals had high prestige value, but the advent of lead and tin alloying after 2000 B.C. led to widespread use of bronze artifacts for farming and as weapons of war. The adoption of bronze-edged weapons had momentous consequences for Sumerian life, for their appearance in local armies can be linked directly to a rising penchant for using war as a means of attaining political ends.

Sumerian Civilization Develops (c. 3250 B.C. onward)

Writing and metallurgy were symbols of a rapidly changing Near Eastern world. By 3300 B.C., expanding trade networks linked dozens of cities and towns from the Mediterranean to the Persian Gulf, and from Turkey to the Nile valley. By this time, states small and large flourished not only in Egypt and Mesopotamia, but in the coastal Levant and in highland Iran. Each of them depended on the others for critical raw materials such as metal ore or soapstone vessels, for timber or even grain. In northern

Mesopotamia, east of the Tigris, and in the Levant, expanding trade and a host of important technological innovations resulted, also, not only from basic economic needs, but from the competitive instincts of a new elite. All, however bitter their enmity, depended on their neighbors and more distant trading partners.

Sumerian civilization came into being as a result of a combination of environmental and social factors. The Sumerians lived in a treeless, low-land environment with fertile soils, but no metal, little timber, and no semiprecious stones. They obtained these commodities by trading with areas where such items were in abundance. Sumerian rulers controlled not only large grain surpluses that could be moved in river craft but also a flourishing industry in textiles and other luxuries. The trade moved up and down the great rivers, especially the placid Euphrates. Ancient over-land trade routes linked the Tigris and Euphrates with the distant Levant cities and ports. Even as early as Sumerian times, caravans of pack animals joined Anatolia to Euphrates, the Levant to Mesopotamia, and Mesopotamia to isolated towns on the distant Iranian highlands to the east.

By 2800 B.C. Mesopotamia was home to several important city-states, states that were in contact with the Levant and the Iranian Plateau, even, sporadically with the Pharaohs of Egypt. As the Mesopotamian delta became an environment increasingly controlled by human activities and the volume of long-distance trade increased dramatically, so competition over resources intensified. Both clay tablets and archaeological finds tell of warfare and constant bickering between neighbors. Each state raised an army to defend its water rights, trade routes, and city walls. The onerous tasks of defense and military organization passed to despotic kings suppos-edly appointed by the gods. Such city-states as Erech, Kish, and Ur had periods of political strength and prosperity when they dominated their neighbors. Then, just as swiftly, the tide of their fortunes would change and they would sink into obscurity.

Some Sumerian cities nurtured powerful and wealthy leaders. When Sir Leonard Woolley excavated a royal cemetery at Ur, he found the remains of a series of kings and queens who had been buried in huge graves with their entire retinue of courtiers. One tomb contained the remains of 59 people. Each wore his or her official dress and regalia and had lain down to die in the correct order of precedence, after taking a fatal dose of poison (Figure 9.4).

Inevitably, the ambitions of some of these proud Sumerian leaders led them to entertain bolder visions than merely the control of a few city-states in the lowlands. They were well aware that the control of lucrative sources of raw materials and trade routes was the secret of vast political power. In about 3400 B.C., a monarch named Lugalzagesi boasted of overseeing the entire area from the Persian Gulf to the Mediterranean. This boast was probably false. It is likely that Sumerian cities dominated the overland routes that linked Mesopotamia, Turkey, and the Levant, but their influence was never permanent, their control probably illusory.

Lugalzagesi and others were characteristic of a tradition of Mesopota-

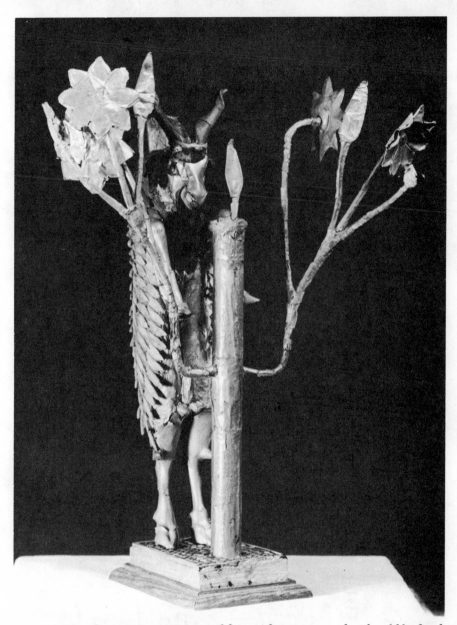

Figure 9.4 Royal cemetery at Ur. A wood figure of a ram covered with gold leaf and lapis lazuli. The body is in silver leaf, the fleece in shell.

mian civilization: the combination of trade, conquest, ruthless administration, and tribute to create large, poorly integrated, and highly volatile empires. Each sought to control an enormous territory between the Mediterranean and the Persian Gulf. And these efforts brought the successors of the Sumerians, the Babylonians, into conflict with another major power — Egypt.

ANCIENT EGYPTIAN CIVILIZATION (c. 3050 B.C. to after 1070 B.C.)

The Nile River slashes through the northeast African desert like a green dagger pointed at the Mediterranean. Here, too, simple farming communities flourished on fertile soils flooded each year by the Nile. The river served as a natural highway for hundreds of miles, for a laden boat could drift and row downstream with the current or sail long distances from the Mediterranean with the prevailing north winds.

The pre-Dynastic Egyptians of 3500 B.C. lived in villages and small towns spaced along the river, which, like Mesopotamian settlements of the day, were clustered under the rule of local leaders. These were the individuals who controlled trade in finely made pottery, alabaster vessels, and in faience (locally made glass) beads. The proportion of luxury goods to functional commodities rose steadily, as the Egyptians learned about metallurgy from Asian sources and started importing copper from Sinai and lead, tin, and silver from Asia.

The same trade brought another innovation: writing. It seems likely that writing was first developed in Mesopotamia, then imported into the Nile valley, where isolated Mesopotamian cuneiform seals have come to light. Egyptian scribes developed their own hieroglyphic (Greek: sacred carving) script. Commonly thought to be a form of picture writing, in fact Egyptian hieroglyphs are a combination pictographic (picture) and phonetic (representing vocal sounds) script, not only written on papyrus reed rolls but also carved on public buildings and painted on clay or wood (Figure 9.5). Early hieroglyphs played an important role in trade and record keeping, but they may also have evolved as a way of conveying the meaning of funerary rituals on painted pots deposited in cemeteries with the dead.

During the fourth millennium B.C., more important villages became the focal points of different chiefdoms, which in later times became the

Figure 9.5 Egyptian writing. The top line shows formal hieroglyphs. Below it are the cursive and shorthand versions of the same script.

nomes, or provinces, of the Egyptian state. The nomarchs (nome leaders) were those who gradually forged a single state along the banks of the Nile from ever-larger regional chiefdoms.

Unification

The process of unification took several centuries, as large-scale, more lasting alliances made increasing economic and political sense. Population densities rose gradually, and there was some intensification of irrigation, although the technology for lifting water was so rudimentary that large-scale agricultural schemes were out of the question. The final stages of unification may have involved considerable fighting. Egypt was finally unified under the Pharaoh Narmer at Hierankonpolis in about 3050 B.C. The resulting civilization survived through many vicissitudes for over 2,500 years.

Fertile soils, river floods and simple irrigation, long-distance trade and emerging social ranking—the same kinds of ecological and social dynamics that formed state-organized societies in Mesopotamia also founded ancient Egyptian civilization. But the Egyptian state was far larger than all the Sumerian city-states combined, a circumstance both of geography and of highly centralized administration.

The supreme ruler, the Pharaoh, was a divine leader. He was responsible for the success of the harvest, in an environment where simple technology prevented him from controlling the success of irrigation. A Pharaoh was thought of as a god incarnate, the earthly embodiment of the god Horus. He was the champion of the cosmic order, priest of all the deities of Egypt, who maintained the power of the gods. As administrator, he was responsible for the economic well-being and ordered life of the people. As soldier, he repelled Egypt's enemies and guaranteed the continuance of ordered life, if necessary by force. Over the centuries, the Pharaohs had to maneuver the cumbersome apparatus of the state to respond to crop failures, threats of invasion, and local insurrection by reorganizing irrigation works, raising armies, and redistributing land. Small wonder there were prolonged periods of political instability and unrest through ancient Egyptian history. Yet the basic adaptation to a changeable floodplain environment persisted until centuries of harsh exploitation of commoners by a rapacious elite ended in social collapse.

The Old Kingdom (3100 B.C. to 2181 B.C.)

Egyptologists conventionally divide ancient Egyptian civilization into four broad periods, separated by at least two intermediate periods of political change and instability (Table 9.1). The most striking feature of this long-lived civilization is, however, its conservatism. Many of the artistic, religious, and technological features of Old Kingdom Egypt persisted intact into Roman times.

Table 1.1.   Ancient Egyptian Civilization

Years B.C./B.P.	Period	Characteristics
30 B.C.	Roman occupation	Egypt an imperial province of Rome
332 to 30	Ptolemaic period	The Ptolemies bring Greek influence to Egypt, beginning with conquest of Egypt by Alexander the Great in 332 B.C.
1085 to 332	Late period	Gradual decline in pharaonic authority, culminating in Persian rule (525 to 404 and 343 to 332 B.C.)
3517 to 3035 B.P.	New Kingdom	Great imperial period of Egyptian history, with pharaohs buried in Valley of Kings; pharaohs include Rameses II, Seti I, and Tutankhamun, as well as Akhenaten, the heretic ruler
3736 to 3517	Second Intermediate period	Hyksos rulers in the delta
3941 to 3736	Middle Kingdom	Thebes achieves prominence, also the priesthood of Amun
c. 4131 to 4123	First Intermediate period	Political chaos and disunity
4636 to 4131	Old Kingdom	Despotic pharaohs build the pyramids and favor conspicuous funerary monuments; institutions, economic strategies, and artistic traditions of ancient Egypt established
5050 to 4036	Archaic period	Consolidation of state
5050	Unification of Egypt under Narmer-Menes	

The Old Kingdom saw four dynasties of Pharaohs governing Egypt from a royal capital at Memphis. Some of these rulers had reputations as cruel despots and it was they who embarked on a brief flurry of pyramid building. The pyramids with their elaborate mortuary temples and enclosures were the houses and tombs for the Pharaohs in eternity, symbols of the permanence of Egyptian civilization. The notion of the pyramid as a royal burial place originated centuries earlier in small, walled enclosures surrounding an earthen mound. In about 2680 B.C., Djoser built a six-step pyramid surrounded by a veritable town of buildings and shrines. The step pyramid is a somewhat hesitant structure, but the royal pyramids built over the next century show increasing confidence. They culminate in the brilliant assurance of the pyramids of Giza near Cairo, with their perfect pyramid shapes (Figure 9.6). The Great Pyramid of Khufu, built in 2600 B.C., covers 13.1 acres (5.3 ha) and is 481 feet (147 m) high. Just under two centuries later, the Pharaohs stopped building huge pyramids and diverted their organizational talents to other public works.

Figure 9.6 The Pyramids of Giza.

There is something megalomaniacal about the pyramids, built as they were with an enormous expenditure of labor and energy. The structure was redolent with religious symbolism. The Pharaoh in his sarcophagus had returned to the earth of the Primeval Mound, the land. The tall pyramid that pointed toward heaven was the means by which his soul broke free from the constrictions of the primeval earth and ascended to the divine kingdom of light. In material terms, the bureaucratic organization and labor required to construct even a single pyramid was enormous. For generations, Giza was a giant construction site, where thousands of commoners labored moving stone in exchange for rations during the slack farming months, while many others worked year-round trimming and quarrying boulders. The state used growing food surpluses to employ thousands of people on lavish public works, putting pressure on the farmer to produce even more grain. In ancient Egyptian civilization, the state became the great provider.

A massive, hereditary bureaucracy effectively ruled the kingdom. Its records tell us that much energy went into tax collection, monitoring harvest yields, and administration of irrigation. An army of 20,000 men, many of them mercenaries, was maintained at the height of Egypt's prosperity.

A vast gulf separated the tiny literate population from the commoners. The life of an Egyptian farmer, given good harvests, was easier than that of a Mesopotamian villager, although the state required occasional periods of forced labor to maintain irrigation canals or other public works. Many minor artisans and unskilled laborers lived more regimented lives, working on temples and Pharaohs' tombs and often living in special villages. Like other early states, the Egyptians depended on slave labor for some public works and much domestic service.

The New Kingdom (1520 B.C. to 1085 B.C.)

The Old Kingdom ended in about 2180 B.C. and was followed by a brief period of political instability when some Asian invaders entered the delta. In 2130 B.C. the city of Thebes in Upper Egypt became the capital, where a series of energetic and less despotic Pharaohs ruled until 1736 B.C., expanding trade and consolidating the worship of the sun-god Amun at Thebes. A second period of instability resulted from quarrels over the royal succession. These disputes were so serious that some Asian nomads, the Hyksos, actually ruled over the delta until they were thrown out in about 1520 B.C.

Then dawned the New Kingdom, the most glorious period of ancient Egyptian civilization. Ahmose the Liberator threw out the Hyksos and became the first of a series of illustrious Theban Pharaohs who ruled Egypt from the delta to Nubia in the south. His successors became symbolic of the power of ancient Egypt: Tutmosis, Amenophis, Seti, and Rameses II. The latter extended the Egyptian empire far beyond the narrow confines of the Nile valley deep into Nubia and into the Levant. By this time, political events in the Near East involved a delicate balance of diplomatic and military power between the Hittites in Anatolia to the north and the Mesopotamians to the south. All three powers sought to control the lucrative trade routes of the eastern Mediterranean.

For centuries, the Pharaohs gradually extended their control over irrigation and food distribution. The New Kingdom saw the development of much more effective water-lifting devices such as the animal-powered waterwheel, still used in Egypt today, also the introduction of a summer crop, sorghum. The result was much higher agricultural productivity and higher population densities. The population of Egypt rose from less than a million in 3000 B.C. to approximately 5 million during the New Kingdom.

New Kingdom rulers adopted new burial customs and abandoned conspicuous sepulchers. Their mummies were buried in the desolate Valley of Kings on the west bank of the Nile. Despite every precaution, nearly all their tombs were robbed by the ancient Egyptians themselves soon after burial. Only the rock-cut sepulcher of an obscure Pharaoh named Tutankhamun survived intact until modern times. The discovery

Figure 9.7 The Antechamber of Tutankhamun's tomb.

and clearance of Tutankhamun's tomb ranks among the greatest archaeological finds of all time. It gives us an impression of the incredible wealth of the New Kingdom Pharaohs' courts (Figure 9.7).

With the death of Pharaoh Rameses III in 1085 B.C., Egypt entered a period of prolonged political weakness that saw foreign armies invade the hitherto sacrosanct Nile valley. Its conservative rulers were slow to adapt to the rapidly changing eastern Mediterranean world. Nubians, Assyrians, Persians, and the Ptolemies, Pharaohs of Greek ancestry, and finally the Romans, ruled over Egypt for varying periods of time.

HITTITES AND SEA TRADERS (1650 B.C. to 1200 B.C.)

The New Kingdom Pharaohs ruled over the Nile at a time when economic ties between different regions of the Near East were becoming ever-closer. This economic interdependency persisted regardless of political changes or intermittent warfare. At the center of what was now a much more durable economic system lay the strategic Levant, a coastline with few natural harbors but with important trade routes to Mesopotamia, Anatolia, and the Nile.

During the second millennium B.C., the eastern Mediterranean coastlands were divided up between a network of small but prosperous states. They lived in the shadow of the great kingdoms that lay inland: Egypt to the south, Mitanni to the east of the Euphrates, and Hatti, the Hittite state of Anatolia. The three states competed directly in the Levant, which was a regular military and diplomatic battleground for its powerful neighbors.

The Hittites were the newest and most able diplomatic players. Their leaders were newcomers from north of Anatolia, who seized power on the inland plateau in about 1650 B.C. by a combination of astute political maneuvering and conquest. All this diplomatic and military activity on the part of the great kingdoms was aimed at the control of the lucrative gold, copper, and pottery trade of the Levant. It was the hub of interlocking trade routes that spanned the entire Mediterranean world.

This land and sea trade was in the hands of traders from the Levant, Cyprus, the Aegean Islands, and Greece. The famous Bronze Age shipwreck at Kas off southern Turkey has given dramatic insights into this commerce (Figure 9.8). The merchantman sank in a storm during the fourteenth century B.C., carrying 200 copper ingots, each weighing about 60 pounds (27 kg), enough metal to equip a small army with weapons and armor. A ton of resin was transported in two-handled jars made by people in the Levant; it was used, so Egyptian records tell us, as incense for religious rituals. There were dozens of blue glass ingots being sent to

Figure 9.8 Excavations on the Bronze Age wreck at Kas, Turkey.

Egypt from Tyre. The ship's hold also contained hardwood, Baltic amber from northern Europe, tortoise shells, elephant tusks and hippopotamus teeth from Africa, ostrich eggs, jars of olives, and even large jars full of stacked lots of pottery from the Levant and mainland Greece. The Kas ship's cargo included items from Africa, Egypt, the Levant, the Greek mainland, the Aegean, Cyprus, and even copper from Sardinia. It is a dramatic reflection of the truly international status of eastern Mediterranean trade in the second millennium B.C.

The maritime trade expanded dramatically during Hittite times and played a major role in the diffusion of iron tools and weapons over the eastern Mediterranean before 1000 B.C. Iron is thought to have been first smelted in the middle of the first millennium B.C., perhaps in the highlands immediately south of the Black Sea. The new metal had many advantages, for its tough, sharp edges were invaluable for weapons and for farming and carpentry. Iron ore was plentiful, too, unlike copper and tin, so tools and weapons made of the new material soon became plentiful over a wide area of Europe and the Near East.

Eastern Mediterranean trade extended far west of Greece, to Sardinia, North Africa, and Spain. But the main western frontier lay in the Aegean Islands and on the Greek islands, where the Minoan and Mycenaean civilizations flourished during the second millennium B.C.

MINOANS AND MYCENAEANS (c. 1900 B.C. to 1200 B.C.)

Aegean Farmers and Seafarers (6500 B.C. to 2000 B.C.)

Parts of the Greek mainland and Aegean Islands were settled by farming peoples as early as 6500 B.C., but it was not until considerably later that village communities sprang up throughout the region. This development coincided with the cultivation not only of cereals, but of olives and vines. By 3500 B.C., the inhabitants of the Aegean and Greece were exploiting local ores to make fine metal tools and precious ornaments.

The Aegean abounds in sheltered bays and many straits, allowing even primitive, heavily laden seagoing vessels to take shelter and sail from island to island. The interisland trade expanded rapidly, not only in metal objects but in olive oil and wine carried in fine pots, also in marble vessels and figurines. A constant flow of new products and ideas flowed across the region. By 2500 B.C., numerous small towns housed farmers, traders, and skilled artisans on the mainland and the islands. The beginnings of town life fostered considerable cultural diversity in the Aegean, a diversity fostered by constant trading connections and increasingly complex political and social organization.

Minoan Civilization (1900 B.C. to 1400 B.C.)

Minoan civilization developed out of earlier indigenous farming cultures by 1900 B.C. It is best documented at the famous Palace of Minos at Knossos near Heraklion on the north coast, a site first settled as early as

6000 B.C., at about the same time as Çatal Hüyük was flourishing on the Turkish plateau. In about 1700 B.C., the first royal residence on the site was destroyed by an earthquake, just as Minoan civilization reached the height of its powers. The palace that rose in its place was an imposing structure that rambled around a central courtyard (Figure 9.9). Some buildings had two stories; the plastered walls and floors were painted with brightly colored geometric designs, with landscapes, dolphins, and other sea creatures. The most remarkable art depicted dances and religious ceremonies, including acrobats leaping vigorously along the backs of prancing bulls. Part shrine, part royal residence, part storehouse, and part workshop, the Palace of Minos at Knossos was the hub of predominantly rural civilization centered on large country houses and chieftains' residences.

The dramatic flowering of Minoan civilization resulted from intensified trading contacts throughout the Aegean and as far afield as Egypt and the Levant. The Minoans were expert seafarers and middlemen in international trade. Their ships handled all manner of cargos. But this time, olive and vine cultivation had added welcome diversity to local village farming economies, as well as providing valuable export commodities. This led to the development of distribution systems organized and controlled by important leaders, who controlled ships, shipping lanes, and market-

Figure 9.9 The Palace of Minos at Knossos, Crete.

places, and lived in palaces large and small. Minoan society developed from entirely local roots, which was an adaptation to a mountainous environment where population densities were never high and much wealth came from the export trade.

We know little of Minoan society, or of the religious beliefs that sustained it. It seems likely that the roots of later classical Greek religion with its many deities lie in Bronze Age civilizations like those of the Minoans and mainland Mycenaeans. There are signs at Knossos of the worship of the bull, an animal later associated with Poseidon, the god of the ocean, and of sacrifices of young children, perhaps part of a fertility rite associated with the Cretan Zeus, father of the gods, and the Earth Mother.

A major event during the later stages of the Minoan civilization was the massive volcanic explosion on the island of Santorini, a Minoan outpost 70 miles (113 km) north of Crete during the late seventeenth century B.C. This cataclysmic eruption caused massive tidal waves and ash falls that mantled many Minoan fields, but Knossos continued to flourish long afterward. The Santorini disaster may have accelerated the decline of Minoan civilization. Some time later, many Minoan sites were destroyed and abandoned. Warrior farmers, probably from mainland Greece, established sway over Minoan domains and decorated the walls of Knossos with military scenes. In about 1400 B.C., the great palace was destroyed by fire. By this time, the center of the Aegean world had shifted west to the Greek mainland, where Mycene reached the height of its power.

Mycenaean Civilization (1600 B.C. to 1200 B.C.)

Mycenaean civilization, centered on the fertile plain of Argos in southern Greece, developed in about 1600 B.C. The chieftains who ruled over the walled fortress of Mycenae gained their wealth and economic power not only from their warrior skills, but from far-flung trading contacts in the Aegean and further afield.

Mycenaean kings were expert charioteers and horsemen, whose material culture and lifeway are immortalized in Homer's epic poems, the *Iliad* and *Odyssey*. These epics were written many centuries after the Mycenaeans themselves had become folk memories. Nevertheless, they give a splendid impression of the wealth and glitter of Bronze Age Greek life. So do Mycenaean graves. Mycenae's rulers and their relatives took their wealth with them to the next world. They were buried in spectacular shaft graves wearing fine gold face masks modeled in the likeness of their owners, and weapons adorned with copper, gold, and silver (Figure 9.10).

Mycenaean commerce took over where Minoan left off. Much of the rulers' prestige was based on their contacts in the metal trade. Minerals, especially tin for alloying bronze, were in constant demand in eastern Mediterranean markets. Both copper and tin were abundant in Turkey

Figure 9.10 Golden funerary mask of a Mycenaean ruler, Mycenae, Greece.

and central Cyprus, so Mycenaean traders became middlemen, developing the necessary contacts in both areas and in the Aegean to obtain regular supplies.

So complex did their trading relationships become that the Mycenaeans found it necessary to establish their own writing system. They refined a simple pictographic script known to archaeologists as Linear A, which had been used by the Minoans, and wrote it in the Greek language, creating what scholars call Linear B. Large numbers of clay tablets from a Mycenaean palace at Pylos in western Greece show that the script was used for inventories and records of commercial transactions, ration issues, and so on, for the daily affairs of estate administration.

Like Minoan civilization, Mycenaean was based on small towns and palaces where the elite lived, and where trade, centralized food storage, and major religious ceremonies took place. Mycenae itself was a formidable citadel ringed with a defense wall of large boulders. The main entrance passed under a portico carved with two seated lions and led up the hill to the stone-built palace with its magnificent views of the Plain of Argos. Everything was set up for storage and defense. There was a water cistern within the defense walls and rows of clay storage jars held large quantities of olive oil, with storerooms for many foodstuffs and the wealth of the palace. The rulers and their immediate relatives were buried in a circular enclosure to the west of the gate, but the Mycenaeans also used beehivelike communal burial chambers outside the citadel for many of their dead.

Mycenae continued to dominate seaborne eastern Mediterranean trade routes until about 1200 B.C., when its power was destroyed, probably as a result of warrior incursions from the north. In the same century, other northern barbarian raids overthrew the Hittite kingdom in Turkey. These incursion were the result of unsettled political conditions and over-population in Europe, and threw the eastern Mediterranean world into confusion.

COLLAPSE AND RECOVERY: SEA PEOPLES AND PHOENICIANS (1200 B.C. to 800 B.C.)

The Hittite civilization collapsed during a period of political upheaval, but the myriad trade routes that joined states large and small continued to link every corner of the Mediterranean world. Even in these troubled days, relatively tiny cities like Ugarit in the northern Levant enjoyed great prestige because of their commercial importance. The ruler of Ugarit was a merchant potentate, who controlled vast supplies of gold and a fleet of more than 150 ships. Ugarit's merchantmen sailed to Cyprus, where they traded with Mycenaean vessels. When the Hittite kingdom dissolved into small, competing states, the entire eastern Mediterranean world fell into chaos, but Ugarit was still very influential.

The imperial powers and petty kingships that had made up much of the economic world of 1200 B.C. were governed by highly centralized palace bureaucracies. These bureaucracies controlled very specialized activities such as trade in glass ingots and ivory ornaments, which allowed significant economies of operation and dense population concentrations. When the Hittite and Mycenaean civilizations came apart in an almost

dominolike effect and Egypt declined at the same time, centralized bureaucracies lost their power over economic activities. The infrastructure
for controlled, specialized trade came apart and the power of urban elites
declined. For 300 years, there was a political vacuum, a period of widespread suffering and piracy, much of it at the hands of warlike bands,
known to archaeologists as the Sea Peoples.

In the Levant, many rural groups moved to the highlands, loosening
their dependence on trading cities like Ugarit and becoming herders and
farmers. Some of them formed loose federations of towns, villagers, and
nomadic bands to preserve their sovereignty in the face of new and
aggressive outside powers like the Assyrians of northern Mesopotamia.
One such federation became the state of Israel, which acquired its own
monarchy after 1000 B.C. and protected itself with a network of walled
cities. By this time, eastern Mediterranean trade was recovering and the
hillside federation expanded into the lowlands, circumscribed by the sea
and the desert and by the still-powerful Egyptian and Mesopotamian
civilizations on either side.

A slow economic recovery during the first millennium B.C. came at the
hands of the Phoenicians. At first, they acted as middlemen in the Cyprus
and Aegean trade. Their ships were soon carrying Lebanese cedarwood to
Cyprus and the Nile, copper and iron to the Aegean. Powerful cities like
Byblos, Sidon, and Tyre extended their trading as far as the copper and tin
mines of Spain. Phoenician merchants made enormous profits from purple
dye extracted from seashells and much used for expensive fabrics. By 800
B.C., Phoenician merchants were everywhere in the Mediterranean, as
Assyria became the dominant power in the Levant. Their need for a highly
accurate record-keeping system played a significant part in the development of the western alphabet.

ASSYRIANS AND BABYLONIANS (900 B.C. to 539 B.C.)

The city of Assur on the Tigris River in northern Mesopotamia had been a
major force in the eastern Mediterranean world since Sumerian times.
The merchants of Assur controlled strategic desert and river trade routes
and commerce downstream to Babylon and beyond. The Assyrian empire
expanded dramatically in the ninth century B.C., when a series of despotic,
grandiose kings expanded their domains with relentless annual campaigns.
These were absolute monarchs, who boasted of their conquests on their
palace walls, living in magnificent splendor. They were well aware of the
value of conspicuous display. When King Assurnasirpal completed his
palace at Nimrud on the Tigris he threw a party for the 16,000 inhabitants
of the city, 1,500 royal officials, "47,074 men and women from the length
of my country," and 5,000 foreign envoys. The king fed this throng of
more than 69,000 people for ten days, during which time his guests ate
14,000 sheep and consumed more than 10,000 skins of wine.

The last of the great Assyrian kings was Assurbanipal, who died in approximately 630 B.C. Eventually, the Assyrian capital, Nineveh, fell to Persian and Babylonian warriors. For 43 years, the mighty King Nebuchadnezzar of Babylon ruled over Mesopotamia and turned his capital into one of the showpieces of the ancient world. His double-walled city was adorned by huge mud-brick palaces with elaborate hanging gardens, a great processional way, and a huge ziggurat. It was to Babylon that a large contingent of Jews were taken as captives after Nebuchadnezzar's armies sacked Jerusalem. This event is immortalized in Psalm 137:1: "By the waters of Babylon we sat down and wept."

The Babylonian Empire did not long survive the death of Nebuchadnezzar in 556 B.C. The armies of Cyrus of Persia took Babylon in 539 B.C. The eastern Mediterranean world came under the sway of much larger empires than ever before. These were the centuries of classical Greece, when Rome began to emerge as a major power, when the basic foundations of Western civilization were laid. They came from a Mediterranean world that had been evolving economically, politically, and socially for thousands of years. What had begun as an adaptation to the realities of living in arid, but fertile floodplain environments had developed into a web of economic and political interdependency that was far larger than anything the world had seen before—the remote forerunner of the vast global economic system of today.

Chapter
10

Asians and Africans

A.D. 1950 —

A.D. 1 —

15,000 B.P. —

50,000 B.P. —

100,000 B.P. —

500,000 B.P. —

1.0 Million —

2.5 Million —

W hile the world's first states did indeed develop in the Near East, state-organized societies soon developed quite independently in south Asia and the Far East (Figure 10.1). Later, they appear in Southeast Asia and sub-Saharan Africa. We must now describe these societies and the relationships between them. The central theme of this chapter is interconnectedness, of both temporary and more lasting ties between societies that were often at considerable distance from one another. Thus, there is a heavy emphasis on trade in the pages that follow, an emphasis that reflects this increasing interconnectedness, but one that does, at times, mask complex processes of cultural change that were occurring in the same parts of the world. However, the length of this book prevents extended discussion of these changes. Rather, this chapter focuses on trade and long-distance connections, as they give a good impression of the complex forces that created much larger world economic and political systems in historic times.

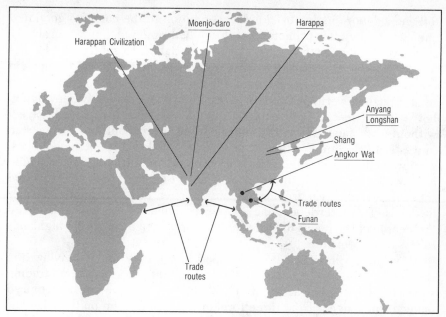

Figure 10.1 Map showing Asian sites and societies mentioned in Chapter 10.

SOUTH ASIA: HARAPPAN CIVILIZATION
(c. 2700 B.C. to 1700 B.C.)

The Indus River, on the banks of which Indian civilization began, rises in the snow-clad Himalayas of southern Tibet and descends 1,000 miles (1609 km) through Kashmir before debouching onto the Pakistani plains. Here, as in Mesopotamia and the Nile valley, fertile floodplain soils played an important role in the development of state-organized society. Between June and September each year, the spring runoff from the distant mountains reaches the plains, inundating thousands of acres of good farming land and depositing rich flood-borne silts as a natural fertilizer, on soil soft enough to be cultivated without the aid of metal artifacts.

Hundreds of village settlements were scattered across the Indus valley plains by 3000 B.C. Many of them were small fortified towns with carefully laid out streets, built above the highest flood level but as close to the river as possible. The next five hundred years saw irrigation canals and flood embankments transform the Indus valley environment into an artificial landscape. The obvious leaders for these new communities were the chieftains, traders, priests, and kin leaders, who acted as intermediaries between the people and their gods. Theirs was a philosophy that humans were part of an ordered cosmos that could be maintained by unremitting toil and a subordination of individual ambition to the common good. No one knows when this primordial philosophy developed, but it is probably as old as farming itself, always a risky undertaking in subtropical lands.

The Harappan civilization, named after the ancient city of Harappa in the Indus valley, developed by 2700 B.C. The first Harappans lived in small villages covering only a few acres. Their environment was low-lying, hot, without metals, and one that could not be cultivated effectively without trade far to the north into the highlands of southern Baluchistan in western Pakistan. For thousands of years, the farmers obtained metals, semiprecious stones, and timber from the highlands, trading cotton, grain, and textiles for these luxuries. Each winter, too, large herds of goats and sheep traveled down from mountain summer pastures to the warmer lowlands. This interdependency between highlands and lowlands linked the people of the plains to trade routes that passed through the highlands to the Plateau of Iran.

Harappan village society developed into a fully fledged civilization with remarkable speed between 2700 and 2500 B.C. as Sumerian trading patterns shifted significantly. After 2500 B.C. the Mesopotamians acquired many of their needs from three foreign states—Dilmun on the island of Bahrain in the Persian Gulf, Magan, a port further east, and distant Meluhha. Perhaps Meluhha was in the Indus valley region, a place where the Sumerians traded for carnelian, furniture, gold, ivory, oils, and silver, among other commodities. They exchanged these goods for cereal grain, cedarwood, cloth, and leather. This expanding trade, which carried goods from both the Indus valley and the highlands, was a major factor in the emergence of the Harappan civilization.

We know of at least five Harappan cities, all of them laid out with carefully organized citadels and street grids. The two largest were Harappa and Moenjo-daro, both built on artificial mounds high above the flood levels of the nearby Indus, each housing as many as 40,000 people. Both offer dramatic contrasts with the jumbled urban environments of walled Sumerian cities. A high citadel stands at the west end of each city, dominating the streets below. Here lived the rulers, protected by great fortifications and floodworks. Moenjo-daro's towering citadel rises 40 feet (12.2 m) above the plain, protected by massive flood embankments and a perimeter wall with towers. The public buildings on the summit include a pillared hall almost 90 feet (27.4m) square, perhaps a precinct where the ruler gave audience to petitioners and visiting officials.

The rulers of each city looked down on the north-south street grid laid out in city blocks. The widest east-west thoroughfares were only 30 feet (9.1m) wide, the cross streets only half as wide and unpaved. Hundreds of drab, standardized houses presented a blind brick facade to the streets and alleys they lined (Figure 10.2). Some more imposing houses had two or even three stories with wooden balconies overlooking the courtyard rather than the street, as was the case at Sumerian Ur. There were bazaars, complete with shops. Here bead makers, coppersmiths, cotton

Figure 10.2 A street at Moenjo-daro, Pakistan.

weavers, potters, and other specialists manufactured their wares. The city authorities provided row after row of standardized, two-room houses for commoners who labored on the many routine, but essential tasks that kept the labor-intensive civilization running. With so many unskilled hands and abundant food supplies, there was no incentive for technological innovation, nor, apparently, did the religious philosophies of the day encourage culture change. Harappan society was organized in distinct social classes, and, perhaps, in a hierarchy of castes that restricted upward mobility and provided a wider identity outside the confines of the family. This caste system was to survive in Indian society until modern times.

We do not know the names of Harappan rulers, for they left almost no portraits and never boasted of their deeds. A limestone figure from Moenjo-daro depicts a thick-lipped, bearded man staring at the world through slitted eyes (Figure 10.3). He seems to be withdrawn in meditation, perhaps detached from worldly affairs. The only clue to his status is that one shoulder is uncovered, a sign of reverence during the Buddha's lifetime more than 1,000 years later. There is nothing of the ardent

Figure 10.3 The bearded man from Moenjo-daro.

militarism of Assyrian kings or of the slavish glorification of the Pharaohs
here.

The Indus valley may have been the focus of Harappan civilization,
but it was only part of a much larger, more varied society, whose influences extended over a vast area of both the lowlands and highlands of
what is now Pakistan. It was a civilization not of cities but of village
farmers, which was part of a huge network of regional trade routes. These
routes stretched deep into Afghanistan and the Plateau of Iran, into Turkish Armenia and over sea routes to the Persian Gulf.

The Decline of Harappan Civilization (1700 B.C.)

The Harappan civilization reached its height in about 2000 B.C., just
before the dawning of the New Kingdom in Egypt. Three centuries later,
Harappa and Moenjo-daro were abandoned. We do not know the reasons
for the collapse, which coincided with an explosion of village settlement
in areas to the south. Perhaps it was the result of changing trading activities, or simply a lack of dynamism among the city's rulers that made it
difficult for them to adjust to new circumstances—but these are merely
intelligent guesses. The rural components of Harappan civilization flourished in outlying areas for two centuries or so. Then, in 1500 B.C., Aryan

nomads swept down on the Indus valley from the north, disrupting low-land society. By that time, the Harappans had passed on a priceless legacy of beliefs and philosophies that formed one of the mainstreams of all subsequent Indian history.

The Harappan civilization rose in part because of local political, social, and economic conditions, and also in response to the growing trade with Mesopotamia. Even as early as 2000 B.C., south Asia formed part of a wider economic and political world that stretched from the Aegean to the Indian subcontinent, connected to it by ever-changing fluctuations in the demand for a multitude of luxuries and raw materials. Far to the north and west, another world of competing states was coming into being, the realm of the Shang civilization of northern China.

CHINA: SHANG CIVILIZATION (c. 1766 B.C. to 1122 B.C.)

Ancient Chinese legends tell us that the celebrated Yellow Emperor Huang Di founded civilization in the north in about 2700 B.C. At the time, the local farmers lived under the rule of a series of competing noble families descended from much earlier village chiefs. Their warlike local rulers lived in walled towns near the Huang-Ho River. Xia, Shang, and Zhou — each royal family was related to its competitors by marriage and closely woven alliances and kin ties. Each rose to prominence, then gave way to its neighbors. For example, legends tell of Xia ruler named Yu the Great, who gained power through his military prowess and his knowledge of flood control in about 2200 B.C.

Shoulder Blades and Diviners (2700 B.C.)

Can we clothe the legends with archaeological fact? By 2700 B.C., a few villages in the north and south became important centers ruled by powerful kin leaders like Yu the Great. There are signs that a new social order existed, for some settlements of the time contain elaborate burials adorned with jade ornaments and ceremonial weapons. Some of them were warriors, who raided their enemies and deposited their corpses in village wells. But their authority was probably based on their great spiritual authority, for they were experts at predicting the future and communicating with the ancestors.

As population densities rose and agricultural techniques became more sophisticated in both north and south, the various regional farming cultures of China were linked through complex trading arrangements that exchanged raw materials, luxury goods, and other commodities over long distances. As in the Near East, this interdependence between regions spurred similar cultural and technological developments in many parts of China. These innovations included copper and bronze metallurgy (developed independently of the west), construction of stamped-earth town walls, and widespread use of fortifications. New, powerful rituals spread widely through the country, among them a cosmology based on animals and birds and the use of divination to communicate with the ancestors and foretell the future.

At Longshan on the Huang-Ho River, archaeologists found dozens of cracked ox shoulder blades used in divination rituals (Figure 10.4). When a question was posed to the ancestors, the diviner would apply a metal point to the bone, causing the surface to crack. The response of the ancestors was read from the fissures. A skillful diviner could control the

Figure 10.4 Shang oracle bones.

extent and direction of the cracks. Thus, divination provided an authoritative leader with a useful and highly effective way of giving advice. He could regard disagreement as treason. Some scholars believe that some common forms of divination cracks became the prototypes for a simple Chinese script that evolved into the elaborate writing of later times.

Such divinations became a vital part of village, and later state, government. All official divinations were addressed to the royal ancestors, who acted as intermediaries between the living and the ultimate ancestor and supreme being, the ruler of heaven and the creator Shang Di. The king was the head of all family lines that radiated from his person to the nobility and then to the common people. These actual and imputed kinship ties were the core of early Chinese civilization, for they obligated the peasants to provide food and labor for their rulers.

Shang Civilization (1766 to 1122 B.C.)

The Shang dynasty of rulers presided over China's first civilization between about 1766 and 1122 B.C. Oracle bone and other historical sources tell us that the Shang rulers lived in at least seven capitals, situated near the middle reaches of the Huang Ho River. Ao, the best known of these royal compounds, was occupied in about 1560 B.C. It was a vast earth-walled precinct that enclosed an area of 2 square miles. It would have taken 10,000 laborers working 330 days a year no less than 18 years to erect the fortifications alone.

In about 1400 B.C., the capital moved to the Anyang area, where it remained until the fall of the Shang Dynasty more than 250 years later. The new royal domain was a network of compounds, palaces, villages, and cemeteries extending over an area of more than 120 square miles. The core of this so-called capital was at Xiao-tun, where 53 rectangular clay and timber long-houses served as residences for noble families. An elevated area in the royal precinct formed two rows of temples associated with a series of five ceremonial gates. The builders buried animals, humans, and even chariots nearby, perhaps to dedicate the shrines.

In the 1930s, Chinese archaeologists excavated eleven royal graves near the compound. The best-known grave is a cross-like pit approximately 33 feet (10 m) deep with slightly sloping walls. Four ramps lead from the surface to each side of the pit. The coffin of the unknown ruler lay inside a wooden chamber (Figure 10.5). He was accompanied by superb bronze vessels and shell, bone, and stone ornaments. Slaves and sacrificial victims accompanied the dead man to the next life, many of them decapitated, their heads lying in one place, their bodies in another. Dozens of people were beheaded, dismembered, or mutilated, then buried in small graves nearby.

Every early Chinese ruler stayed in power by virtue of a strong army. Shang society was organized along military lines, so that the royal standing army could be supplemented with thousands of conscripts at short

Figure 10.5 Chariot burial from the royal Shang tombs near Anyang. The wooden parts of the chariot were excavated by following discolorations in the soil left by the rotting wood.

notice. The kings were frequently at war, suppressing rebellious rivals, protecting their frontiers, or raiding for prisoners of war to serve as sacrificial victims. Graves reveal that foot soldiers carried a bow and arrows, a halberd, shield, small knife, and sharpening stone. Shang armies boasted of wooden chariots with spoked wheels held together with sinew lashings and pulled by two horses. The charioteer rode in a wicker and leather car measuring between 3 and 4 feet (0.9 to 1.2 m) across.

The Shang Dynasty fell in about 1100 B.C. at the hands of the neighboring Zhou. The conquerors did not create a new civilization; rather they took over the existing network of towns and officials and incorporated them into their own state, thus shifting the focus of political and economic power to the south and west, away from Anyang into the fertile Wei Valley near the modern city of S'ian. By this time, the influence of what may loosely be called Shang civilization extended far to the south, into the rice-growing areas of the south and along the eastern Chinese coast. The Zhou divided their domains into various almost independent provinces, which warred with one another for centuries.

It was not until 221 B.C. that the great Emperor Huang Ti unified China into a single empire. By Roman times, Chinese civilization had been flourishing for more than 2,000 years. By then, aggressive merchants were expanding Chinese influence far into Southeast Asia, where its interests collided with those of Indian merchants trading eastward from their homeland.

CHINA, INDIA, AND SOUTHEAST ASIA (A.D. 200 to 1500)

By 2000 B.C., state-organized societies flourished in many parts of the Near East, in south Asia, and in China. The political and social institutions of these societies varied greatly from one area to the next, but all of them shared a tendency toward greater political integration over much larger regions. This trend culminated in the Roman Empire in the west, in the vast empire of Chandragupta in India that linked the Indus and Ganges valleys in a single kingdom, and in the unification of China under Emperor Huang Ti. These three empires were well aware of one another. The Romans traded with India and maintained outposts there and Chinese silk reached the Mediterranean. The economic, political, and religious influences of these various empires extended far beyond the confines of their own domains. Among the regions affected were Southeast Asia and sub-Saharan Africa.

The Rise of States in Southeast Asia (A.D. 200 to 600)

Rice cultivation and bronze metallurgy were well established throughout Southeast Asia by the time Shang civilization emerged in northern China. But it was not until about A.D. 200 that state-organized societies appeared in the region, for reasons that are still obscure. Much of Vietnam came under the domination of China's Han emperors in 111 B.C. At the same time, the busy sea-trading networks of Southeast Asia were incorporated into the vast oceanic trade routes from China in the east to the shores of the Red Sea and the east coast of Africa in the west.

No one people controlled the whole of this enormous trade. Beyond India, the trade was dominated by Indian merchants who penetrated deep into the Southeast Asian archipelago. There they were in contact with Chinese mariners, who carried luxuries to the south China coast. These contacts came about as the Roman Emperor Vespasian prohibited the export of precious metals from his empire in A.D. 70, commodities that were vital to India's rulers for their religious and economic value. As a result, the Indian gold and spice trade with Southeast Asia expanded dramatically in the centuries that followed.

The influx of Indian merchants to Southeast Asia brought not only foreign products but new philosophical, social, and religious beliefs. Inevitably, the chieftains of trading villages adopted many customs from the foreigners. Within a few centuries, kingdoms appeared with governments run according to Hindu or Buddhist ideas of social order and divine kingship.

Numerous city-states soon flourished throughout Southeast Asia. The most powerful was Funan, a mercantile empire of the third to sixth centuries A.D. that extended along the Mekong Delta in Vietnam and inland into Cambodia. Chinese histories speak of a "port of a thousand rivers," of a rich trade in bronze, gold, silver, and spices. They also tell of vast drainage and irrigation works that rapidly transformed much of the Mekong delta from barren swamps into rich agricultural land. Most Funans lived in large island cities in lakes fortified with great earthworks and moats swarming with crocodiles. Each major settlement was a port connected to the ocean and its neighbors by a network of artificial canals. In the sixth century, Indian Brahmans brought from Funan the cult of Shiva, the god who was to become a compelling symbol of divine kingship.

Khmer Civilization (A.D. 600 to 1500)

With the collapse of Funan, economic and political power shifted to the Great Lake region of central Cambodia. For much of the year, the lake is a series of muddy pools drained by the Tonle Sap River that flows into the Mekong River. Between July and January, floodwaters reverse the river's course and turn the swamps into a huge lake. The Great Lake was such a favorable environment for rice farming and fishing that its shores supported a far higher population density than even the irrigated delta where Funan had flourished. Here the state of Chenla prospered for two centuries after A.D. 611, until the first of a series of ambitious Khmer kings seized power and proclaimed themselves god-kings.

The first of these rulers, Jayavarman II, was crowned in 802. Everyone, whether noble, high priest, or commoner, was expected to subordinate his or her ambitions to the need to perpetuate the existence of the god-king on earth and in the next life. Jayavarman's strategy of kingship was so successful that he ruled for 45 years. For three centuries, each of Jayavarman's successors presided over a tightly controlled state that supervised every aspect of Khmer life, from agriculture to warfare, economic life, and the rituals of public and private worship. The Khmers' unique form of divine kingship produced, instead of an austere civilization like that of the Harappans, a society with a blind faith in powerful kings who carried the cult of wealth, luxury, and self-aggrandizement to amazing lengths. Thousands of their subjects toiled to build fabulous temples and palaces purely for the king's pleasure.

Of all these royal edifices, the most famous is Angkor Wat, built in 1200. At 500 feet by 4000 feet (152 by 1219 m) across, it is the largest religious building in the world, greater even than Vatican City (Figure 10.6). Angkor Wat was built in three rising squares, approached by a 500-foot (152 m) paved causeway across a wide moat. Four miles (6.4 km) of masonry walls enclose the temples! The squares of buildings consist of towers, pavilions, stairways, and central chambers surrounded by long, open galleries adorned with more than 4,000 feet (1219 m) of polished reliefs. Here 2,000 temple dancers cavort, hundreds of elephant-mounted soldiers march to war, and the god-king rides on a royal elephant surrounded by slaves and warriors. Every detail of this extraordinary building reproduces part of the heavenly world, the highest tower depicting the cosmic mountain, *Meru*, where the gods lived, the moat the ocean that surrounded the world.

The cost of building Angkor Wat and the nearby capital, Angkor Thom, was so high that it exhausted the Khmer. After 1218, a fatigued society built no more stone temples. There were no longer the resources to support armies or maintain the great irrigation works of Tonle Sap. Once the image of the divine king was challenged by rebellious neighbors,

Figure 10.6 Angkor Wat, Cambodia.

the empire was doomed. Angkor Thom fell to alien armies in about 1430, and the divine kings and their works were soon just a shadowy memory.

The maritime trade routes that had sustained the Khmer empire and its predecessors linked widely spaced parts of the ancient world in loosely interdependent ways. There were always merchants and governments seeking new markets and fresh sources of precious metals and other luxuries. The same trade networks that had brought Indians to Southeast Asia and Chinese to the island of Sri Lanka carried merchandise across the Indian Ocean to the Persian Gulf, Arabia, and the east coast of Africa. Sub-Saharan Africa soon became an active partner in international trade.

ANCIENT AFRICAN KINGDOMS (900 B.C. to A.D. 1600)

During the late Ice Age, sub-Saharan Africa's peoples evolved in isolation, separated from the Mediterranean world by the arid wastes of the Sahara. Yet, in sharp contrast, it was in North Africa that one of the world's oldest civilizations flourished, that of the ancient Egyptians (Figure 10.7).

The ancient Egyptians were a valley people, living within the narrow confines of a fertile, well irrigated floodplain. They belonged culturally and politically to the Mediterranean world. To the south was Nubia, hotter, drier, and less hospitable than Egypt itself. The Sahara effectively isolated the peoples of sub-Saharan Africa from the Nile world. To the south of the desert lay an enormous, environmentally rich and diverse continent, peopled by Stone Age hunter-gatherers. Some cattle herders did penetrate south from Ethiopia into the high grasslands of East Africa as early as 1000 B.C., but farming, towns, and cities were unknown in sub-Saharan Africa until well after the heyday of ancient Egypt.

Meroe (900 B.C. to 200 B.C.)

Despite claims that the ancient Egyptians were black Africans, there is no archaeological or historical evidence whatsoever that the Pharaohs or their subjects had any direct contact with sub-Saharan Africa. Nubia was an important source of elephant ivory and of black slaves, a frontier buffer zone between the familiar homeland and unknown desert to the south.

In about 900 B.C., an unknown governor of the southernmost part of Egypt founded his own dynasty at the town of Napata and ruled a string of small settlements extending far south into what is now the Sudan. The Napatans' herds overgrazed their riverside grasslands, so they founded a new capital called Meroe on a fertile floodplain between the Nile and Atbara Rivers. There they created their own modest urban civilization, which was in touch with people living far to the west on the southern edges of the Sahara (Figure 10.8).

Meroe prospered on its sporadic contacts with the Mediterranean world to the north, trading copper, gold, iron, and ivory with the Red Sea

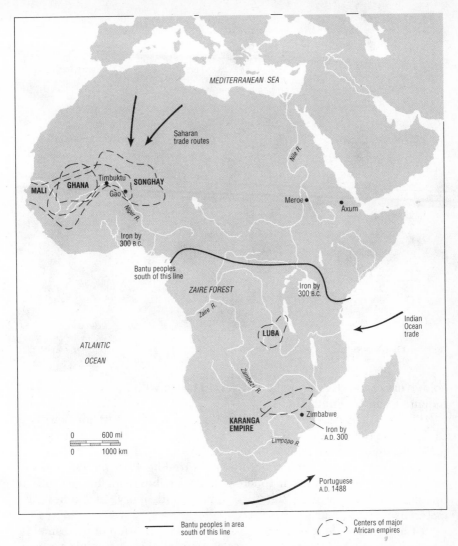

Figure 10.7 African states and archaeological sites mentioned in Chapter 10.

area. Some of Meroe's prosperity was based on ironworking, for rich deposits lie in its territory, to the point that some early scholars called Meroe the Birmingham of Africa. The isolation of sub-Saharan Africa did indeed begin to break down during Meroe's heyday, but it seems likely that the new chapter in Africa history was the result of contacts from two very different directions—North Africa and the Indian Ocean.

Camels and Dhows

The cultural isolation of sub-Saharan Africa finally broke down during the early Christian era. The insatiable demands of its neighbors for copper,

Figure 10.8 Meroe.

gold, ivory, and slaves brought Africans in touch with Mediterranean and Indian Ocean trading systems.

The North African coast had long been a staging post for maritime traders from the eastern Mediterranean, especially the Phoenicians. It was they who founded port-colonies in what are now Algeria and Morocco. The colonists came in contact with nomads trading salt from deep in the Sahara. They, in turn, were in touch with black tribes living to the south of the desert, who bartered salt for copper, gold, ivory, and other raw materials.

At first this trade was sporadic, but the domestication of the camel in Roman times revolutionized contacts across the desert. Camels are perfectly adapted to desert travel, so much so that North African merchants could organize regular caravans that crossed the Sahara like clockwork from the Mediterranean to tropical West Africa. By the time of Christ, the Saharan trade was linked to that of the Mediterranean world. African gold and ivory became important sources of Medieval European wealth.

No one knows when mariners discovered the cycles of the Indian Ocean monsoon winds. The northeast monsoon brings sailors to Africa in winter. Then, in summer, the northwest monsoon returns them to their destination. These cycles are so regular that a sailing vessel can travel from India to Arabia or East Africa and back within 12 months. The monsoon winds were known to Egyptian and Greek navigators by A.D. 100, by which time the Indian Ocean was part of the vast trading net-

Figure 10.9 Indian Ocean dhow under sail.

works that linked China with the Southeast Asian and Mediterranean worlds. There was an insatiable demand for African ivory, gold, silver, iron, and slaves in Arabia and India.

Arabian dhows, downwind sailing vessels, brought cargoes of Indian cotton, strings of cheap glass beads, Chinese porcelain, and other exotic goods to the East African coast (Figure 10.9). There they traded them for ivory and other raw materials brought to coastal ports and towns like Manda, Lamu, and Kilwa. From the coast, small parties of traders traveled far into the interior, along intervillage paths, developing trading contacts and relationships that were to endure for many centuries. By A.D. 300, isolated strings of Indian glass beads were worn by villagers in the heart of central Africa, more than 600 miles from the Indian Ocean.

The Spread of Iron (before 300 B.C. to A.D. 250)

It was the Saharan trade that brought iron and ironworking south of the desert for the first time, as early as the fourth century B.C. More a utilitarian than a decorative metal, and ideal for tropical forest clearance and agriculture, iron spread rapidly through sub-Saharan Africa as agricultural economies took hold for the first time. Farmers had settled in the great East African lakes region by the last few centuries B.C. and to the banks of the Zambezi and Limpopo Rivers in the early Christian era. The newcomers absorbed, eliminated, or pushed out the indigenous hunter-gatherers. Today, hunter-gatherer populations survive only in areas that are too arid for farming such as the Kalahari Desert in southern Africa.

The farmers used simple agricultural methods that required careful selection of fertile soils and a large amount of land. African tropical soils are, for the most part, of only moderate fertility and many areas of the continent are infested with tsetse fly, an insect whose bite is fatal to cattle and dangerous to humans. These two factors ensured that most of Africa's farming land was taken under cultivation relatively quickly. These agricultural populations were the ancestors of the many present-day Bantu-speaking cultures of tropical Africa such as the Tonga of Zambia and Sotho of Zimbabwe. They were relatively egalitarian village societies, organized on kinship lines.

The Kingdoms of Ghana, Mali, and Songhay (c. A.D. 800 to 1550)

Throughout the first millennium A.D., the Saharan gold trade continued to expand gradually, especially with the spread of a major new religion — Islam. Its founder, the prophet Muhammad, died in A.D. 632, having founded a religious creed that inspired his successors to great conquests. They swept through Egypt and into North Africa within half a century of the prophet's death. The Saharan trade passed into Islamic hands at the end of the first millennium A.D., a development that brought literate and much-traveled Arab geographers to the lands south of the Sahara. There the geographer al-Bakri described the Kingdom of Ghana, so rich in gold that "it is said that the king owns a nugget as large as a big stone."

The Kingdom of Ghana straddled the northern borders of the gold-bearing river valleys of the upper Niger and Senegal. No one knows when it first came into being, but the kingdom was described by Arab writers in the eighth century A.D. The Ghanians prospered off the gold, ivory, and salt trade. They also exported kola nuts (used as a stimulant) and slaves. In return they, and their successors, received cloth, leather goods, glass beads, and weapons. This was a powerful state. The King of Ghana was said by al-Bakri to be able to "put 200,000 men in the field, more than 40,000 of whom were bowmen." The figure sounds impressive, but the ruler probably presided over a loosely knit alliance of minor chiefs and small towns and had little real power.

Ghana dissolved into its constituent chiefdoms during the eleventh century. Two centuries of incessant squabbling ensued, until the Kingdom of Mali came into being at the hands of an able ruler named Sundiata. Sundiata came to power in about 1230 and founded his new capital at Mali on the Niger River. A century later, the Kingdom of Mali extended over much of sub-Saharan West Africa. The fame of the Mali kings spread all over the Islamic world. The city of Timbuktu on the fringes of the western Sahara became not only a famous caravan center but a celebrated place of Islamic scholarship. All this prosperity was based on the gold and ivory trade. Malian gold underpinned not only much of the Islamic world, but the treasuries of European kings, too. Before Columbus sailed to the New World, Mali and its lesser neighbors provided no less than two-thirds of

Europe's gold. The precious ingots and dust passed north across the Sahara from places like Gao and Timbuktu to Fez in Morocco and then on to Spain, and through Tripoli to Italian ports. The gold supply was sporadic and slow in arriving, but for some centuries Mali, and its successor Songhay, controlled the western world's gold supplies.

Mali's Islamic rulers governed with supreme powers granted by Allah and ruled their conquered provinces with carefully selected religious appointees, or even through clever slaves, chosen for their loyalty and political acumen. Islam provided a reservoir of thoroughly trained, literate administrators, who believed that political stability resulted from efficient government and sound trading practices. So confident was the Malian king Mansa Musa that he left his kingdom and crossed the Sahara on a long pilgrimage to Mecca in 1324. He and his wealthy entourage spent so freely in Cairo that the price of gold was depressed for several years.

About a year later, Mansa Musa brought the great trading center at Gao on the Niger River under his control. The leaders of Gao resented Malian control and threw off its yoke in 1340, founding a rival kingdom, Songhay. The new state prospered as a series of able rulers expanded their domains. Most famous among them was Sonni Ali, who expanded Songhay's frontiers far into the Sahara and deep into Mali country between 1464 and 1494, monopolizing much of the gold and ivory trade at the same time.

Songhay was at the height of its powers when Columbus landed in the New World. When it invaded the Americas, Europe acquired new sources for precious metals that trebled the amount of gold and silver circulating in Europe in half a century. The annual output from America was ten times that of the rest of the world. The Saharan gold trade declined sharply. Cities like Gao and Timbuktu, a well as the Kingdom of Songhay, crumbled into relative obscurity. By 1550, Songhay had collapsed, as the center of political power moved south, into the tropical forests and coastal regions that are now Ghana, Nigeria, and the Ivory Coast, where European ships traded for gold, ivory, and slaves.

Zimbabwe and Karanga Kingdoms (A.D. 1100 to 1500)

The staple commodity of the Indian Ocean trade was elephant ivory. African ivory is softer and more easily carved than the brittle tusk of the Indian elephant. Tusks fed a flourishing market for Hindu bridal ornaments throughout India. This ancient commerce was well established by the late first millennium A.D. and continued to prosper long after the discovery of the Americas. By 1100 A.D., a string of small Islamic towns flourished along the coast from Somalia in the north to Kilwa in southern Tanzania in the south. They formed a distinctive coastal civilization that was based entirely on the Indian Ocean trade. From places like the islands of Kilwa and Zanzibar, small caravans set off for the interior, carrying bundles of cotton, glass beads, and thousands of seashells from Indian Ocean beaches. These latter were prized as ornaments in the far interior. This trade was very one-sided in strict monetary terms, for the glass beads, cheap cloth, and other luxuries perceived as prestigious in the African interior were worth a fraction of the gold dust, copper ingots, ivory, and slaves that fueled the maritime trade of an entire ocean.

Much East African gold came from the highlands between the Zambezi and Limpopo Rivers in southern Africa. The major trading port was in Sofala, just south of the Zambezi River delta. The coastal traders bartered with the Karanga peoples of the interior plateau, who were farmers and cattle herders organized into several powerful kingdoms headed by major hereditary rulers. These chiefs acquired and held political power by controlling sources of copper, gold, and ivory, and redistributing imports from the coast to their subjects. Karanga chiefs were also important spiritual leaders, who acted as intermediaries between the people and their ancestral spirits. They were often shamans, individuals with important rain-making powers.

One such chief built an imposing stone capital at Zimbabwe (Figure 10.10). His Great Enclosure with massive free-standing masonry walls lay in the shadow of a low hill at the head of a valley that brought moist winds and mist up from the distant Indian Ocean. It was here that the chief and his priests performed rain-making ceremonies and interceded with the ancestors. Here, too, the chief traded with occasional parties of visiting coastal traders, probably men who were part Arab, part African. There is

Figure 10.10 Zimbabwe ruins.

no evidence that the Zimbabwe chiefs embraced Islam. Zimbabwe was the center of a truly indigenous African kingdom.

At least five stages of occupation have been recognized at Zimbabwe, the earliest dating to the fourth century A.D. The first settlement was a humble village, the four remaining occupations the work of Karanga peoples who built progressively more complicated stone enclosures and retaining walls. The heyday of Zimbabwe was between 1350 and 1450, just before Europeans arrived on the coast. The site was abandoned sometime after 1450, when the local grazing grass and farming land became depleted.

All these indigenous African kingdoms developed in response to economic and political opportunities from outside. But their political, social, and economic institutions were always adapted to local conditions and were logical developments of earlier farming cultures.

After the fifteenth century A.D., Africa was exploited not only for its raw materials, but for its slaves. The tentacles of the international slave trade touched not only African coasts, but reached into the deepest strongholds of the interior. It was not until the nineteenth century that Victorian explorers, in pursuit of elusive geographical prizes like the source of the Nile, revealed to a horrified world the full extent of the slave trade and its catastrophic effect on late prehistoric Africa.

Chapter
11

Mesoamerican Civilizations

A.D. **1950** —

A.D. **1** —

15,000 B.P. —

50,000 B.P. —

100,000 B.P. —

500,000 B.P. —

1.0 Million —

2.5 Million —

*I*n 1519, Spanish conquistador Hernan Cortes and his men gazed down on the Aztec capital Tenochtitlan in the Basin of Mexico. The white buildings and temples of the great capital gleamed in the bright sunlight. The Spaniards marveled at the extraordinary sight, at a city as sophisticated as Constantinople or Seville. They wandered through a market that sold products from throughout Central America, and climbed pyramids dedicated to bloodthirsty, totally alien gods. Aztec civilization was ruled by Moctezuma, a mighty lord who presided over the fate of more than 5 million people. Aztec civilization was the culmination of more than 3,000 years of continuous state formation in Mesoamerica, a process that began while Shang civilization was flourishing in China and as Egypt's New Kingdom Pharaohs were at the height of their power. Here, as in the Near East and Asia, the appearance of state-organized societies was an entirely indigenous development (Figure 11.1).

VILLAGE FARMERS (before 2000 B.C. to 1500 B.C.)

Many centuries elapsed between the beginnings of village life and the appearance of state-organized societies in Mesoamerica. The first signs of political

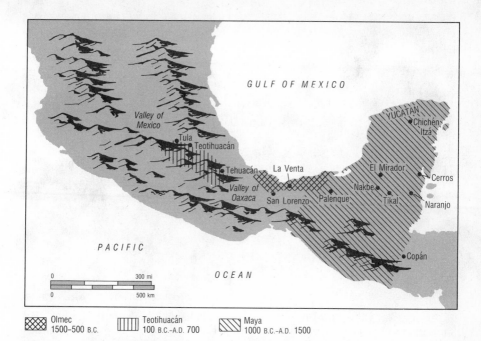

GULF OF MEXICO

Valley of Mexico

Tula
Teotihuacán

Tehuacán   La Venta

Valley of Oaxaca   San Lorenzo   Palenque

YUCATÁN
Chichén Itzá

El Mirador
Cerros
Nakbe
Tikal
Naranjo

PACIFIC

OCEAN

Copán

| 0 | 300 mi |
| 0 | 500 km |

| Olmec 1500–500 B.C. | Teotihuacán 100 B.C.–A.D. 700 | Maya 1000 B.C.–A.D. 1500 |

Figure 11.1 Map showing sites and states mentioned in the text.

and social complexity appear between about 2000 and 900 B.C. In many regions, small but often powerful chiefdoms headed by a chief and a select elite appeared. These few families dominated economic, political, and religious life and ruled over large commoner populations.

There was no one region where this emerging political and social complexity occurred first. Rather, it was a development that took place more or less simultaneously in many regions of Mesoamerica, not in isolation, but with each region, whether in highlands or lowlands, interacting with the others. The most famous of these newly complex societies was that of the Olmec.

THE OLMEC (c. 1500 B.C. to 500 B.C.)

The Olmec people lived on the Mexican south Gulf Coast from about 1500 to 500 B.C. Their homeland was low-lying, tropical, and humid with fertile soils. The swamps, lakes, and rivers are rich in game and fish. The origins of the Olmec are a complete mystery, but the culture undoubtedly has strong local roots in the lowlands. It was in this region that the Olmec created a highly distinctive art style executed in sculpture and relief. The artists concentrated on natural and supernatural beings, the dominant motif being the were-jaguar, or humanlike jaguar. Many jaguars were given infantile faces; drooping lips; and large, swollen eyes, a style also applied to human figures, some of whom resemble snarling demons (Fig-

Figure 11.2 An Olmec lord from La Venta sits below a schematic jaguar pelt. He emerges from a niche or cave holding a rope that binds prisoners carved on either side of the throne.

ure 11.2). In time, these art styles, associated with new and powerful religious beliefs spread widely through Mesoamerica.

The earliest traces of Olmec culture are well documented at the famous San Lorenzo site, first occupied before 1250 B.C. Here, Olmec people lived on an artificial platform in the midst of frequently inundated woodland plains. They erected ridges and mounds around their platform, where they built pyramids and placed elaborate monumental carvings overlooking the sacred precinct. Some of them were large heads, perhaps portraits of powerful rulers. Some wear helmets, which appear to bear as yet undeciphered name glyphs (symbols) (Figure 11.3).

The first monumental sculpture appears at San Lorenzo just as the inhabitants were beginning to construct raised gardens in nearby swamps in organized efforts to intensify agricultural production. By this time, too, San Lorenzo was an important trade center that attracted obsidian and other semiprecious stones from all over Mesoamerica. At the height of its prosperity, this important Olmec center housed more than 2,500 people.

About 900 B.C. San Lorenzo went into decline and was surpassed by La Venta, another major center closer to the Gulf of Mexico. The Olmec built La Venta's ceremonial precinct on a small island in the middle of a swamp. An earthen mount 393 feet long by 229 feet wide (120 m by 70 m) dominates the island. Long, low mounds surround a rectangular plaza in front of a large mound, faced by walls and terraced mounds at the other end of the plaza. Like San Lorenzo, La Venta was a major trade center

Figure 11.3 Colossal head from San Lorenzo, with parrotlike glyph on the headdress.

that attracted jade, obsidian, serpentine, and other materials from as far away as Costa Rica. Every stone for sculpture and temples had to be brought in from at least 60 miles (96 km), a big undertaking since some of the stone blocks at the site weigh more than 40 tons. Vast, monumental sculptures litter La Venta, including some large heads with flared lips. There are ceremonial thrones, too, bearing scenes of rulers at the gateway to the underworld, symbolizing their role as intermediaries between the living and spiritual realms (Figure 11.2). This role of spiritual intermediary was to assume dominant importance in later Mesoamerican civilizations such as that of the Maya. La Venta flourished for about 400 years and was then destroyed in about 400 B.C., at which time many of its finest monuments were intentionally defaced.

The earliest Olmec were organized in a series of chiefdoms along the Gulf Coast of Veracruz and Tabasco, which may have exercised some influence over adjacent areas of Chiapas and Central Mexico. Later, Olmec society flourished during a period when art motifs, religious symbols, and ritual beliefs were shared between developing chiefdoms in many regions. This sharing came about as a result of regular contacts between neighboring leaders and through day-to-day trade.

Between 300 B.C. and A.D. 250 common religious ideologies and practices unified large areas of Mesoamerica. These ideologies were much refined versions of ancient village beliefs that revolved around the close relationships between the living and spiritual worlds. Animals like the jaguar played a powerful role in these beliefs. The jaguar is the most feared predator in Central and South America, an animal of great physical strength, cunning, and endurance. Jaguars are highly adaptable beasts that flourish on land, in water, and in the upperworld of trees. Their hunting behavior resembles that of humans. The jaguar is aggressive and fearsome like a brave warrior, emits a thunderous roar like a violent thunderstorm, and is reputed to have great sexual prowess. These are impressive, resourceful beasts, who, like human shamans, cross boundaries between different environments.

Inevitably, the jaguar became a potent symbol of kingship in Mesoamerican civilization, as primordial village beliefs became transformed into an intricate, pervasive philosophy of kingship and statehood. Leaders sit in the mouths of human-jaguars, their open jaws perhaps symbolizing the route to the underworld. Everything reinforces the notion that the rulers had a close relationship to the supernatural.

The new religious beliefs developed and spread with the aid of complicated symbolism depicted in art and public architecture. As in Egypt and Mesopotamia, the leaders of the new order validated their rule and their authority in elaborate public ceremonies conducted in the midst of spectacular settings of pyramids and plazas. The great Maya ceremonial centers, the city of Teotihuacan of the highlands, the central precinct of Aztec Tenochtitlan, all were symbolic landscapes of the spiritual world depicted in earth, stone, and stucco. Here supreme lords would appear in trance, and cross the threshold between the realms of the living and the gods in carefully staged public rituals. They ruled over complicated worlds, regulated by increasingly precise astronomical calendars that measured the endless cycles of days and years.

TEOTIHUACAN (200 B.C. to A.D. 750)

By the time the classic Mesoamerican civilizations arose in the second century A.D., dynasties of elites had been ruling parts of Mesoamerica for more than 1,000 years. Some of their small villages and towns became great city-states, like rivals Monte Alban in the Valley of Oaxaca and Teotihuacan in the highland Valley of Mexico.

By 200 B.C., different areas of the Valley of Mexico and other parts of the lowlands and highlands were linked by increasingly sophisticated trading networks and by an emerging market economy, centered on rapidly growing towns and religious centers. One of these, Teotihuacan, was

Figure 11.4 The city of Teotihuacan, the Pyramid of the Moon in the left foreground, showing the Avenue of the Dead, the Pyramid of the Sun at left.

destined to become one of the largest cities in the world of its day. In 200 B.C. Teotihuacan was little more than a handful of villages, at least one of which specialized in obsidian manufacture. A century later, the hamlets had become a town of about 600 people.

By A.D. 150, the town had become a city covering more than 5 square miles (13 km) and housing more than 20,000 people. Obsidian manufacturing and trade were expanding rapidly and a vast ceremonial precinct was rising in the core of the city. Between A.D. 150 and 750, Teotihuacan grew explosively. It became a huge metropolis laid out on a north-south axis, centered on the Avenue of the Dead (Figure 11.4).[1] The entire city was dominated by an artificial mountain, the Pyramid of the Sun, a gargantuan structure of earth, adobe, and piled rubble 210 feet (64 m) high and 650 feet (198 m) square with a wooden temple at its summit. The pyramid rose above a cave that was a symbolic entrance to the Otherworld, an important feature of Mesoamerican religious belief.

The Avenue of the Dead passes the west face of the pyramid, leading to the Pyramid of the Moon, the second largest structure at Teotihuacan. The Avenue is lined with civic, palace, and temple buildings that were once brightly painted, while side streets lead to residential areas. To the

---

[1]It should be noted that the names for the Avenue of the Dead and the major pyramids at Teotihuacan are modern.

south of the pyramid complexes lies a large palace and temple complex dedicated to the Feathered Serpent god Quetzalcoatl, one of the major figures in the divine pantheon worshipped at Teotihuacan.

By any standards, Teotihuacan was a major city, one which once housed up to 120,000 people. The grandiose pyramids, plazas, and avenues give an overwhelming sense of wealth and power. They were built to impress, to dwarf even the large crowds that gathered on major festival days. The residential areas sprawled around the central precincts, priests and crafts workers living in dwellings around small courtyards, commoners in large compounds of rooms connected by narrow alleyways and patios. There were even quarters where foreign traders from places like Oaxaca lived.

The lords of Teotihuacan controlled large areas of the Valley of Mexico and exercised vital trade monopolies, both of which brought in great quantities of food and other essentials and luxuries under the close control of a tiny minority, the nobility. They turned Teotihuacan into a major manufacturing center, with a huge market that sold goods from all over Mesoamerica. The elite may have controlled some highly strategic and economically significant areas of the highlands, but Teotihuacan was no imperial capital. It was a powerful city-state bound to other city-states like Monte Alban by uneasy alliances and tribute exchanges.

By A.D. 600, Teotihuacan probably was governed by a secular ruler who was looked on as some kind of divine king. A growing class of nobles headed up the many kin groups that organized the thousands of commoners in and around the city. Teotihuacan, like other Mesoamerican civilizations, was organized in a rigid social pyramid. The minority controlled the majority through a combination of economic monopoly and institutionalized social inequality that was validated by elaborate religious ceremonies and by force.

Teotihuacan collapsed with dramatic speed after A.D. 650, when much of the city was burned to the ground. Only 50 years later, its population was scattered in a few villages. Much of the population settled in surrounding regions. No one knows exactly why Teotihuacan collapsed, but its conservative and powerful leaders may have been oblivious of threats from outside, their authority weakened by drought and environmental degradation. More aggressive, less tradition-bound states in the Valley of Mexico may have moved against their ancient neighbor and toppled her powerful lords.

Just as in the eastern Mediterranean the great powers of Egypt, Mesopotamia, and Anatolia vied for control of the Levant, so in Mesoamerica states like Teotihuacan influenced states and peoples far from home. Teotihuacano merchants ventured far afield, to the southern highlands and to all parts of the lowlands, carrying not only goods but ideas with them. The greatest legacy of Teotihuacan was not merely its religious beliefs, architecture, art, and trade networks, but a new interconnectedness between the many societies of prehistoric Mesoamerica, including the famous Mayan civilization of the lowlands.

MAYA CIVILIZATION (1000 B.C. to A.D. 900 and beyond)

Maya civilization flourished in the Mesoamerican lowlands long before, and long after, Teotihuacan rose to prominence on the highlands. It was centered on the densely forested Yucatan and Peten, which have yielded some of the most spectacular archaeological discoveries in the Americas.

Origins

Between 1000 and 600 B.C., as the Olmec people flourished, large numbers of farmers moved into the lowlands from higher ground, perhaps in response to a growing demand by highland nobles for such tropical products as jaguar pelts and brightly colored tropical bird feathers, which figures prominently in religious regalia. As the volume of trade between highlands and lowlands increased, so did lowland populations, especially at major ritual and trade centers.

Between 600 and 400 B.C., the inhabitants of Nakbe in the southern lowlands were building elaborate complexes of finely finished stone buildings that stood on huge platforms. Within a few centuries, Nakbe's leaders were commissioning beautiful masonry work and plaster masks of gods and ancestors for their temples. These temple facades bear motifs that seem to foreshadow what the Maya called *Ch'ul Ahau*, the notion of divine kingship.

By far the largest of the preclassic Maya centers was El Mirador, built between 250 and 50 B.C. El Mirador grew to cover about 6 square miles (16 sq. km), lying on low, undulating land, many acres of which flooded during the rainy season. Archaeologists from Brigham Young University in Utah have uncovered more than 200 buildings at El Mirador, among them great complexes of pyramids, plazas, causeways, and buildings (Figure 11.5). The Dante pyramid at the east end of the site dominates El Mirador. It rises from a low hill more than 210 feet (70 m) high. The western face of the hill is sculpted into large platforms surmounted with buildings and temples. A little over a mile (2 km) west rises the Tigre complex, a pyramid 182 feet (55 m) high surrounded by a plaza, a small temple, and several smaller buildings. The Tigre complex covers an area a little larger than the base of Teotihuacan's Pyramid of the Sun. El Mirador was an elaborate city, probably controlled by a highly organized elite that presided over a hierarchical society of artisans, priests, architects, and engineers, as well as traders and thousands of commoners.

This stupendous city was at the height of its power while Teotihuacan

Figure 11.5 Reconstruction of the ceremonial precinct at El Mirador.

on the highlands was still a series of small villages. But it suddenly collapsed at the beginning of the Christian era, for reasons that are a mystery. Similar collapses on a smaller scale occurred at other preclassic centers, where the new institution of kingship came into being and was then abandoned some generations later.

Maya Kingship: Sacred Space and Time

The leaders of El Mirador and other early Mayan centers are anonymous. They left no record of their names or personal histories. Their only legacy to their successors was a distinctive architectural tradition — plazas, pyramids, and temples that were symbolic replicas of the sacred landscape created by the gods at the beginning. The architecture replicated forests, mountains, and caves as columns, pyramids, and temple openings. The rituals performed in the midst of these symbolic settings, at the entrances of temples set on high pyramids, were so central to Mayan belief in the spiritual world that the places where they were conducted became more and more sacred as successive rulers built new temples on the same spot.

Maya civilization was also embedded in a matrix of unfolding, cyclical time. Mayan priests grappled with the cycles of the cosmos by studying the movements of planets and stars. They maintained both sacred and secular calendars, time scales of vital importance to daily life. Each day on the endless cycle of time had a position in all the permutations of cyclical time. Each Mayan king developed a precise relationship to this constantly

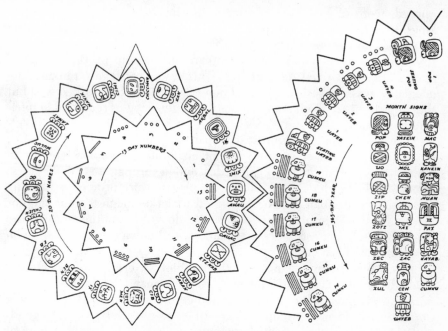

Figure 11.6 The Maya calendar, showing the two interlocking cycles. The left wheel is the 260-day *tzolkin*, the sacred calendar with 13 day numbers (inner wheel) and 20 day names (outer wheel). The right hand wheel is the *haab*, the secular cycle, with 18 months of 20 days each.

moving time scale (Figure 11.6). Such events as dates of accession to the throne, important histories, and royal births and deaths left their marks on the calendar.

Mayan rulers linked their actions to those of the gods and the ancestors, sometimes legitimizing their descent by claiming that it reenacted mythical events. In a real sense, Mayan history was linked to the present and to the Otherworld, and to the legendary Olmec civilization of the past. Society was embedded in a matrix of sacred space and time.

The king believed himself to have a divine covenant with the gods and ancestors, a covenant that was reinforced again and again in private and public rituals. The ruler was often depicted as the World Tree, the conduit by which humans communicated with the Otherworld. Trees were the living environment of Mayan life and a metaphor for human power. So the kings of the Maya were a forest of human World Trees within a natural, forested landscape.

The Maya developed a hieroglyphic script used for calculating calendars and regulating religious observances. The script was also much used for recording genealogies, king lists, conquests, and dynastic histories. The symbols are fantastically grotesque, consisting mostly of humans, monsters, or gods' heads. These hieroglyphic scripts, only partially deciphered, were of cardinal importance in Mayan life. The institution of kingship was based on the principle that the royal crown passed from generation to generation, in a line that led back to a founding ancestor. From there, families and clans were carefully ranked by their distance from the central royal descent line. This system of family ranking and allegiance was the basis of political power, a system that worked well but that depended on careful documentation of genealogies recorded in intricate glyphs.

The ceremonial structures at Copan, an important Mayan frontier city, include a ball court used for an elaborate ceremonial contest in which sacrificial victims and rulers descended through a symbolic abyss into the Otherworld (Figure 11.7). The players wore protective padding and used a rubber ball, which they aimed at markers such as stone rings or macaw heads set into the side walls. We do not know the rules of the game, but ball contests were associated with human sacrifice and much pomp and circumstance.

The lives of Mayan kings and their subjects were interconnected in vital, dynamic ways. The king was state shaman, the individual who enriched everyone's life in spiritual and ceremonial ways. His success at organizing trade and agriculture gave all levels of society access to goods and commodities. The great ceremonial centers built by the labors of hundreds of commoners were the setting for rituals and ceremonies that validated the rulers as divine kings.

Figure 11.7 The ball court at Copan.

Political History

Maya civilization varied greatly through the lowlands. It was a complicated mosaic of states, large and small, linked by common religious beliefs, calendars, and written script. Untangling Mayan political history is
like fitting together the pieces of an intricate jigsaw puzzle. Since Mayan
states were in a state of constant political flux as a result of frequent
warfare and ever-shifting diplomatic alliances, it is hard indeed to trace
even an outline of Classic Mayan history. It should also be noted that the
histories that come down to us were written as a form of political propa-
ganda and should therefore be treated as somewhat self-serving and
unreliable.

As El Mirador declined in the lowlands, important new centers came
into prominence at Tikal and Uaxactun nearby. Less than 12 miles (20 km)
apart, the two kingdoms were bitter rivals, each headed by powerful
dynasties of kings. In January A.D. 378, Great-Jaguar-Paw of Tikal's armies
defeated Uaxactun. His successors transformed Tikal into a powerful
kingdom of some 360,000 people living over an area of 956 square miles
(2000 sq. km) (Figure 8.3).

Tikal's dominance ended in about A.D. 560, when it was conquered by
neighboring Caracol. The diplomatic and military landscape changed constantly, as the balance of power shifted between Dos Pilas, Palenque,
Tikal, and other centers. With no standing armies, Mayan lords could not
garrison conquered towns, nor did they ever develop any form of effective
imperial government that would have enabled them to rule over very
large areas of the lowlands. The lowlands were never unified during the
centuries of Classic Maya civilization. What Mayan lords did share was a
set of highly complex traditions and a network of contacts between rulers
that transcended the local interests of individual states. Only when a few
aggressive, successful leaders emerged at places like Palenque and Tikal
did larger, multicenter kingdoms appear. These tended to disintegrate
within a few generations.

There are some parallels between the Classic Mayan and early Mesopotamian civilizations. The Sumerians were governed by independent
rulers with important ritual powers. Their small city-states were in a
constant state of change and interaction. The city-state remained the
practical political unit until long after a ruler named Sargon created a
theoretically unified Mesopotamia in about 2400 B.C. Just as in the Mayan
lowlands, larger political units forged by exceptionally able leaders soon
fragmented back into their component city-states.

Collapse (c. A.D. 900)

Maya civilization reached it peak after A.D. 600. Then, at the end of the
eighth century, the great centers of the Peten and the southern lowlands

were abandoned, the long-count calendar was discontinued, and the structure of religious life and the state decayed.

No one has been able to explain the collapse of Classic Maya civilization satisfactorily. It began at some sites early in the ninth century. Major centers were abandoned, monumental inscriptions and major public works ceased, and urban populations declined rapidly. Within a century, huge sections of the southern lowlands were abandoned, never to be resettled. At Tikal, perhaps the greatest Mayan center, the elite vanished and the population declined to a third of its earlier level. The survivors clustered in the remains of great masonry structures and tried to maintain a semblance of their earlier life. All this is not to say that Maya civilization vanished completely. New centers may have emerged in neighboring areas, taking in some of the displaced population. Maya civilization continued to flourish in the northern Yucatan.

A multiplicity of factors led to catastrophe in the southern lowlands. Archaeologist Patrick Culbert has studied population densities and the potential for agricultural production in the southern lowlands. He has shown that population densities rose to as high as 77 persons per square mile (200 per sq. km) during the late Classic over an area so large that it was impossible for people to adapt to bad times by moving to new land or emigrating. He believes that failure of the agricultural base rather than social malfunction was an important factor in the collapse equation.

Culbert theorizes that long-term environmental degradation was an important factor, for short-term gains in productivity were followed by catastrophic declines. For example, as populations rose, the length of time farming land was left fallow to recover fertility had to be shortened. The result was lower levels of plant nutrients and declining crop yields, something that is commonplace in many parts of the Third World today. We do not know what the Maya did to counteract these trends. Perhaps they mulched their fields or planted soil-restoring plants. In any case, widespread deforestation resulting from forest clearance and soil erosion may have ruined many fields, for the Maya did not adopt any soil conservation strategies.

In some ways, the Maya collapse may have been the result of too much success. An expanding Mayan population was ruled by powerful lords who made no allowance for the impact of long-term trends such as soil erosion or declining fertility of the land. There was a fundamental conflict between the leadership's responsibility to maintain the environment and the need to intensify agricultural production to maintain their increasingly elaborate kingdoms, thereby causing further, permanent damage. Environmental degradation hit home just at a moment when Maya civilization was expanding in a frenzy of warfare and political activity. Mayan kings had always depended on the labor of commoners and commanded their subjects' loyalty by their ability to intercede with the gods and ancestors and to bring prosperity to their people. When the moment of environmental collapse came, the elite lost their support as the commoners found it to their advantage to branch out on their own, to live in small, dispersed villages, as their ancient predecessors had always done.

Chichen Itza and Mayapan (A.D. 900 to 1500)

By A.D. 900 the classic period had ended in the southern lowlands, although Maya civilization continued uninterrupted in the northern Yucatan. The long tradition of lowland civilization continued, although religious beliefs changed somewhat and political leadership became less despotic. War and violence assumed great importance as militaristic leaders vied for control of strategic resources and trade routes.

In the northern Yucatan, Mayan leaders were more receptive to changes that flowed to the Yucatan from the highlands. Chichen Itza in northeast Yucatan was an important ceremonial center in postclassic times (Figure 11.8). In the ninth century, Chichen came under some form of highland influence. Its rulers controlled the two great resources of the northern Yucatan: a talented, well-organized population and massive salt fields along the coast. Chichen Itza became the center of an important regional state, which survived until the thirteenth century. Then the center of power passed to Mayapan, a walled settlement clustered around a ceremonial center ruled by the powerful Cocom family. Maya civilization enjoyed a resurgence in this area until constant civil wars weakened Mayapan in the fifteenth century. The Spanish found the Yucatan ruled by numerous petty chiefs and the great ceremonial centers of the past became just a memory.

Figure 11.8 The Castillo at Chichen Itza, the largest pyramid at the site.

THE TOLTECS (A.D. 900 to 1160)

The fall of Teotihuacan and the collapse of southern lowland Maya civilization left a political vacuum in the highlands. Many small groups vied for control of central Mexico. Eventually, however, the militaristic and aggressive Toltecs achieved dominance in the ninth century.

If later Aztec legends are to be believed, the Toltecs came to the Valley of Mexico from the northwest frontiers of Mesoamerica. They settled at Tula, 37 miles (57 km) north of the Valley of Mexico, where they built an imposing ceremonial center dedicated to the Feathered Serpent, Quetzalcoatl. Richly adorned stone warriors with elaborate breastplates supported the roof of the god's temple (Figure 11.9). The Toltecs assumed an almost mythic role in Aztec history, for these warlike people were considered to be the ancestors of their nobility. It was the Toltec qualities of bravery in war, of ardent militarism and human sacrifice, that were passed on to the leaders of the societies that arose in later centuries.

Aztec legends tell of strife at Tula between the followers of the warlike god Tezcatlipoca and those of the more peaceful Quetzalcoatl.

Figure 11.9 Toltec stone warriors supporting roof of the Temple of Quetzalcoatl at Tula, Mexico.

The Tezcatlipoca faction prevailed. Quetzalcoatl and his priests fled from Tula to the Gulf Coast. There "he fashioned a raft of serpents. When he had arranged the raft, there he placed himself, as if it were his boat. Then he set off across the sea," vowing, we are told, to return in the year "One Reed." By grotesque historical coincidence, conquistador Hernan Cortes landed in Mexico in the very year "One Reed." It was hardly surprising that the Aztecs greeted him with the regalia of a god.

The Toltec ruled from Tula for some two-and-a-half centuries, before some newcomers from the north captured their capital and destroyed the temples. Another period of political chaos ensured in the Valley of Mexico as more small groups from the north maneuvered and fought for land and political power. One of these small tribes was that of the ragtag Aztecs, or Mexica, as they called themselves. Two centuries later, these insignificant farmers were the rulers of the Mesoamerican world.

AZTEC CIVILIZATION (c. A.D. 1325 to 1521)

The Aztecs arrived in the Valley of Mexico during the twelfth century. They were a politically weak but aggressive group who barely retained their own identity. After years of constant harassment, they fled into the swamps of Lake Texcoco in 1325. There they founded a small hamlet named Tenochtitlan, "The place of the Prickly Pear Cactus." When Hernan Cortes gazed down on their capital just under two centuries later, it was the largest city in the Americas.

Tenochtitlan soon became an important market center. Through judicious diplomacy, discreet military alliances, and strategic royal marriages, the Aztec quietly became a major force in the Valley. Then, in the fifteenth century, a series of brilliant leaders embarked on a ruthless campaign of long-term military and economic conquest. Soon the Aztec controlled a loosely connected network of minor states and cities that extended far outside the Valley of Mexico.

The real inspiration behind this change was a counselor and general named Tlacaelel, who was adviser to a succession of aggressive supreme rulers. It was he who promoted the worship of an obscure but ambitious god named Huitzilopochtli, a sun deity. He encouraged the use of terror and human sacrifice as a means of controlling conquered neighbors. It was he and his masters who developed tribute collection to a fine art. A defeated neighbor was allowed to live in peace, provided regular tribute payments in local products were made on time. These payments were carefully calculated on the basis of local productivity, with collection enforced by bands of tax collectors. Obedience was obtained through the knowledge that an army would descend and inflict harsh punishment if payments were not made on time.

The rich tribute from conquered cities and states made Tenochtitlan the center of the Mesoamerican world. It became the hub of an economic

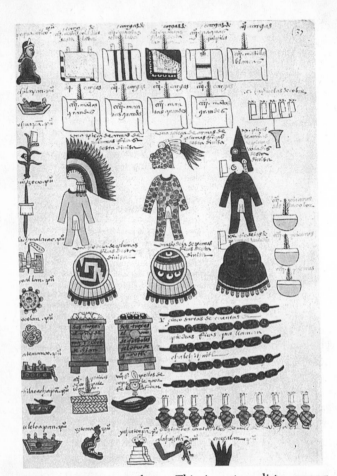

Figure 11.10 Aztec tribute. This inventory lists, among other items from the province of Tochtepec: "1600 rich mantles, 800 striped red, white and green mantles, 400 warrior' tunics and shirts. . . ." The tribute included colored bird feathers, cacao, and tree gum.

and political confederacy that extended from near the Pacific Ocean to the Gulf of Mexico and from northern Mexico as far south as Guatemala. All these riches and tribute payments flowed to the center, for the benefit of a tiny nobility, the elite of Aztec society (Figure 11.10).

Tenochtitlan

Tenochtitlan itself grew to become a city of more than 200,000 people by the early sixteenth century. Thousands of farmers labored in vast swamp field systems to produce food for the capital and outlying communities. Tenochtitlan's market sold every form of foodstuff and provided every

Figure 11.11 An artist's reconstruction of the ceremonial precincts at Tenochtitlan.

luxury and service. A complex hierarchy of government officials regulated not only agriculture and the market, but every aspect of Aztec life.

Tenochtitlan was a magnificent city set in a green swathe of country surrounded by clear lake water, with a superb backdrop of snow-capped volcanoes. Six major canals ran through the capital and there were three causeways that connected it with the mainland. At least 20,000 canoes provided convenient transport for the people of the city, which was divided into 60 or 70 residential wards organized by kin groups or occupations. Tenochtitlan was certainly larger, and probably cleaner, than many European cities of the day.

The principal streets of Tenchtitlan were of beaten earth and the central precincts contained at least 40 pyramids adorned with fine, decorated stonework (Figure 11.11). Large residential areas surrounded the central pyramids and plazas, and houses with chinampas lay on the outskirts of the city. The hub of the city was the great temple of the sun-god Huitzilopochtli and the rain deity Tlaloc. The temple has recently been excavated and restored by archaeologist Matos Moctezuma. He peeled off successive layers of the temple as far as a shrine built in 1390, discovering human skulls, sacrificial offerings, and precious artifacts from all over the Aztec empire in its foundations.

Social Classes in Aztec Society

Inevitably, the changes in Aztec society wrought by warlike leaders led to the development of a rigid, highly stratified class system. The supreme ruler was revered as a demigod and had virtually despotic powers. He was elected from a tiny class group of *pipiltin*, nobles. Under the nobles were classes of priests, artisans, professional merchants (*pochteca*), and others.

According to Aztec oral traditions collected after the Spanish Conquest, warriors formed a large class of society, ranked according to the number of people they had killed and captured in battle (Figure 8.4). Most people were, of course, free commoners, organized into groups of lineages called *calpulli* (large house). These provided the basis for military levies and compulsory labor levies. Landless farmers, prisoners, and slaves were the lowest class of society.

Aztec civilization, like its predecessors, depended on social inequality for survival, on the labors of thousands of anonymous people working for the common good. Conformity was considered a fundamental attribute of society, conformity carefully structured by education, compulsory military service, and elaborate religious ceremonies that included human sacrifice.

Human Sacrifice and Cannibalism

The Aztecs worshipped an elaborate pantheon of gods. Principal among them were the bloodthirsty, ambitious sun-god Huitzilopochtli, and the rain-god Tlaloc. Huitzilopochtli had presided over the expansion of the Aztec empire through conquest and yet more conquest. Every ruler embarked on ambitious wars not only to obtain more tribute, but also to feed the insatiable appetite of the sun-god for life-giving blood from human sacrifices. To die in war or as a captured prisoner under the sacrificial knife was a supreme honor for Aztec warriors, a fate known as the Flowery Death.

By the time Hernan Cortes arrived at Tenochtitlan in 1519, Aztec society was functioning in a state of frenetic and bloody violence, which flourished at the behest of arrogant, imperial rulers. The Aztecs had learned the art of terror as a political instrument and regularly staged elaborate public ceremonies in Tenochtitlan to which subject leaders were invited. It was then that the ruler displayed his fabulous wealth and when many sacrificial victims died, marched in lines to the summit of the great temple. They were laid over a sacrificial stone and their still-beating hearts ripped out with a sharp obsidian knife, to be smeared against the image of Huitzilopochtli or Tlaloc (Figure 11.12). The still twitching body was tumbled down the pyramid steps, where it was dismembered and parts of it sometimes consumed in private rituals. No one knows exactly how many people were sacrificed annually throughout the Aztec empire, but Cortes' secretary estimated about 20,000 people, a figure that has been widely accepted, but which may be too high.

The Aztecs have acquired a formidable reputation because of their penchant for human sacrifice and cannibalism. That they were addicted to human sacrifice is certain, the cannibalism less so. Some believe that Aztec nobles ate human flesh to compensate for a lack of meat in their diet, but the beans they ate as a staple were more than sufficient as a protein source. It seems more likely that Aztec nobles and priests engaged

Figure 11.12 Human sacrifice. A victim's heart is torn out at the Temple of Huitzilopochtli.

in occasional ritual cannibalism as part of their intensely symbolic religious beliefs.

The Fall of Aztec Civilization

By 1519, Aztec civilization was in danger of being torn apart. The demands for tribute from subject states and from the free people of Tenochtitlan itself became ever larger and more exacting. There may well have been intense philosophical disagreements between the militant priests and warriors, who advocated conquest and human sacrifice, and other more sophisticated Aztecs who believed in a gentler, less aggressive world. It is interesting to speculate what might have happened had Cortes not landed in Mexico. Given the past history of Mesoamerican civilization, it seems likely that Aztec civilization would have collapsed suddenly, to be replaced in due time by another state much like it. In truth, Aztec society had reached a level of complexity that was beyond the capacity of its rulers to control and administer. This level of complexity was something that Old World civilizations had eventually brought under control. We can be certain that the successors of the Aztecs would eventually have done so, too.

The Aztecs were the dominant political force in Mesoamerica when the Spaniards first set foot in what was to become New Spain. From coastal villages in the lowlands, they heard stories of their fabulously wealthy kingdom in the high interior. Soon Hernan Cortes and his army of Spaniards pressed inland, their numbers swelled by Indian warriors from subject kingdoms rebelling against harsh Aztec rule. The supreme ruler, Moctezuma II, had been troubled for some years by constant omens of pending doom and predictions that the Feathered Serpent Quetzalcoatl, traditionally depicted with a white face, would return to claim his homeland. When white-faced Spaniards appeared off the Gulf Coast, Moctezuma assumed immediately that the god had indeed returned—in the very year One Reed that legends predicted.

Thus it was that on November 8, 1519 Hernan Cortes and Moctezuma met on a causeway leading to Tenochtitlan. "Thou hast come to arrive on earth. Thou hast come to govern thy city of Mexico; thou hast come to descend on thy mat . . . which I have guarded for thee. . . . And now it hath been fulfilled; thou hast come," proclaimed the Aztec ruler in puzzled confusion. Once challenged and put on the defensive, Aztec civilization collapsed like a deck of cards. Tenochtitlan fell in 1521. By 1680, the 1.2 million people living in the Aztec heartland had been reduced by smallpox, slavery, war, overwork, and exploitation to a mere 70,000. Mesoamerica as a whole lost between 85 and 95 percent of its indigenous population during that 160-year period. Only a few fragments of the fabulous Mesoamerican cultural tradition survived to become part of the fabric of today's Mexico.

Chapter
12

Andean Civilizations

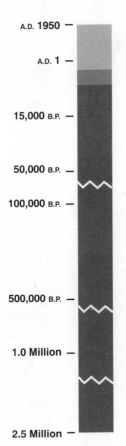

A.D. 1950 —

A.D. 1 —

15,000 B.P. —

50,000 B.P. —

100,000 B.P. —

500,000 B.P. —

1.0 Million —

2.5 Million —

*I*n 1532, Spanish conquistador Francisco Pizarro encountered the Inca empire, a vast preindustrial state known as Tawantinsuyu, The Land of the Four Quarters. Tawantinsuyu was centered in what is now Peru. Its domain extended from high-altitude mountain valleys through plains to foothills to coastal deserts, some of the driest landscapes on earth. This extraordinary state was the culmination of nearly 4,000 years of increasingly complex Andean civilization (Figure 12.1).

THE MARITIME FOUNDATIONS OF ANDEAN CIVILIZATION

Andean civilization evolved in many different ways, for each environment of the highlands and lowlands presented radically different climatic conditions. The rugged central Andean mountains are second only to the Himalayas in height, but only 10 percent of their rainfall descends to the Pacific watershed. The foothill slopes and plains at the western foot of the mountains are mantled by one of the world's driest plains, which extends virtually from the equator to 30 degrees south, much of it along the Peruvian coast. The cultivation of this dry landscape re-

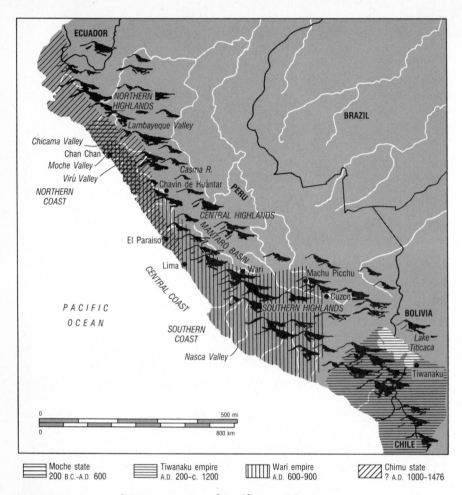

Figure 12.1 Sites and States mentioned in Chapter 12.

quires controlling the runoff from the Andes with large irrigation systems that use long canals built by the coordinated labors of hundreds of people. Only 10 percent of this desert can be farmed, so the inhabitants rely heavily on the Pacific. The richest fishery in the Americas hugs the Pacific shore, yielding a bounty of small schooling fish such as anchovies and also many larger species.

Archaeologist Michael Moseley believes that the unique maritime resources of the Pacific coast provided sufficient calories to support rapidly growing, sedentary populations, which clustered in large communities. In addition, the same food source produced sufficient surplus to permit the construction of large public monuments and temples, work organized by the leaders of newly complex coastal societies.

The Moseley hypothesis runs contrary to conventional archaeological thinking, which regards agriculture as the economic basis for state-organized societies. On the Andean coast, according to Moseley, it was fishing, not agriculture that characterized the society. For thousands of years coastal populations rose and their rise preadapted them to later circumstances, under which they would adopt large-scale irrigation and maize agriculture. Large fish and mollusks were vital resources on the coast, but it may have been anchovies and other small schooling fish that made the critical difference. Anchovies can be easily netted from small canoes throughout the year and could be dried and ground into fine meal. Judging from modern yields, if prehistoric populations had lived at 60 percent of the carrying capacity of the fisheries and eaten nothing but small fish, the coast would have supported more than 6.5 million people. That is not to say that it did, but the figures make the point that the exploitation of small fish would have provided a more than adequate economic base for the emergence of complex hunter-gatherer societies on the coast.

Moseley believes that the reliance on maritime resources led to large, densely concentrated populations, whose leaders were able to organize the labor forces needed not only for building large ceremonial centers but also for transforming river valleys with sizable irrigation schemes. Under this scenario, large-scale farming was in the hands of a small number of individuals, who took advantage of existing simple technology and local populations to create new economies. The transformation, based as it was on maize agriculture and a maritime diet, acted as a kick for radical changes in Andean society.

The main criticisms of the Moseley hypothesis come from those who argue that large coastal settlements could not have been supported by maritime resources alone. Most of these critiques tend to ignore the abundance of anchovy, which has only recently been recognized as being the important staple that it was. The critics also point to the El Niño phenomenon, periodic changes in Pacific currents that reduce the fisheries to a shadow of their normal selves for several years at a time. In fact, Moseley responds, El Niño brings unfamiliar fish species to the coast, albeit in smaller numbers, as well as violent rainfall.

Overall, the maritime foundations hypothesis has stood the test of time well, provided that it is seen as a component in a much broader evolutionary process. The same process of cultural change took place inland, in the highlands, and elsewhere where the width of the coastal shelf prevented extensive anchovy fishing. What was of critical importance, according to archaeologist Richard Burger, is that changing dietary patterns increased demand among highland farmers for coastal products. These included salt, fish, and seaweed. Seaweed is rich in iodine and was an important medicine in the highlands, used to combat endemic goiter and other conditions. The formation of states in both lowlands and highlands may have been fostered by continuous, often highly localized interchanges between the coast and interior.

THE RISE OF COMPLEX SOCIETY (2500 B.C. to 1800 B.C.)

Sometime between 2500 and 1800 B.C., maize agriculture came to the Peruvian coast. Many fishing villages were now relocated inland, by which time some of them were much larger communities with highly organized social institutions and temple mounds as much as 80 feet (24 m) high. These seven centuries saw new religious beliefs permeate Andean societies. They manifested themselves in a wave of monumental construction in both lowlands and highlands.

By 2400 B.C., the inhabitants of the Casma Valley on the coast were building the huge stone-faced platform of Sechin Alto. The mound — 130 feet high (40-m), nearly 1000 feet (300 m) long, and over 800 feet (250 m) wide — formed the base of a huge U-shaped ceremonial center with sunken courts, plazas, and flanking mounds. A vast sprawl of houses and platforms lies around this ceremonial center, the largest on the coast. The center was elaborately decorated.

El Paraiso (c. 1800 B.C.)

The shrines at Sechin Alto employ one of the persistent themes of ceremonial architecture in the Andes and on the coast, that of artificially raising or lowering sacred spaces relative to one another. People entered the forecourt of a sacred complex at ground level, descended into a sunken court, and then climbed to the summit of the temple platform. The U-shaped architecture so characteristic of early Andean temples was part of this theme. It is well represented at El Paraiso, located near the mouth of the Chillon River near Lima (Figure 12.2). This vast site consists of at least six large buildings constructed of roughly shaped stone blocks cemented with unfired clay and grouped around elongated U-shaped patios. The people painted the polished clay-faced outer walls in brilliant hues. Each complex consisted of a square building surrounded by tiers of platforms reached by stone and clay staircases. The largest is more than 830 feet (250 m) long and 166 feet (50 m) wide, standing more than 30 feet (10 m) above the plain. The rooms were covered with matting roofs supported by willow posts.

El Paraiso's vaguely U-shaped layout coincides with the appearance of similarly shaped ceremonial centers in the interior, at a time when coastal peoples began to consume much larger quantities of maize and potatoes, to make pottery, and to shift their settlements inland to fertile river valleys. Perhaps these developments coincided with the introduction of large-scale canal irrigation to grow not only maize but also cotton for fine textiles, a staple of lowland-highland trade.

These were the seven centuries when Andean society became more complex. The many ceremonial centers on the coast suggest that different kin groups commemorated their identities by erecting their own shrines, perhaps competing with one another in doing so. There were probably

Figure 12.2 El Paraiso.

several larger domains extending over several river valleys, such as the Casma Valley, but the identity of those who ruled them is a mystery.

CHAVIN DE HUANTAR (900 B.C. to 200 B.C.)

Chavin de Huantar lies in a small valley 10,170 feet (3100 m) above sea level, midway between the Pacific coast and tropical rainforest. The climate is wet and the soils are well suited to growing maize, potatoes, and other crops. The local farmers had access to several distinct ecological zones, all within easy walking distance. There were irrigated fields in the valley bottoms, potato gardens on the slopes, and high altitude grasslands for grazing llamas and alpacas.

Between about 850 and 550 B.C., Chavin de Huantar was but a small shrine, located at a strategic river crossing point for routes from the Andes to the coast. By 500 B.C. the town was growing rapidly. It eventually covered about 103 acres (42 ha), with a resident population of between 2,000 and 3,000 people. Chavin de Huantar was now a major religious shrine and a highly organized trade and production center where artisans manufactured ceramics and all manner of ritual objects.

The Old Temple is a group of rectangular buildings, some standing up to 40 feet (12 m) high. The U-shaped temple, inspired, almost certainly, by El Paraiso and other ancient architectural traditions of the coast, encloses a rectangular court on three sides, but is open to the east, the direction of the forest and the sunrise. Inside, the buildings are a maze of passages, galleries, and small rooms, ventilated with numerous small shafts. The effect is somewhat like a labyrinth, a tangle of stone-walled, narrow defiles and chambers with stone-slab roofs.

No one knows what rituals unfolded in the depths of the Old Temple, in the presence of the white granite monolith in a cruciform chamber near the central axis of the oldest part of the shrine. The lancelike figure stands on its original position, perhaps erected before the building was constructed around it. Some 15 feet (4.5 m) high, it depicts an anthropomorphic being. The eyes gaze upward, the feline mouth with its great fangs snarls. The left arm is by the side, the right raised, with clawlike nails.

Figure 12.3 Artist's rendering of the "Lanzon" figure, Chavin de Huantar.

Snarling felines stare in profile from the elaborate headdress. A girdle of small feline heads surrounds the waist. This is the famous Lanzon (Lance), so-named on account of its elongated shape. Its pose is that of a mediator between opposing forces, as a link between the living and spiritual worlds (Figure 12.3).

Chavin Art and Ideology

Chavin art is dramatic, strangely exotic, filled with mythical and living beasts and snarling humans. The imagery is compelling, some of the finest from prehistoric America, an art style with a strong Amazonian flavor. Chavin de Huantar lies high in the Andes, but the animals in its shrines are jaguars and caymans, snakes, and tropical birds. Most of the Chavin animals come not from the Andes but from the humid tropical forest on the eastern slopes of the mountains. Powerful beliefs from lowland Amazon cosmology came to Chavin, perhaps through the journeys of highland shamans into exotic forest environments, where they communed with people schooled in very different spiritual worlds, acquiring unfamiliar knowledge in the process.

The exterior walls of the temple at Chavin de Huantar were once decorated with intricately carved stone heads of beings that were part-human, part-feline. Writhing serpents often formed their hair and eye-brows. They present the stages of drug-induced transformation that a shaman underwent from human to jaguar or other mythical beast (Figure 2.1). Some sculptures depict contorted faces with round eyes and copious mucus flowing from their nostrils. Two other groups of portraits show humans in process of transformation into animals, and the head of a jaguar with mucus dripping from its nostrils. It is the green, slimy mucus that gives the clue, for the irritation of the nasal membrane by hallucinogenic snuff is a characteristic sign of a mind-altering trance. "They take these powders, and put them in their noses and which, because they are pungent, make the mucus flow until it hangs down to the mouth, which they observe in the mirror, and when it runs straight down it is a good sign," wrote seventeenth-century Friar Pedro Simon of the Muisca Indians of Columbia.

Chavin ideology centered on the relationship between jaguars and humans. It was an ideology born of both exotic tropical forest and coastal beliefs, one so powerful that it spawned a lively, exotic art style that spread rapidly over a wide area of the highlands and arid coast. Chavin was also the catalyst for many technological advances throughout the Andean area, among them the painting of textiles, many of which served as wall hangings with their ideological message writ large in vivid colors. These powerful images, in clay, wood, and gold, on textiles and in stone, commemorated the complex symbolism of age-old beliefs centered around a pantheon of mythical and actual beasts. They were a powerful unifying factor in later Andean society.

IRRIGATION AGRICULTURE

The development of irrigation agriculture on the coast involved hundreds, if not thousands, of people. At first each family may have irrigated its own sloping gardens at the edge of the valley. Organized irrigation perhaps began as many minor cooperative works between individual families and neighboring villages. These simple projects eventually evolved into elaborate public works that embraced entire inland valleys. Those who organized such works and controlled trade became powerful rulers. They lived in large ceremonial centers such as El Paraiso and Huaca Florida 8 miles (121.8 km) inland, built somewhat later in 1700 B.C.

Huaca Florida consists of an imposing mound of adobe and boulders, a great platform more than 840 feet (252 m) long, 180 feet (54 m) wide, and 100 feet (30 m) high. The site lies in the midst of an artificial environment created by large-scale irrigation. It was maize agriculture more than fishing that supported this inland settlement. Perhaps the rulers devised a forerunner of the *mit'a* tax employed 2,000 years later by the Inca. *Mit'a* obligated people to work a certain number of days a year for the state, as either construction laborers or farmers. When one labored for the state, pay was given in food and shelter, sometimes in the form of a share of the yield from state land.

MOCHE CIVILIZATION (200 B.C. to A.D. 600)

From the Initial period on, the Andean region witnessed an extraordinary array of state-organized societies that displayed a remarkable diversity of culture, art, organization, and religious belief.

One such state was that of the Moche, which originated in the Chicama and Moche valleys in about 200 B.C. By this time, irrigation works had developed on a very large scale on the coast, so much so that some settlements covered more than a square mile. Much of the cultivated land lay along the terraced edges of the valley, where the soils were better drained and easily planted with simple wooden digging sticks, just as they are to this day. Just like today, the farmers must have diverted seasonal flood waters into side canals by building dams of stakes and boulders into the streams. Moche irrigation canals wound along the sides of the valleys, a series of narrow channels approximately 4 feet (1.2 m) wide, set in loops and S-shaped curves, watering plots approximately 70 feet (21.3 m) square.

Like other ancient American states, Moche society was headed by a tiny but immensely powerful and wealthy elite, who lived at imposing centers marked by enormous adobe brick mounds and platforms. At Sipan about 420 miles (680 km) northwest of Lima, Peruvian archaeologist Walter Alva uncovered an unlooted burial chamber in an adobe platform which contained a plank coffin and the skeleton of a man in his thirties lying on his back with his arms along his sides. The Lord of Sipan wore gold nose and ear ornaments, gold and turquoise bead bracelets, and copper sandals. A ceremonial rattle, crescent-shaped knives, scepters, spears, and exotic seashells surrounded the body. Three young women, each about 18 years old, lay at the head and foot of the coffin, two males in their mid-thirties on either side. A dog, two sacrificial llamas, and hundreds of clay vessels lay in the grave. Archaeologist Christopher Donnan has identified the man as a warrior priest. Such individuals are shown on Moche vessels presiding over sacrifices of prisoners of war. They served as war leaders and formed a powerful elite in Moche society.

In the earliest level of the same platform, Alva has also unearthed the richly decorated burial of an even earlier warrior priest, an older man with a gold funerary mask, a magnificent necklace of golden spiders atop their webs, and a gilded copper crab effigy of a deity more than 2 feet (6 m) tall that was once mounted on a fabric banner.

Beautifully painted and modeled Moche clay vessels tell us much about this society of fisherfolk and farmers. The potters depicted men clubbing seals, women giving birth attended by midwives, wives carrying babies on their backs in shawls and in wooden cradles suspended by nets. Men wore short loincloths or cotton breeches underneath tunics fastened around the waist with colorful woven belts. Women dressed in loose tunics that reached the knee, went bareheaded or draped a piece of cotton cloth around their heads. The potters also showed artisans at work and priests wearing puma-skin headdresses and with felinelike fangs set in their mouths.

Without question, the Moche elite ruled not only on account of their exceptional spiritual powers but by force. Moche paintings show a ruler with a fine feather headdress seated on a pyramid, while a line of naked prisoners parades before him. A decapitated sacrifice at the base of one painting reminds us that human sacrifice may have been their fate. There are warriors, too, complete with shields and war clubs, well-padded helmets, and colorful cotton uniforms, sometimes charging their opponents with raised clubs.

The Moche people were remarkable not only for their fine pottery, but also for their metalwork. The coastal people had been expert metalworkers for some time, but the Moche carried the art of metallurgy to new heights. They panned for gold in streambeds, then hammered it into fine sheets and embossed it to make raised designs. Moche smiths learned how to anneal gold, making it possible to soften the metal and then hammer it into more elaborate forms. They used gold as a setting for turquoise and shell ornaments, crafted crowns, circlets, necklaces, pins, and tweezers.

When possible, the Moche extended their ambitious irrigation schemes to link several neighboring river valleys and then constructed lesser centers as a basis for secure administration of their new domains. Moche influence extended far south beyond the core area and their traders were in contact with the north and the southern Peruvian coast as well.

In about A.D. 600, the Moche people moved their center of administrative activity north to the Lambayeque Valley. By this time, their southern centers had been abandoned, perhaps as a result of drought and El Niño flooding, as the political and economic influence of the southern highlands and coast rose.

TIWANAKU AND HUARI (?A.D. 200 to c. 1200)

The Moche civilization did not flourish in isolation, for there were other powerful kingdoms on the coast and in the highlands at the same time. By A.D. 600, as Moche civilization was in decline, the rulers of Tiwanaku near Lake Titicaca at the southern end of the central Andes became a dominant force in the Andean world.

The high, flat country around Lake Titicaca, often called the Altiplano, is fine llama country. The local people maintained enormous herds of these beasts of burden and were also expert irrigation farmers. They reclaimed swamplands and turned them into raised fields where they harvested several crops of potatoes a year. These plots were surrounded with small canals, which protected them from the harsh frosts that ruined crops on dry lands. (It is interesting to note that raised-field agriculture was forgotten when Tiwanaku collapsed in about A.D. 1000, and only reintroduced when archaeologists showed the local people how the ancients had cultivated the soil.)

By A.D. 200, Tiwanaku on the eastern side of Lake Titicaca was a major population center and an important economic and religious focus for the region (Figure 12.4). Four centuries later, Tiwanaku controlled

Figure 12.4 A great sunken court at Tiwanaku, Bolivia.

much of the trade between the highlands and the southern coast. Its llama caravans carried textiles, wool, and other products along well-trodden routes to the Pacific.

Tiwanaku itself centered around the great enclosure of Kalasasaya, dominated by a large earth platform faced with stones. Nearby, a rectangular enclosure is bounded with a row of upright stones and there is a doorway carved with an anthropomorphic god, believed to be the creator deity, Viracocha. The art that adorns Tiwanaku incorporates a powerful iconography (pictorial representation of any topic). Jaguars and eagles and anthropomorphic gods are attended by lesser deities or messengers. Similar motifs occur over much of southern Peru, also in Bolivia and the southern Andes. Tiwanaku's religious beliefs, delivered by compelling iconography, went hand-in-hand with its economic and political power. Such was her rulers' influence that there was a serious political vacuum in the south after A.D. 1200, when the great center inexplicably collapsed into obscurity.

Huari in the Ayacuchu region to the north is another important ceremonial center that stands on a hill, associated with huge stone walls and many dwellings that cover several square miles. Like their southern neighbors, the Huari people seem to have revered a Viracocha-like being. By A.D. 800, their domains extended from Moche country in the Lambayeque Valley on the north coast into the highlands south of Cuzco. The Huari leaders were expert traders, who probably expanded their domains through conquest, commercial enterprise, and perhaps religious conversion.

Both Huari and Tiwanaku vanished at the end of the first millennium A.D., but they were a turning point in Andean history, being the first states that controlled peoples living in dramatically different highland and lowland environments. Their rulers held sway over many small regional states, which they conquered and integrated into much larger empires. By controlling major trade routes and careful manipulation of powerful religious iconographies, the leaders of both states were able to forge much larger political units out of smaller ones. These processes of integration and interaction were to intensify in later centuries.

CHIMU CIVILIZATION (?A.D. 1000 to 1476)

The collapse of the Moche state left a political vacuum on the north coast. Eventually, the Chimu became the dominant force in the rich and fertile Lambayeque Valley. The Chimu inherited ancient traditions of kingship and empire and refined them still further. Their rulers were probably the descendants of the once-powerful Moche nobles whose silent *huacas* (shrines) dotted the sandy coastal plain. They chose to live at Chan Chan, close to the Pacific (Figure 12.5).

As always on the coast, the first priority was a secure food supply.

Figure 12.5 Chan Chan, the Chimu capital.

Beginning in about 850, the lords of Chimor invested heavily in an elaborate complex of sunken gardens, which extended inland from the ocean for 3 miles (5 km). They also used *mita* labor to build enormous canal systems that watered flatlands north and west of the city. So effective were these irrigation works that the Chimu controlled more than 12 river valleys, all of them farmed with hoes and digging sticks. After 1200, land reclamation near Chan Chan itself required too much labor, so Chimor sought to acquire land by conquest. Eventually, the lords of Chan Chan controlled more than 700 miles (1,126 km) of the north coast.

At the height of its power, Chan Chan's urban sprawl covered more than 4 square miles (10.2 sq. km). Only nobles, artisans, and other skilled workers lived within the city limits. As many as 26,000 people lived in humble dwellings of mud and cane along the southern and western edges of the civic center, expert metal smiths and weavers for the most part, who intermarried and were buried in separate cemeteries. Another 3,000 lived close to their royal employers' compounds, and some 6,000 nobles and officials occupied detached adobe brick enclosures nearby.

The mud-brick walls of the royal compounds lie in a broken rectangle at the center of Chan Chan. They once stood as high as 33 feet (9.9 m) and covered areas as large as 670 by 2,000 feet (202 by 600 m). The walls were not constructed for defense, but to provide privacy and some shelter from winds sweeping off the Pacific. Each enclosure had its own water supply, a ceremonial precinct that served as the royal burial place, and lavishly decorated residential quarters. The enclosure that served as a royal palace in life became the residence of the same ruler in death.

The Chimu rulers adopted an institution that was to become of paramount importance to their Inca successors — that of split inheritance. This custom had the royal title passing from father to son, while at the same time, the dead leader retained not only his compound, but all his lands and material possessions. Meantime, the new leader had to acquire lands and great wealth for himself, which in turn remained with him after death. This institution gave the Chimu rulers a strong incentive to expand their domains, to embark on wars of conquest and new trading ventures.

The Chimu elite had access to a huge labor pool. They soon learned the value of efficient communications, of officially maintained roadways that enabled them to move their armies rapidly from one place to the next. They constructed roads that connected every valley in their domains. In densely populated valleys, Chimu roads were between 15 and 25 feet (4.5 and 7.5 m) across. These were the roads that carried gold ornaments and fine, hammered vessels to Chimu and textiles and fine, black vessels throughout the empire. The traveler would encounter heavily laden llamas carrying goods to markets and luxuries to Chan Chan, but most loads were carried on peoples' backs, for the Chimu never developed the wheeled cart. All revenues and tribute passed along the official roadways.

For all its wide-ranging military activities and material wealth, the Chimu empire was very vulnerable to attack. The massive irrigation works of the northern river valleys were easily disrupted by an aggressive conqueror, for no leader, however powerful, could hope to fortify the frontiers of an entire empire. The Chimu were vulnerable to prolonged drought, too. Perhaps, too, the irrigated desert soils became too salty for agriculture after many seasons of watering, so that crop yields fell drastically at a time when population densities were rising sharply.

This conquest came at the hands of the Inca of the highlands, who overthrew the leaders of Chan Chan in the 1460s and installed their own puppet ruler instead. Many of Chan Chan's expert gold workers and skilled artisans were taken to Cuzco in the highlands where they worked for the Inca royal court.

INCA CIVILIZATION (?A.D. 1400 to 1534)

Like the Aztecs, the Incas liked to think of themselves as people who had risen from the proverbial rags to riches. They were born into a world of quarrelsome, constantly competing petty chiefdoms, their homeland lying northwest of Lake Titicaca in the area round Cuzco, high in the Andes. They were a small-scale village farming society, organized in kin groups known as *ayllus*, groups claiming a common ancestry and also owning land in common. Each ayllu's land was protected by its ancestors, so the Incas always revered their mummified forebears.

The earliest Inca rulers were probably minor war leaders (*sinchi*), elected officials. To stay in office, they had to be politically and militarily adept so that they could both defeat and appease their potential rivals. The official Inca histories speak of at least eight (probably legendary) rulers between 1200 and 1438. At the beginning of the fifteenth century, a sinchi named Viracocha Inca rose to power. Unlike his predecessors, he turned from raiding neighbors to a strategy of permanent conquest. He soon presided over a small state centered on Cuzco. Viracocha now proclaimed himself a living god, associated with the supreme ancestor, the sun-god.

Split Inheritance

Around 1438, a brilliant warrior named Cusi Inca Yupanqui was crowned Inca. He immediately assumed the name Pachakuti ("He Who Remakes the World") and set about transforming Inca society into a highly centralized state. Pachakuti combined the age-old Andean reverence for the dead and the institution of split inheritance into a new and powerful system of imperial kingship.

According to Inca accounts collected after the Spanish conquest, the new system worked as follows. A dead ruler was mummified. His palace, servants, and possessions were still considered his property and were maintained by all his male descendants except his successor, normally one of his sons. The deceased was not considered dead, however. His mummy attended the great public ceremonies of state and would even pay visits to the houses of the living. Those entrusted to look after the dead Inca ate and talked with him just as if he were alive. This element of continuity was extremely important because it made the royal mummies some of the holiest artifacts in the empire. Dead rulers were visible links with the gods, the very embodiment of the Inca state.

Meanwhile, the ascending ruler was rich in prestige but poor in possessions. The new Inca had to acquire wealth so he could live in perpetual royal splendor during his reign and after death—and the only wealth in the highland kingdom was taxable labor. The split inheritance system meant that all taxes levied by their predecessors went to them and not to the living king. He had to develop a new tax base and could do so only in two ways: by levying more labor from existing taxpayers or by conquering new lands. Since the Inca rulers needed land to provide food for those who worked for them and the earlier kings owned most of the land near Cuzco, the only way a new Inca could obtain his own royal estates was by expansion into new territory. The conquest had to be permanent, the conquered territory controlled and taxed, and everyone had to be convinced the conquest was worthwhile. A highly complicated system of benefits, economic incentives, rewards, and justifications fueled and nourished the Inca conquests.

Conquest and Administration

These successful ideologies provided a critical advantage for the Incas over their neighbors. Within a decade of Pachakuti's accession, they were masters of the southern highlands. In less than a century the tiny kingdom taken over by Pachakuti had become a vast empire. Topa Yupanqui (1471–1493) extended the Inca Empire into Ecuador, northern Argentina, parts of Bolivia, and Chile. His armies annexed the Chimu state, whose waters Topa already controlled. Another king, Huanya Capac, ruled for 34 years after Topa Inca and pushed the empire deeper into Ecuador.

The Incas divided the resulting Land of the Four Quarters into four provinces, known as *suyu* (quarters), each divided in turn into smaller subdivisions, some of them coinciding with the boundaries of conquered states. All the important government posts in their highly stratified society were held by Inca-born nobles with close ties to the Inca himself. Conquered peoples within the empire were ruled by leading members of local families, a form of secondary nobility. In this way, the Inca left much administration in local hands, while retaining the real strings of power in their own hands.

The Inca rulers realized that the essence of efficient government in such varied environments and landscapes was an effective road system. Their road engineers commandeered a vast network of centuries-old Indian highways from the states they conquered. They linked them in a coordinated system with rest houses at regular intervals so that they could move armies, trade goods, and send messengers from one end of the empire to the other in short order (Figure 12.6). Indeed, it was said after the Spanish conquest that runners could take a message from Cuzco to Lima along Inca roads faster than a European messenger on horseback.

All this organization, and the sheer volume of tribute, taxed labor, and trade, required an accurate record keeping system. The Incas relied not on a written script, but on knotted strings, or *quipus*. These *quipus* were a complex and sophisticated record-keeping system that was so efficient that it more than made up for the lack of writing. They were not only the computers of Inca life, but were invaluable for enforcing social conformity, codifying laws, and providing data for tax inspectors, who regularly visited each household to ensure that everyone was engaged in productive work and living in sanitary conditions. Everything about the Inca lifeway stressed conformity and the need to obey and respect the Inca and the central government.

NOBIENBRE
AIA·MARCAI
quilla
la fiesta delos defuntos

Figure 12.6 Inca ancestor worship. Seventeenth-century Native Andean chronicler Felipe Guaman Poma de Ayala.

The Collapse of the Inca Empire

At the time of the Spanish Conquest, the Incas controlled the lives of as many as 6 to 12 million people, most of them living in small villages dispersed around religious and political centers. But despite its glittering facade of fine buildings, gold, and silver, Tawantinsuyu was ripe for collapse by the 1520s (Figure 12.7). One villain was the very institution of split inheritance that fueled constant military conquest. The need for more and more conquests caused great military, economic, and administrative stress. Moreover, although Inca tactics were well adapted to open country, where their armies were invincible, the rulers eventually had to start fighting in forest country, where they fared badly. Meanwhile, the empire had grown so large that communication with the center of government at Cuzco became a lengthier and lengthier process, compounded by the great diversity of people living within the Inca domain (Figure 12.8). Also, the increasing number of high ranking nobles devoted to dead rulers' interests led to constant quarreling over the succession and other critical policy matters that further weakened the empire.

In the end, the Inca Empire was overthrown by chronic factional quarreling, civil war, and by a combination of devastating smallpox epidemics and outside interference. In 1532, a small party of rapacious Spanish conquistadors led by Francisco Pizarro landed on the coast of northern Peru. When Pizarro arrived, the Inca state happened to be in political disarray, its people already decimated by epidemics of smallpox introduced by the very first Spanish visitors some years earlier. Huanya

Figure 12.7 Inca architecture was based on closely fitted stone blocks. They were moved by human hands as Andean llamas could only carry loads of about 100 pounds (45 kg).

Figure 12.8 Machu Picchu, an Inca settlement high in the Andes.

Capac had died in such an epidemic in 1525, plunging the empire into a civil war between his sons Atahuallpa and Huascar. Atahuallpa prevailed and was journeying to Cuzco when he met Pizarro.

The Spaniards were bent on plunder and conquest. Pizarro captured Atahuallpa by treachery, ransomed him for a roomful of gold, and then brutally murdered him. A year later, the Spaniards captured Cuzco with a tiny army. They took over the state bureaucracy and appointed Manco Inca as puppet ruler. Three years later, he turned on his new masters in a bloody revolt. Its ruthless suppression finally destroyed the greatest of the Andean empires.

Chapter
13

Epilog

Our journey through the long millennia of prehistory ends on the very threshold of modern times. It ends with the so-called Age of Discovery that saw European explorers sailing ever further from their homeland, in search of gold and spices, to serve God, or simply out of compelling curiosity.

Western Europe was born three thousand years ago. For thousands of years it had been a geographical outpost of Asia, on the fringes of civilizations and empires based in the Near East and Mediterranean lands. Twenty-five centuries ago, Europe became a western peninsula with a consciousness and identity all its own. This consciousness was born of Greek civilization, and matured still further in much later European victories against Huns, Turks, and Moors. It was a Christian peninsula, driven by doctrines that encouraged a deep sense that the individual was as important as the state. A growing sense of individualism and adventure bred an intense curiosity about the outside world. What peoples lived south of the endless sands of the Sahara Desert? Were there distant lands beyond the boundless horizons of the western ocean?

During the 1420s and 1430s, Henry the Navigator, Prince of Portugal, organized annual voyages of exploration southward from Europe deep into tropical latitudes. His captains coasted down the west coast of Africa and rounded the great western bulge in 1433. Then, in 1488, Bartolemeu Dias rounded the southern tip of Africa. He came in contact with the Khoi Khoi, simple cattle herders who appeared to wander aimlessly with their herds. The Khoi Khoi made a profound impression on the Western mind, for they appeared more primitive in their customs than any other people on earth. For centuries, the Khoi Khoi were thought of as half-apes, half-humans, lower on the Great Chain of Being than other human beings. They vanished a mere 70 years after European settlement at the Cape of Good Hope in 1652, their herding adaptation destroyed by encroaching white farmers.

Dias was followed by Vasco da Gama in 1497, who sailed up the east African coast to what is now Kenya, then followed the trade winds to India. Thus, Europeans found an alternative route to the rich gold and spice markets of south and southeast Asia. They sailed along ancient seaborne roots that linked Africa, with its seemingly inexhaustible exports of gold, ivory, and slaves, with markets that had an insatiable demand for such commodities. In the centuries that followed, Africa was exploited for human and material wealth not only by European nations, but by Islam. The burgeoning international slave trade decimated African populations far from the continent's familiar coastlines. European explorers did not penetrate the far interior until the nineteenth century, by which time Africa was already part of a vast and complex world economic system.

As Dias and da Gama explored African shores, so did Christopher Columbus sail west to the "Indies" in 1492. He thought he was at the threshold of Asia. In fact he revealed a New World teeming with new species of animals and plants and a great diversity of American Indian societies. As we have seen, the great civilizations of Mexico and Peru collapsed rapidly in the face of the conquistadors, while epidemics of smallpox and other exotic diseases decimated native American populations within a few generations of the first European visitors wherever they appeared.

With the rounding of the Cape of Good Hope and the discovery of the Americas, the final chapter of human prehistory began, a complex and long drawn-out clash between increasingly elaborate Western civilization and a myriad of non-Western societies in all parts of the world. The basic scenario was relived again and again. A small party of European explorers would arrive, as did Captain James Cook in Tahiti and New Zealand, or French voyager Marion du Fresne in Tasmania, Australia. Almost invariably the first encounter was a fleeting kaleidoscope of curiosity, sometimes horrified fascination, and often romantic excitement. Sometimes spears were thrown and muskets fired. At others there was friendly trading of furs for cheap glass beads and other trinkets. Almost invariably, however, there was total incomprehension on both sides.

Sometimes the people thought that their strange visitors were gods, as did Moctezuma with Hernan Cortes at the gates of Tenochtitlan. An elderly Maori chief in New Zealand told a nineteenth-century official that the priests had told him the whites were spirits with eyes in the backs of their heads, an apparent reference to Cook's oarsmen facing the stern in their boats. All too soon, and wherever they appeared, the strangers proved not to be gods, but to be only too human — aggressive, warlike, and acquisitive.

At first the contacts were brief ones. But soon Europeans came in larger numbers to trade for furs, to refit their ships, or to search for gold. Then the missionaries arrived, seeking to convert the heathen and to save their souls. Australia became a dumping ground for convicts, many of whom escaped and brutalized Australian aboriginal groups. In many places the early visitors were followed by a flood of colonists, often impoverished, land hungry farmers from Europe who sought a better life in the fertile soils of the African interior, British Columbia, New Zealand, or Tasmania.

These were permanent residents, people with iron tools and firearms in search of new homes and lush acreage. They competed with the indigenous populations for prime land, elbowing them aside, sometimes hunting them down, or often acquiring large farms through shady land sales or illegal treaties. Almost inevitably, the indigenous population lost their land, territory that had often been vested in the same kin groups for centuries, if not millennia. They had few options open to them, except to retreat onto remote, marginal lands where they preserved a shadow of their former culture and lifeway, if they were able to survive at all. The only alternative was to assimilate themselves into the newcomers' society, where they almost always lived on the margins, often employed as agricultural laborers or domestic servants.

The spread of Western civilization around the world has accelerated dramatically since the Industrial Revolution of the late eighteenth century. This revolution was another catalyst in human history, which created industrial societies driven not by human hands but by fossil fuels. It fostered insatiable demands for raw materials of all kinds, gave birth to the steamship and the railroad, and led to large-scale human migrations from Europe to America, from Asia to all parts of the Pacific and North America on an unprecedented scale. The mass population movements of recent times have had catastrophic effects on non-Western societies large and small.

Today, there are no parts of the world where prehistoric lifeways survive untouched by modern civilization. There are a handful of groups deep in the Amazon Basin and in highland New Guinea who have still not come into sustained contact with industrial civilization. These are endangered societies, as rainforests are felled and landscapes modified beyond recognition by the insatiable maw of industrial civilization. To all intents and purposes, however, the prehistoric world, which began over 2.5 million years ago in Africa, has vanished into near-oblivion except insofar as we know it from modern scientific research.

Guide to Further Reading

The references that follow have been selected as ways of exploring the topics covered in this short book in more detail. The emphasis is on general works, all of which contain comprehensive bibliographies that summarize the specialist literature. For more detailed information, please consult one of the major summaries listed here or ask a specialist. The emphasis here is on English-language sources, simply because most readers are English-speaking.

GENERAL WORKS AND JOURNALS

Two major college texts offer more comprehensive summaries of world prehistory. My *People of the Earth*, 7th ed. (New York: HarperCollins, 1992) is a much expanded version of this book. Robert Wenke's *Patterns in Prehistory*, 2nd ed. (New York: Oxford University Press, 1984) has an authoritative evolutionary perspective. John Gowlett, *Ascent to Civilization* (New York: Random House, 1992) is excellent for the Stone Age.

The best atlas of archaeology for the general reader is Chris Scarre (ed.), *Past Worlds: The Times Atlas of Archaeology* (London: Times Books, 1988). A good dictionary: Warwick Bray and David Trump, *A Dictionary of Archaeology* (London: Penguin Press, 1970).

There are dozens of local, national, and international journals that cover the subject matter of this book, most of them aimed at specialists. Among those carrying popular articles are *National Geographic Magazine*, *Natural History*, *Smithsonian*, and *Scientific American*. *Archaeology* is a lively magazine for enthusiast, traveler, and professional archaeologist alike. *Antiquity*, *The Journal of World Prehistory*, and *World Archaeology* carry articles of wide interest to serious archaeologists and informed lay people. American archaeologists rely heavily on *American Antiquity* and *American Anthropologist*. Old World archaeologists often publish in *Man* and the *Proceedings of the Prehistoric Society*, while the latest hominid discoveries often appear in *Nature* or *Science*. *The Journal of Field Archaeology* is of high technical value and often contains definitive field reports.

Chapter 1: The Study of World Prehistory

The history of archaeology is widely accessible through the National Geographic Society's *The Adventure of Archaeology* (Washington, D.C.: National Geographic Society, 1985), also through Glyn Daniel, *A Short History of Archaeology* (New York: Thames and Hudson, 1981). For American archaeology, see Gordon Willey and Jeremy Sabloff, *A History of American Archaeology*, 2nd ed. (New York: W.H. Freeman, 1980). Bruce Trigger's *A History of Archaeological Interpretation* (Cambridge: Cambridge University Press, 1989) is definitive.

Method and theory in archaeology are well covered in a series of widely available college texts. These include the companion volume to this work, my *Archaeology: A Brief Introduction*, 4th ed. (New York: HarperCollins, 1991) and a more comprehensive treatment: *In the Beginning*, 7th ed. (New York: HarperCollins, 1991). Robert Sharer and Wendy Ashmore, *Archaeology: Discovering the Past*, 2nd ed. (Palo Alto: Mayfield, 1990) is another useful text. Paul Bahn and Colin Renfrew, *Archaeology* (New York: Thames and Hudson, 1991), is a magisterial handbook of archaeological method and theory that is an essential reference book for any serious student of the past. James Deetz' brief *Invitation to Archaeology* (Garden City, NY: Natural History Press, 1967) is an eloquent, minor classic of archaeology.

Chapter 2: Explaining Prehistory

All the references cited under Chapter 1 will be helpful here, especially Bruce Trigger's *History of Archaeological Interpretation*. Gordon Willey and Phillip Phillips, *Method and Theory in American Archaeology* (Chicago: University of Chicago Press, 1958) is the fundamental work on culture history, especially when combined with V. Gordon Childe, *Piecing Together the Past* (London: Routledge and Kegan Paul, 1956). Later developments in archaeology can be explored with the aid of Lewis Binford's *In Pursuit of the Past* (New York: Thames and Hudson, 1983). A magnificent assessment of contemporary American archaeology appears in David Meltzer, Don Fowler, and Jeremy Sabloff (eds.), *American Archaeology Past and Future* (Washington D.C.: Smithsonian Institution Press, 1986).

The literature of theoretical archaeology is enormous. Anyone navigating through these shark-infested academic waters should read Guy Gibbon's *Anthropological Archaeology* (New York: Columbia University Press, 1984) and P.J. Watson, Steven A. LeBlanc, and C.L. Redman, *Archaeological Explanation* (New York: Columbia University Press, 1984). For evolutionary archaeology and a critique of recent archaeological theory, see Steven Mithen, "Evolutionary Theory and post-processual archaeology," *Antiquity* 63(1989):483–494.

Chapter 3: Origins

The literature is enormous and sometimes polemical. John Pfeiffer, *The Emergence of Man*, 3rd ed. (New York: HarperCollins, 1983) is somewhat outdated, but offers an excellent historical survey for the lay reader. So does Roger Lewin, *Bones of Contention* (New York: Simon and Schuster, 1987). The same author's *Human Evolution*, 2nd ed. (Oxford: Blackwell Scientific Publications, 1990) offers an excellent summary of what we know about human evolution. Donald Johanson and Maitland Edey, *Lucy: The Beginnings of Humankind* (New York: Simon and Schuster) is an excellent popular account of the Hadar finds.

At a more technical level, Robert Foley (ed.), *Hominid Evolution and Community Ecology* (London: Academic Press, 1984) offers some extremely intelligent essays on early human evolution. Nicholas Toth and K.D. Schick, "The First Million Years: The Archaeology of Protohuman Culture," *Advances in Archaeological Method and Theory* 9(1986):1–96, is an excellent summary of recent thinking on the archaeology of human origins. Richard Klein, *The Human Career* (Chicago: University of Chicago Press, 1989) is an advanced, noncommittal text.

Chapter 4: Out of Africa

There are few general summaries of the long millennia covered by this chapter, except for the outdated account in John Pfeiffer's *Emergence of Man*, which is particularly good on the controversies over big-game hunting. My *The Journey from Eden* (New York: Thames and Hudson, 1990) is a more recent popular account of the origins of modern humans, which also discusses earlier developments.

More specialist contributions include J. Desmond Clark and Jack Harris, "Fire and Its Roles in Early Hominid Lifeways," *African Archaeological Review* 3(1985):3–28, and F. Clark Howell and J. Desmond Clark, *Acheulian Hunter-Gatherers of Sub-Saharan Africa* (New York: Viking Fund Publications, 36). See also F. Clark Howell, "Observations on the Earlier Phases of the European Lower Palaeolithic," *American Anthropologist* 68(2)(1966):111–140. Robert Foley, "Hominid Species and Stone-Tool Assemblages: How Are They Related?" *Antiquity* 61(1987):380–392 is a provocative essay on the relationship between stone tools and biological evolution. For bamboo and archaic humans, Geoffrey Pope,

"Bamboo and Human Evolution," *Natural History* 10(89):49–56. Chris Stringer and Paul Mellars (eds.) *The Human Revolution*, 2 vols. (Edinburgh: Edinburgh University Press, 1989, 1990) provides authoritative essays on the controversies surrounding the origins of modern humans, including an important essay by Gunter Brauer, whose work is cited in our narrative. Anthony Marks, "The Middle to Upper Palaeolithic Transition in the Levant," *Advances in World Archaeology* 2(1983):51–98 covers the technological changeover associated with modern humans.

Chapter 5: Diaspora

The Journey from Eden carries a basic summary of the material in this chapter, which can be amplified from numerous references of both a general and more specialist nature. Australia and New Guinea are well summarized by J. Peter White and James O'Connell, *A Prehistory of Australia, New Guinea, and Sahul* (Sydney: Academic Press, 1982). However, this is somewhat outdated by new discoveries, well summarized by Jim Allen, "When did Humans first Colonize Australia?" *Search* 20,5(1989):149–154. The Cro-Magnons have been described by many popular authors. Randall White, *Dark Caves and Bright Visions* (New York: American Museum of Natural History, 1986) is a useful summary, especially when amplified by Paul Bahn and Jean Vertut, *Images of the Ice Age* (New York: Viking, 1988), which is an invaluable analysis of Stone Age art.

Olga Soffer and Clive Gamble (eds.) *The World in 18,000 B.P.* (Edinburgh: Edinburgh University Press, 1991) contains useful articles on the late Ice Age, as does Soffer's edited *The Pleistocene Old World* (New York: Plenum Press, 1985). The same author's monograph *The Upper Palaeolithic of the Central Russian Plains* (New York: Academic Press, 1985) describes Mezhirich in detail. For the controversies surrounding the first settlement of the Americas and the Clovis people, see Brian Fagan, *The Great Journey* (New York: Thames and Hudson, 1987). Some recent essays on the same subject appear in Tom Dillehay and David Meltzer (eds.), *The First Americans: Search and Research* (Boca Raton: CRC Press, 1991).

Chapter 6: The First Farmers

This chapter was written from many specialist sources, for there are few general accounts that incorporate fully up-to-date information. For hunter-gatherer archaeology and the issue of social complexity among them, see R.L. Bettinger, "Archaeological Approaches to Hunter-Gatherers," *Annual Review of Archaeology* 16(1987):121–142. Paul Martin and Richard Klein (eds.), *A Pleistocene Revolution* (Tucson: University of Arizona Press, 1984) summarizes evidence for extinction of big-game in many parts of the world. Douglas Price and James Brown (eds.), *Complex-*

ity among Prehistoric Hunter-Gatherers (Orlando: Academic Press, 1985) contains valuable essays on the issue of social complexity. Douglas Price, "The Mesolithic of Western Europe," *Journal of World Prehistory* 1(3)(1987):225–305 describes complex hunter-gatherers in Europe, while Stuart Struever and Felicia Holton, *Koster: Americans in Search of Their Past* (New York: Anchor Books, 1979) is a popular account of that famous site. Further descriptions of Archaic cultures in North America, and of the Chumash Indians of California, can be found in my *Ancient North America* (New York: Thames and Hudson, 1991).

The classic theories surrounding the origins of agriculture are gathered in Stuart Struever's anthology *Prehistoric Agriculture* (Garden City, NY: Natural History Press, 1971). David Rindos, *The Origins of Agriculture: An Evolutionary Perspective* (New York: Academic Press, 1984) summarizes the evolutionary perspective. Kent Flannery et al., *Guila Naquitz* (Orlando: Academic Press, 1986) is essential reading, if nothing else for its hypothetical dialogs, which contain a multitude of wisdoms about archaeology and archaeologists. Andrew Moore, "The Development of Neolithic Societies in the Near East," *Advances in World Archaeology* 4(1985):1–70 contains much of value on Abu Hureyra and is authoritative. European agriculture: Graham Barker, *Prehistoric Farming in Europe* (Cambridge, Eng.: Cambridge University Press, 1985). For American agriculture, see Barbara Stark's "Origins of Food Production in the New World," in David Meltzer, Don Fowler, and Jeremy Sabloff (eds.), *American Archaeology Past and Future*, pp. 277–322 (Washington D.C.: Smithsonian Institution Press, 1986). Richard I. Ford (ed.), *Prehistoric Food Production in North America* (Ann Arber: University of Michigan Museum of Anthropology, 1985) offers insights into the origins of maize and other crops.

Chapter 7: Ocean Voyagers, Pueblos, and Moundbuilders

For Pacific voyaging, the interested reader can do no better than start with David Lewis' fascinating account of traditional Polynesian navigational techniques: *We the Navigators* (Honolulu: University of Hawaii Press). Peter Bellwood, *Man's Settlement of the Pacific* (Oxford, Eng.: Oxford University Press, 1979) and *The Polynesians* (New York: Thames and Hudson, 1979) summarize the first colonization of the Pacific Islands. Patrick V. Kirsch, *The Evolution of the Polynesian Chiefdoms* (New York: Cambridge University Press, 1984) describes complex societies in the Pacific. New Zealand archaeology: Janet Davidson, *The Prehistory of New Zealand* (Auckland: Longman Paul, 1984).

Southwestern archaeology is well analyzed by Linda Cordell, *The Prehistory of the Southwest* (Orlando: Academic Press, 1984). S.H. Wills, *Early Prehistoric Agriculture in the Southwest* (Santa Fe, NM: School of American Research Press, 1989) covers the introduction of maize, as does Richard Ford's *Early Food Production*, already cited. For the Eastern Woodlands, see an excellent summary by Bruce Smith, "The Archaeology of the Southeastern United States: From Dalton to de Soto, 10,500 to 500 B.P.," *Advances in World Archaeology* 5(1986):1–92. Also my *Ancient North America*, Chapters 19 and 20.

Chapter 8: State-Organized Societies

Charles Redman, *The Rise of Civilization: From Early Farmers to Urban Society in the Ancient Near East* (San Francisco: W.H. Freeman, 1978) critiques theories up to the late 1970s. See also: Kent Flannery, "The Cultural Evolution of Civilizations," *Annual Review of Ecology and Systematics* (1972):399–426, and Elizabeth Brumfiel, "Aztec State Making: Ecology, Structure, and the Origin of the State," *American Anthropologist* 85(2)(1983):261–284.

Chapter 9: The Mediterranean World

Two books summarize the Sumerians admirably. Samuel Kramer, *The Sumerians* (Chicago: University of Chicago Press, 1963) is a well-deserved popular classic. Harriett Crawford, *Sumer and the Sumerians* (Cambridge: Cambridge University Press, 1991) is an up-to-date synthesis.

The ancient Egyptians have attracted an enormous literature. Three volumes provide a good general summary. Cyril Aldred, *The Egyptians* 2nd ed. (New York: Thames and Hudson, 1986) is a concise account, while Barry Kemp, *Ancient Egypt: The Anatomy of a Civilization* (London: Routledge, 1989) is destined to become a classic. Nicholas Reeves, *The Complete Tutankhamun* (New York: Thames and Hudson, 1990) is a magnificent tour of the golden Pharaoh's sepulcher.

The Hittites: J.G. MacQueen, *The Hittites* (New York: Thames and Hudson, 1987). For later events, see K.W. Whitelaw and R.B. Coote, *The Emergence of Israel in Historical Perspective.* (Sheffield, Eng.: Almond Press, 1987). The Assyrians are described in Nicholas Postgate, *The First Empires* (Oxford: Phaidon, 1977). The Minoans: Sinclair Hood, *The Minoans.* (New York: Thames and Hudson, 1973). Mycenaean Civilization: Lord William Taylour, *The Mycenaeans*, 2nd ed. (New York: Thames and Hudson, 1990). See also Colin Renfrew, *The Emergence of Civilization* (London: Methuen, 1973).

Chapter 10: Asians and Africans

Mortimer Wheeler, *The Indus Civilization*, 2nd ed. (Cambridge, Eng.: Cambridge University Press, 1962) is still a major source on the Harappan Civilization. Gregory Possehl (ed.), *The Harappan Civilization* (London: Aris and Phillips, 1982) provides an update, as does Bridget and Raymond Allchin, *The Rise of Civilization in India and Pakistan* (Cambridge, Eng.: Cambridge University Press, 1983). Chinese prehistory is well summarized by K-C Chang, *The Archaeology of Ancient China*, 4th ed. (New

Haven, CT: Yale University Press, 1986) and the same author's *Shang Civilization* (New Haven, CT: Yale University Press, 1980) is authoritative. David Keightley (ed.), *The Origins of Chinese Civilization* (Berkeley and Los Angeles: University of California Press, 1983) contains much useful material. Paul Wheatley, "Urban Genesis in Mainland Southeast Asia," in R.B. Smith and W. Watson (eds.), *Early Southeast Asia* (Oxford, Eng: Oxford University Press, 1979), pp. 288–303, deals with the origins of southeast Asian civilization. For southeast Asia generally, Charles Higham, *The Archaeology of Mainland Southeast Asia* (Cambridge, Eng.: Cambridge University Press, 1989).

Roland Oliver, *The African Experience* (London: Weidenfeld and Nicholson, 1991) provides a summary of early African history. More specific works include Graham Connah, *African Civilizations* (Cambridge, Eng.: Cambridge University Press, 1987), Nehemiah Levetzion, *Ancient Ghana and Mali* (London: Methuen, 1971), and Peter Garlake, *Great Zimbabwe* (New York: Thames and Hudson, 1973).

Chapter 11: Mesoamerican Civilizations

A good starting point is Kent Flannery (ed.), *The Early Mesoamerican Village* (New York: Academic Press, 1976), which also contains a rich foundation of wisdom about archaeology generally. For the Olmec, Michael Coe and Richard Diehl, *In the Land of the Olmec* (Austin: University of Texas Press, 1980), also Nick Saunders, *People of the Jaguar* (London: Souvenir Press, 1989), which is excellent on jaguar cults. Teotihuacan is well described in Rene Millon, R.B. Drewitt, and George Cowgill, *Urbanization at Teotihuacan* (Austin: University of Texas Press, 1974), while William Saunders, Jeffrey Parsons, and Robert Santley, *The Basin of Mexico* (New York: Academic Press, 1979) describes the comprehensive archaeological surveys carried out in this highland region.

The Mayan literature is rich and often contradictory. Linda Schele and David Freidel, *A Forest of Kings* (New York: Morrow, 1990) is a popular synthesis of Maya history based on both archaeology and glyphs, which is seminal. Norman Hammond, *Ancient Maya Civilization* (New Brunswick, NJ: Rutgers University Press, 1982), and Jeremy A. Sabloff, *The New Archaeology and the Ancient Maya* (New York: Scientific American Library, 1990) are useful summaries, while the latter's *The Cities of Ancient Mexico* (New York: Thames and Hudson, 1989) provides a guide to major Mesoamerican sites. Michael Coe, *The Maya*, 4th ed. (New York: Thames and Hudson, 1987) is another widely read summary.

The Toltecs are summarized by Richard Diehl, *Tula, the Toltec Capital of Ancient Mexico* (New York: Thames and Hudson, 1983). The Aztecs are analyzed by Geoffrey W. Conrad and Arthur A. Demarest, *Religion and Empire* (Cambridge, Eng.: Cambridge University Press, 1984), their civilization described in Francis Berdan, *The Aztecs of Central Mexico: An Imperial Society* (New York: Holt, Rinehart, and Winston, 1982). Inga

Clendinnon, *Aztecs* (Cambridge: Cambridge University Press, 1991) is a valuable analysis of Aztec history. For the Spanish Conquest, see Charles Dibble and Arthur Anderson, *The Florentine Codex* (Salt Lake City: University of Utah Press, 12 vols., 1950–1975).

Chapter 12: Andean Civilizations

Michael Moseley, *The Incas and Their Ancestors* (New York: Thames and Hudson, 1992) is an excellent summary of Andean archaeology for the general reader. George Bankes, *Peru Before Pizarro* (Oxford, Eng.: Phaidon) is a somewhat outdated but clearly written account. Richard Keatinge (ed.), *Peruvian Prehistory* (Cambridge: Cambridge University Press, 1988) contains useful essays covering the general subject. Christopher Donnan (ed.), *Early Ceremonial Architecture in the Andes* (Washington DC: Dumbarton Oaks, 1985) brings together articles on early architecture on the coast and in the highlands. Richard Burger, *The Prehistoric Occupation of Chavin de Huantar* (Berkeley, CA: University of California Publications in Anthropology, 1984) describes excavations at this most important of sites. Nick Saunders, *People of the Jaguar*, already cited, gives a valuable analysis of Chavin iconography. Lawrence Sullivan's monumental excursion into traditional Latin American religions, *Icanchu's Drum* (New York: Macmillan, 1988) is essential for any student of Andean archaeology.

The Moche are well described by Christopher Donnan and Donna McClelland, *The Burial Theme in Moche Iconography* (Washington DC: Dumbarton Oaks, 1987). The National Geographic Society has run a series of well illustrated articles on the Lords of Sipan in recent years, such as: Walter Alva, "Discovering the New World's Richest Unlooted Tomb," *National Geographic Magazine* 174(4)(1989):510–548. Tiwanaku: Alan Kolata, "Tiwanaku: Portrait of an Andean Civilization," *Field Museum of Natural History Bulletin* 53(8)(1982):13–28. See also the same author's "The Agricultural Foundations of the Tiwanaku State," *American Antiquity* 51(4)(1986):748–762. Huari: William Isbell and Katharina Schreiber, "Was Huari a State?" *American Antiquity* 43(1978):372–389. Chimu: Michael Moseley and C. Kent Day (eds.), *Chan Chan: Andean Desert City* (Albuquerque NM: University of New Mexico Press, 1982).

The best starting point for the Inca civilization is Conrad and Demarest's *Religion and Empire*, already cited. John Rowe, *Inca Culture at the time of the Spanish Conquest* (Washington DC: Smithsonian Institution Handbook of South American Indians, vol. 2, 1946) is still the definitive account. John Hemming, *The Conquest of the Incas* (Baltimore: Pelican Books, 1983) describes Pizarro's ravages.

Chapter 13: Epilog

Three books cover the closing centuries of prehistory from different perspectives. John Bodley's *Victims of Progress*, 2nd ed. (Menlo Park:

Cummings, 1982) is a widely consulted college text. My *Clash of Cultures* (New York: W.H. Freeman, 1984) describes contact between Westerners and a series of non-Western societies for a general audience. Eric Wolf, *Europe and the People Without History* (Berkeley and Los Angeles: University of California Press, 1984) is the authoritative account, with a strong anthropological bias.

Acknowledgments

Chapter 1: *Figure 1.1*: Hirmer Photoarchiv. *Figure 1.2*: Kent V. Flannery. *Figure 1.3*: L. Schele and D. Friedel, *A Forest of Kings*, William Morrow, New York, 1990. *Figure 1.5*: Adapted from D. R. Brotherwell and Eric Higgs, *Science in Archaeology*, Thames & Hudson Ltd., London. *Figure 1.9*: Photo by A. L. Smith. Courtesy of the Peabody Museum, Harvard University.

Chapter 2: *Figure 2.1*: Courtesy Gordon Willey. *Figure 2.2*: Gordon Hillman. *Figure 2.3*: Adapted from Colin Renfrew and Paul Bahn, *Archaeology: Theories, Methods, and Practice*, Thames & Hudson Ltd., London, 1991. *Figure 2.4*: Copyright © Werner Forman Archive. Photograph by Lewis R. Bindord. From Gordon R. Willey and Jeremy A. Sabloff, *A History of American Archaeology*, 2nd. ed., W. H. Freeman, New York, 1980.

Chapter 3: *Table 3.2*: Redrawn with permission from David Pilbeam, *The Ascent of Man*, Macmillan, New York, 1972. Copyright © 1972 David Pilbeam. *Figure 3.1(c)*: Redrawn with permission of publisher from Prudence Napier, Bantam, New York, 1972. *Figure 3.3*: Courtesy of Transvaal Museum, South Africa. *Figure 3.4*: Courtesy of Alan R. Hughes, University of the Witwatersrand. *Figure 3.5*: Institute of Human Origins. *Figure 3.6*: Photograph by John Reader, courtesy of Mary Leakey. *Figure 3.7*: Institute of Human Origins. *Figure 3.8*: Copyright © by the National Museums of Kenya, P. O. Box 40658, Nairobi, Kenya. Reprinted by permission. *Figure 3.9*: Robert Foley/Antiquity Publications Ltd. *Figure 3.10*: From *Life Nature Library/Early Man*. Redrawn from Lowell Hess. Copyright © 1980 Time-Life Books Inc. *Figure 3.11*: Henry T. Bunn.

Chapter 4: *Figure 4.2*: Cambridge Museum of Archaeology and Anthropology. *Figure 4.3*: Adapted from J. D. Clark, *Prehistory of Africa*, Thames & Hudson Ltd., London. *Figure 4.4*: Courtesy of F. Clark Howell. *Figure 4.5*: Copyright © Brake, Photo Researchers. *Figure 4.6*: Drawing by Janis Cirulis from William Howells, *Mankind in the Making*, Doubleday, New York. Copyright © 1959, 1967 by William Howells. Doubleday is a division of Bantam, Doubleday, Dell Publishing Group. *Figure 4.7*: Giovanni Caselli.

Chapter 5: *Figure 5.2:* From Karl W. Butzer, *Environment and Archaeology*, 2nd ed., Aldine, Hawthorn, NY, 1971. Reprinted by permission of the author. *Figure 5.4:* Courtesy of Milford Wolpoff. *Figure 5.5:* Courtesy of the Peabody Museum, Harvard University. *Figure 5.7:* Courtesy of Topham/The Image Works. *Figure 5.8:* Courtesy, the Museum of Indian Archaeology (London), an affiliation of the University of Western Ontario, Artist: Ivan Koesis. *Figure 5.10:* University of Arizona Museum.

Chapter 6: *Figure 6.2:* Center for American Archaeology. *Figure 6.3:* Museum of Anthropology, University of Michigan. *Figure 6.4:* Courtesy of Tell Abu Hureyra excavation. *Figure 6.6:* Michael Holoford, London. *Figure 6.7:* Redrawn from James Melaart, *Çatal Hüyük*, Thames & Hudson Ltd., London, by permission. *Figure 6.9:* Redrawn from Stuart Piggott, *Ancient Europe*, Edinburgh University Press, 1965. Used with permission. Copyright © 1965 Stuart Piggott. *Figure 6.10:* Reprinted by permission from Kwang-Chih Chang, *The Archaeology of Ancient China*, 3rd ed., Yale University Press, New Haven, 1977. *Figure 6.11:* Courtesy of the R.S. Peabody Foundation for Archaeology, Andover, MA. *Figure 6.12:* Photo by Thomas F. Lynch.

Chapter 7: *Figure 7.1:* British School of Archaeology in Jerusalem. *Figure 7.3:* Granger. *Figure 7.4:* Courtesy of The British Library. *Figure 7.6:* University of Arizona Museum. *Figure 7.7:* Copyright © Granitsas/The Image Works. *Figure 7.8:* Werner Forman Archive. *Figure 7.9:* Field Museum of Natural History (Neg. #90925), Chicago. *Figure 7.10:* Courtesy of the Museum of the American Indian, Heye Foundation, New York. *Figure 7.11:* Artist's reconstruction by William Iseminger. Photograph courtesy of Cahokia Mounds State Historic Site.

Chapter 8: *Figure 8.2:* Photography by Egyptian Expedition, The Metropolitan Museum of Art. *Figure 8.3:* Copyright © 1986, Menzel/Stock, Boston.

Chapter 9: *Figure 9.2:* From Max E. Mallowan, *Early Mesopotamia and Iran*, Thames & Hudson Ltd., London. *Figure 9.3:* The British Museum. *Figure 9.4:* Courtesy of the University Museum, University of Pennsylvania. *Figure 9.6:* Copyright © Topham/The Image Works. *Figure 9.7:* All rights reserved, The Metropolitan Museum of Art. *Figure 9.8:* Donald A. Frey, Institute of Nautical Archaeology. *Figure 9.9:* Fotoarchiv Hirmer Verlag Munchen.

Chapter 10: *Figure 10.2:* Roger-Viollet Documentation Generale Photographique, Paris. *Figure 10.3:* Scala, Art Resource. *Figure 10.4:* Peabody Museum, Harvard University. Copyright © 1978 President and Fellows of Harvard College. Photo by Hillel Burger (Neg. #N28172). *Figure 10.5:* The China Friendship Society, from Grahame Clark, *World Prehistory*, 3rd ed., Cambridge University Press, p. 306. Copyright © 1977 Cambridge University Press. *Figure 10.6:* Granger. *Figure 10.8:* P. L. Shinnie. *Figure 10.9:* Sassoon, Robert Harding Picture Library. *Figure 10.10:* Granger.

Chapter 11: *Figure 11.2:* Mary E. Miller. *Figure 11.3:* Werner Forman Archive. *Figure 11.4:* Mazzaschi/Stock, Boston. *Figure 11.5:* Rutledge, Copyright © El Mirador Project. *Figure 11.6:* J. E. S. Thompson, *Maya Hieroglyphic Writing*, University of Oklahoma Press, Norman, OK, 1971. *Figure 11.7:* Nelson/Stock, Boston. *Figure 11.8:* Copyright © Alper/Stock, Boston. *Figure 11.9:* Lesley Newhart. *Figure 11.10:* From *Codex Mendoza*. Courtesy of Bodleian Library, Oxford, M. S. Arch. Selden A.1, folio 46. *Figure 11.11:* The American Museum of Natural History. *Figure 11.12:* *Codex Magliabecchi* (facsimile), British Museum. Photo by John Freeman.

Chapter 12: *Figure 12.2:* Photo by Jeffrey Quilter. *Figure 12.3:* Courtesy of Franklin Graham. *Figure 12.4:* Copyright © Saunders, Werner Forman Archive. *Figure 12.5:* Russell, Robert Harding Picture Library. *Figure 12.7:* Copyright © Saunders, Werner Forman Archive. *Figure 12.8:* George Holton/Photo Researchers, Inc.

Index

Abri Pataud rock shelter, France, 102
Abu Hureyra mound, Syria, 126–128
Accelerator mass spectrometry (AMS), 17–18
Acheulian technology, 79–82
Adams, Robert, 170
Adaptation
    adaptive radiation, 66
    culture as, 33–34
    early patterns, 71–72
    early primate, 55–58
    by *Homo erectus*, 77–78
    toolmaking and, 66
Adena culture, 155–156
Aegean agriculture, 195
Africa
    agriculture, 7
    ancient kingdoms in, 214–221
    Ghana, Mali, and Songhay kingdoms, 218–219
    Homo sapiens in, 86–87
    Ice Age glaciation in, 53
    iron and ironworking in, 217–218
    Meroe kingdom, 214–215
    slave trade, 221
    trade, 215–217

Zimbabwe, 219–221
Age of Humanity, 53
Agriculture. *See also* Food production
    Aegean, 195
    in America, 137–141
    in Andes Mountains, 250
    beginnings, 7
    beginnings in Mesoamerica, 222–223
    in China, 135–136
    in East Africa, 217–218
    in Egypt, 129–131
    Pueblo farmers, 149–155
    social and political changes resulting from, 142–145
    spread into Europe, 131–133
    Sumerian 'Ubaid farmers, 181–182
Ahmose the Liberator, 192
Alva, Walter, 29, 250
Amenophis, 192
America. *See also* North America; South America
    early agriculture in, 137–141
    hunting and gathering intensifies in, 120–122
    Pueblo farmers, 149–155
    written records, 14

275